SMOKED

The Inside Story of the Minnesota Tobacco Trial

By **Deborah Caulfield Rybak** of *Minnesota Law & Politics* and
David Phelps of the Minneapolis *Star Tribune*

For Michael and Pat

David Phelps

Deborah Caulfield Rybak

220 South Sixth Street, Suite 500
Minneapolis, MN 55402

Copyright © 1998 by Deborah Caulfield Rybak and David Phelps

DESIGNED BY JULIE DIXON
COVER ILLUSTRATION © 1998 BRIAN BARBER
ADDITIONAL ILLUSTRATIONS BY SCOTT BUCHSCHACHER

Printed in the United States of America

Library of Congress Catalog Card Number 98-67743

ISBN 0-9641908-4-2

Table of Contents

Acknowledgments

As we covered the Minnesota tobacco trial in the winter and spring of 1998, it became clear to us that this case was special. Not only was it historic, but events inside and outside the courtroom added dramatic subplots and twists that made its story even more compelling.

Tom Mason, editor and publisher of *Twin Cities Business Monthly*, proposed the idea of writing a book about the trial, and believed in its value so much that he volunteered his time as editor. He has been a tireless supporter throughout and he has our deepest thanks for providing us with such an opportunity. Dozens of the trial's participants cooperated in our research and provided valuable insights into the events that made headlines and those that escaped the media's attention.

Twelve weeks is an extremely short time to produce such a book. We are sincerely grateful for all the assistance we received and could not have accomplished our task without the support of a wide array of people who believed this story should be told.

Thanks to Minneapolis *Star Tribune* editor Tim McGuire, managing editor Pam Fine and business editor Scott Gillespie for granting David Phelps the time to work on this project and for their encouragement during its development.

We'd also like to acknowledge the assistance of Attorney General Hubert H. Humphrey III and his staff, particularly Lee Sheehy, Tom Pursell, Doug Blanke, Eric Johnson and Leslie Sandberg. Also, Joe Loveland, a former member of the attorney general's office, whose insights were always helpful.

From Blue Cross and Blue Shield of Minnesota, the authors wish to acknowledge the cooperation of Chief Executive Andy Czajkowski, associate corporate counsel Tom Gilde, and spokeswoman Maureen Schriner.

Special thanks also to the tobacco trial team from the firm Robins, Kaplan, Miller & Ciresi, in particular Michael Ciresi, Roberta Walburn, Bruce Finzen, Tara Sutton, Dick Gill, Thomas Hamlin, and Susan Richard Nelson, all of whom patiently recounted trial developments. Also, to Gail Shore, who acted as media liaison for the firm.

We want to thank Greg Little, Thomas F. McKim, D. J. Leary and Scott Williams for their help in opening doors to trial participants on the defense side.

Our particular thanks to defense attorneys Peter Sipkins, Jonathan Redgrave, Jack Fribley, Robert Weber, Peter Bleakley, David Bernick, Peter Biersteker, Gerald Svoboda, David Martin,

Steven Kelley, and David Sasseville for the detailed interviews and observations they provided.

This book wouldn't be complete without the assistance of jurors who participated in the four-month trial. We are grateful for the help of Dorothy Hallen, David Olson, Jill Burton, Jim Otis, James Livingston, and Terry Zaspel, who put a human face on the trial and took the time to discuss the case from their viewpoint.

Our colleagues in the media who covered the tobacco trial also should be recognized for their role in trial coverage and the assistance they provided us, including Karren Mills and Steve Karnowski of the Associated Press, Pat Kessler of WCCO-TV, Lillian McDonald of KMSP-TV, Laura McCallum and Elizabeth Stawicki of Minnesota Public Radio, Tom Watkins of CNN, and Melissa Levy of the Minneapolis *Star Tribune*.

We also wish to acknowledge the contributions of former *Star Tribune* Page One editor Jim Kelly, who provided guidance on journalistic issues, the *Star Tribune's* Graydon Royce, who understood the pressures involved and offered support, and Claude Peck, who deftly edited the newspaper's daily trial coverage for four months.

Kudos to Bill White and Steve Kaplan at *Minnesota Law & Politics* for their friendship, advice, support and creative thinking when it came to naming this book.

Special thanks to Deborah Rybak's former *Los Angeles Times* editor Irv Letofsky (of *Star Tribune* fame as well) for his insight, support, and suggestions in producing a book like this under such tight deadlines. Irv was right. It hurt, but it was worth it. Thanks as well to former *Los Angeles Times* colleagues and published authors Dennis McDougal and Pat Broeske whose suggestions on collaborative writing were invaluable.

Our intrepid researcher Berit Thorkelson performed a host of tasks that enabled us to maintain focus. MSP Business Book's managing editor Brooke Benson marshalled this material for production without once losing her cool. Joan Kanavich's precise and lightning fast proofreading saved us from stylistic embarrassment. Warm thanks to *Twin Cities Business Monthly's* Doug Benson, Dave Elmstrom, and Heather Ehre, and MSP's Pamela Youngberg for their additional support and assistance in getting the book to press.

Last but certainly not least, love and thanks to our families, George and Lyn Caulfield, Frank and Fran Phelps, Nathan Phelps, and especially our spouses, Michael and Pat, for their patience, love and encouragement during an intense period in our lives.

Foreword

I t is possible that I have the best job in the world.

I talk to people, take moving pictures of what they say, and put them on television. Some of them even like it when I do this.

I've listened to murderers, master criminals and petty thieves. I've covered presidents, prime ministers, poets, politicians, priests, farmers, crackheads, eggheads, deadbeat dads, suburban moms, and inner city kids. I've attended labor union rallies, political debates, bridge openings, business closings, prison lockdowns, and welfare protests.

But in 20 years of public affairs reporting, I can count on the fingers of one hand the times I felt—really felt—that the unfolding story I was witnessing had a lasting import beyond the evening news.

The first time I knew: A farmhouse in rural Iowa. Then-candidate Ronald Reagan, speaking from a small flag-bedecked stage surrounded by bales of straw to make it seem more "rural," looked out over several hundred corn farmers in blue jeans and seed caps.

Gripped by nostalgia, the future president spoke not of farm policy, but of a rural pub in the English countryside he visited shortly after World War II.

The pub owner and his wife, Reagan recounted, had grown to love a group of American soldiers stationed nearby during the war.

On many nights, they served home-cooked meals and English ale to the courteous, bashful, strong, and handsome boys.

His voice breaking, Reagan remembered the deep pain of this simple British couple who had come to love these Americans, all of whom were killed in battle and were unable to keep their promise to return.

"Big strappin' lads they was," Reagan, in a near whisper, recalled the old pub owner saying. "From a place called . . . Iowa."

Silence.

To my left and right, these old Iowa farmers, who would have been about the same age, wiped quiet tears from their ruddy cheeks.

And then, great loud cheers as Reagan, smiling, wiped away tears of his own.

At that moment, I felt a page of history turn. From Jimmy Carter to Ronald Reagan. From the 1970s to the 1980s. From helplessness to hope.

Fast forward, 18 years.

All of us have now witnessed—and survived—vast technological and cultural changes: the fax machine, phone pagers, the

Internet, the fall of the Soviet Union, the spread of legalized gambling, and the de-glorification of drunk driving.

That's why the growing legal battles between tobacco companies and state governments have taken on new meaning, and have become the next step in the wrenching of our cultural psyche.

Attorney General Hubert Humphrey III, toiling in the shadow of his famous father's reputation, and famed litigator Mike Ciresi, son of a produce merchant, came up with a new legal theory.

Instead of blaming tobacco companies for causing Uncle Ned's cancer, the Minnesota case would charge that the tobacco companies knew their product was dangerous for Uncle Ned to use, and lied about it.

The best and brightest legal minds in America defended the tobacco industry, and throughout the landmark trial, "Big Tobacco" lawyers showed why. They also demonstrated good humor outside the courtroom with reporters who wanted—what else—pictures of tobacco lawyers smoking.

On some days, the show outside the courtroom was better than the one with the judge presiding.

There was an increasingly hostile public relations battle between trial lawyers, that sometimes bordered on the inane. Attorney Ciresi once admonished tobacco lawyer Robert Weber for not knowing "the legal distinction between sic 'em and bite 'em."

But there was a full-scale war under way in the judge's chambers.

Despite extraordinary efforts by the court to restrict the flow of information, journalists David Phelps and Deborah Caulfield Rybak reveal sometimes startling new information about the judge and jury, as well as the battalions of warrior lawyers for both sides.

Phelps and Rybak pull the curtain back on private meetings in the judge's chambers, the anger and frustration of sequestered jurors, the warrior mentality of attorneys, and tobacco anecdotes ranging from *The Beverly Hillbillies* to court security run amok.

It is an entertaining and important story; a chronicle of one of the most important civil lawsuits in the last 20 years, and perhaps the next 20.

And that's something with significance beyond the evening news.

Patrick Kessler
WCCO-TV

September 1998

Chapter One

Out on a Limb

The view from the Jackson Lake Lodge in Moran, Wyoming, is stunning. But on a July day in 1997, as Minnesota Attorney General Hubert H. Humphrey III stared out of the resort's soaring picture windows at the majestic jagged mountains, his mind was preoccupied with the biggest challenge in his public career. The serenity of the surroundings did not deflect Humphrey's turmoil.

Elsewhere in the lodge, his fellow attorneys general celebrated the news of a $368.5 billion agreement with the tobacco industry to pay for decades of wrongful conduct and the ravages of smoking-related illnesses. Humphrey was not among the back-slappers. He was concerned, very concerned, that the settlement was premature and contained terms far too favorable for the industry.

Humphrey had battled the tobacco industry for the previous three years, often in close coordination with his colleagues from other states. But now he stood alone, worried that the flush of success at the negotiating table masked missing elements of an agreement necessary to fundamentally change the conduct of companies whose product Humphrey considered to be vile and destructive.

It was an emotionally painful and trying position for Humphrey, normally an optimistic and upbeat politician.

Humphrey had come to Wyoming for the annual summer meeting of the National Association of Attorneys General. The meeting was always a highlight for Humphrey, who once served as the organization's president. The attendees were colleagues whose professionalism and friendship he treasured. He shared beers with his compatriots at these meetings and often discussed politics and public policy in the hot tub.

But this year, the beautiful environment and the camaraderie of the gathering were lost on Humphrey as he walked in the long shadow of Mississippi Attorney General Mike Moore, who had just spearheaded the settlement agreement.

Moore, with the help of attorneys general from other states, including Washington, Arizona, Florida, and Connecticut, had completed the proposed settlement just days before, on June 20, and announced it during a nationally televised press conference from Washington, D.C.

Humphrey, who had watched the broadcast from his Minnesota State Capitol office in St. Paul, now quietly observed as Moore and his group accepted accolades from their peers, while his protestations fell on deaf ears.

"Here were all of my friends congratulating each other," Humphrey recalled. "We had meetings to outline the settlement terms. I raised my objections and my concerns and tried to explain what we were doing in Minnesota. But it was 'Boy, isn't this great.' People were literally patting each other on the back."

Humphrey believed the settlement language was too soft on the industry and didn't go far enough to reduce smoking. He thought the financial pain in the agreement was insufficient. Plus, he believed the industry had avoided disclosure of internal documents that would show decades of deceit and denial about smoking and disease.

Moore and Humphrey had been friends and, for a time, allies in the fight with the tobacco industry. Moore, with anchorman good looks, was a new breed of southern politician—more progressive than previous generations—who dressed in Ole Miss chic: tasseled loafers and crisp oxford shirts. Moore had been the first to file a state lawsuit against cigarette manufacturers; Humphrey had been second.

Their paths had crossed regularly because of the issue. Moore, at one point, seemed genuinely fond of his Minnesota counterpart, once asking a visiting reporter from Minneapolis how Humphrey's chances for governor looked.

But their paths on the tobacco issue eventually diverged as Moore followed a settlement strategy and Humphrey became the public health advocate, the hard-liner on financial issues, and a document-obsessed crusader. Humphrey also voiced concerns about Moore's decision to align with a group of private plaintiffs' attorneys, fearing that they were driven more by the prospect of fees than public policy issues.

At the mountain resort, everyone's mood was upbeat, except Humphrey's. The Minnesota attorney general, his staff joked darkly, sat at a table for one at dinner. Even Humphrey referred to himself as "that obstinate fool on the frozen tundra."

Humphrey watched as Moore basked in the media limelight. "I was out walking early one morning, and there was Moore, at 6:30 A.M., being interviewed by CNN. I thought, 'OK, It's his day. He'll have his day and I'll have mine.'"

Humphrey's interest in having his day in court with Big Tobacco was certainly not unprecedented. Tobacco-related lawsuits had washed over the legal landscape in periodic waves since the early 1950s. The first set, filed between 1953 and 1973, was little more than a series of shorebreakers. Lacking definitive scientific links between smoking and disease, smokers had trouble proving their cases in court.

The second wave of lawsuits, filed between 1983 and 1992, was more scientifically substantive. But the industry's well-deployed legal armada sailed through those without a scratch, successfully arguing that smokers knew the risks involved with the habit. By the end of the second wave, the industry was considered to be almost unbeatable. Of 813 claims filed against the industry, 23 had been tried in court. Of those, the industry had lost only two, only to have those reversed on appeal. While many plaintiffs' attorneys had been bankrupted in the process, the industry hadn't paid one cent in damages.

However, new activities and legal theories surfaced in the 1990s. And compared to past actions, a third wave against Big Tobacco loomed like a tsunami on the legal horizon.

Industry whistle blowers Jeffrey Wigand and Merrell Williams were beginning to generate unfavorable publicity for cigarette manufacturers—Williams by his theft of incriminating documents from Brown & Williamson Tobacco Corp. (B&W), and Wigand, a former B&W researcher, with his first-hand knowledge of the industry's efforts to mask the truth about smoking and health.

In California, medical professor Stanton Glantz received an anonymous package containing 4,000 pages of the documents stolen by Williams. The only return address on the Federal Express box was "Mr. Butts," a reference to the cigarette character in "Doonesbury." Glantz immediately realized the significance of the material, which talked about nicotine addiction and strategies for beating back lawsuits.

He placed the documents in the public archives of his college library on the San Francisco campus of the University of California. The library, after defeating an attempt by B&W to seal the material, placed the documents on the Internet and made the collection available on CD-ROM.

In Washington, the Clinton Administration named a virulently antismoking activist, David Kessler, to head the Food and Drug

Administration (FDA). Under Kessler, the FDA began to examine the possibility of regulating nicotine as a drug. On Capitol Hill, Democratic California Congressman Henry Waxman held extensive hearings on smoking and addiction, calling the major industry executives as witnesses. Although the executives denied under oath that nicotine was addictive, evidence to the contrary was closing around them.

And in legal circles, a new theory was touted as the lance that could ultimately pierce Big Tobacco's previously invincible armor. Instead of focusing on individual smokers, this new wave of lawsuits concentrated on recouping billions of dollars paid by states under Medicaid to treat smoking-related illnesses. This new approach attracted a breed of plaintiffs' attorneys whose pockets were deep enough to absorb the massive financial burden Big Tobacco traditionally inflicted. Some formulated massive class-action suits; others turned to state attorneys general to turn on some serious legal juice.

Humphrey's interest began to take shape in early 1994. His staff had a successful track record on consumer fraud issues and they began to look at cigarettes, the use of which included serious health consequences, in terms of state consumer laws. But staff resources were not sufficient to take on the entire tobacco industry.

In the downtown Minneapolis law offices of Robins, Kaplan, Miller & Ciresi, attorneys Mike Ciresi and Roberta Walburn also pondered the prospect of declaring legal war on Big Tobacco, an idea they'd been contemplating for several years. Robins attorney Dick Allyn, a former Humphrey aide, heard about the attorney general's interest and brought the state and the firm together to discuss a strategy for making the tobacco industry pay for the health care of sick smokers.

Walburn also had been having conversations about tobacco with Tom Gilde, associate corporate counsel for Blue Cross and Blue Shield of Minnesota. Gilde was intrigued by the idea. With the disclosure of the Merrell Williams documents, he became even more interested and ran it up the chain of command, eventually bringing it to Blue Cross Chief Executive Andy Czajkowski, who decided it was worth pursuing.

By spring, the parties had been properly introduced and the decision was made to draft a lawsuit, which would recover the cost of treating smoking-related health problems paid through the state's publicly funded insurance programs and Blue Cross' policies. The foundation of the developing lawsuit was consumer fraud and antitrust laws, which were new theories for confronting the tobacco industry.

Ciresi and Walburn were two of Robins' top attorneys and seasoned veterans at complex civil litigation involving corporate misdeeds. They intended to prove that the industry colluded to deceive the public about the health risks of smoking. Humphrey and Czajkowski were on board with this approach and hired the Robins firm to present the case in court for a 25 percent contingency fee arrangement.

Because the size of its potential claim was substantially larger than that of Blue Cross, the state acted as lead plaintiff in the lawsuit.

Ciresi's firm was a formidable choice to head the legal battle. Nearly a third of its cases were on contingency, so the attorneys were financially prepared for the risk involved if there was no award at the end of the trial.

With 230 attorneys on staff, the firm had the resources to tackle large, complicated litigation. Ciresi had built a reputation as a ferocious, take-no-prisoners attorney against corporations such as A. H. Robins, maker of a defective intrauterine device, Japanese camera manufacturer Minolta, and Union Carbide after the Bhopal, India, gas-leak disaster. Walburn had been at Ciresi's side in each of those cases.

For Humphrey, son of the late Vice President Hubert H. Humphrey, the case was the biggest he'd undertaken since becoming attorney general in 1982. A former state senator from the Twin Cities suburb of New Hope, "Skip" Humphrey, as he'd been known since childhood, was a cautious and well-liked politician, but considered less charismatic than his famous father. A run for the U.S. Senate in 1988 failed. Now there was talk that Humphrey was interested in the governor's office.

Humphrey and Blue Cross filed their joint lawsuit in Ramsey County District Court on August 17, 1994. The suit was the first state-filed lawsuit to allege antitrust conspiracy and consumer fraud against the tobacco companies. Earlier lawsuits had chal-

lenged industry conduct and smoking's harm with product liability laws. The suit by Minnesota and Blue Cross contained new,
untested claims that the industry violated consumer fraud laws by
failing to adequately inform smokers about the addictiveness of
nicotine and the health hazards of smoking. The lawsuit also
alleged that the industry had failed to develop a safer cigarette
because it would have constituted an acknowledgment that their
existing product was unsafe. Moreover, the suit claimed the
industry conspired to do all of these things in violation of state
antitrust laws. It was also the first lawsuit to include a private
insurance company as a co-plaintiff.

Named as defendants were Philip Morris, Inc., R. J. Reynolds
Tobacco Company, Brown & Williamson Tobacco Corporation,
B.A.T. Industries P.L.C., British-American Tobacco Company
Ltd., BAT (UK & Export) Ltd., The American Tobacco
Company, Liggett Group, Inc., The Council for Tobacco
Research-USA, Inc., and The Tobacco Institute, Inc.

"Previous lawsuits have said the tobacco companies should pay
because their products are dangerous. This suit says they should
pay because their conduct is illegal, "Humphrey said at a press
conference announcing the lawsuit. "It's time to blow away the
black cloud of conspiracy and collusion, and force the tobacco
companies to clean up and pay up."

The lawsuit represented a risky proposition for Blue Cross, a
nonprofit health care provider created in 1933 by the Minnesota
Legislature to improve health care services offered to state resi-

dents. Its corporate peers were skeptical.

"This was very different from anything we'd done," said Blue Cross counsel Gilde. "This is a health firm, not a law firm that routinely sues people or is in the business of litigation."

"There were a lot of people who questioned my sanity at the time and thought this was really a roll of the dice," said CEO Czajkowski, who unsuccessfully asked Blue Cross providers in other states to take similar action. "A lot of CEOs told me I'd bring a lot of problems to our organization. I really didn't get much support."

Even Czajkowski's 12-member board of directors originally questioned the lawsuit. "There were a lot of concerns," he said. "Certainly the industry had an air of invincibility to it—that it was the boss. It would be a formidable task and there was some concern about the commitment of resources and staff time."

Czajkowski was concerned that the tobacco industry could quietly retaliate against Blue Cross in some form. He'd heard of a western state where an insurer sued the industry and suddenly faced a referendum on health care costs. Czajkowski was aware of the tobacco industry's clout at state legislatures, where tobacco-control legislation was often contested.

But Blue Cross and Czajkowski had long been interested in the issue of smoking, and the impact smoking had on its rate structure and its health care expenditures. In the early 1980s, it became the first health plan in the United States to offer a discount to nonsmokers. It helped found the Minnesota Smokefree

Coalition, an antismoking advocacy group established in 1984. Buildings on its sprawling Eagan campus went smoke free in 1988.

After two sessions with Czajkowski, Blue Cross directors gave their approval to the lawsuit.

It was a big step for Czajkowski, a soft-spoken, small man whose business attire showed a fondness for striped shirts with bone-white collars and cuffs. Czajkowski had been chief executive of Blue Cross since 1983, and planned to retire in 1999. He wasn't even sure the lawsuit would be resolved on his watch.

The case would be shepherded by District Court Judge Kenneth J. Fitzpatrick, a career public servant who'd been on the bench since 1973. Fitzpatrick hadn't been the first choice of either party. Nor did he necessarily want the case. However, after it became clear that other judges either weren't available or weren't willing to take on the gigantic caseload, Fitzpatrick, then chief judge of the Ramsey County bench, offered his services. Both sides agreed. Fitzpatrick had the reputation as a fair, quiet jurist who, in attorneys' lingo, allowed them to "present their cases in court." In short, he would allow both sides to be heard.

From the beginning, there was always a sense that the scope of the lawsuit was enormous, if only from the size of the legal teams. Some three dozen defense attorneys from across the country regularly descended on Fitzpatrick's 13th floor St. Paul courtroom to participate in pretrial hearings.

Conflict immediately marked the case. Less than three months into the proceeding, the defendants attempted to have the

Robins firm disqualified from the case because it once represented the Liggett Group, one of the defendants. The defendants also
challenged the constitutionality of the law firm's contingency fee
arrangement. Fitzpatrick denied the disqualification motion and
upheld the fee arrangement.

The plaintiffs, meanwhile, sought the disqualification of five
Twin Cities firms as representatives of tobacco interests because
of past and current attorney-client relationships with various
divisions of state government. Fitzpatrick denied that motion as
well.

In early 1995, the defendants then attempted to remove Blue
Cross from the case, claiming a private insurer couldn't collect
damages for its individual smoker subscribers. It lost that too, taking unsuccessful appeals up to the Minnesota Supreme Court.

Pretrial discovery began in June 1995. Aware of the volume of
material that would be produced in the case, Fitzpatrick agreed
to create document depositories capable of holding tens of millions of pages of material. He created one in Minneapolis and a
smaller one for the British defendants outside London. But material only trickled in, particularly from the U.S. defendants. Eight
months after the state made its first discovery request, Philip
Morris, the industry leader, had produced just 17 boxes of material.

Delay became common in the case. In one instance,
Fitzpatrick issued eight separate orders over a 14-month period
regarding the production of document indexes before they were

handed over to the plaintiffs. The computerized indexes had been accumulated by industry lawyers during years of previous tobacco litigation and would serve as a road map for the state and Blue Cross. The amount of material required from the industry was enormous. It forced Philip Morris to assign 100 extra attorneys and paralegals to the case to review corporate files.

After the industry lost an appeal to the U.S. Supreme Court, the pace of document delivery to the Minneapolis depository quickened. There, the Robins document team began to uncover evidence that the industry long knew about the addictiveness of nicotine, suppressed research about the link between smoking and disease, and had marketing plans to capture the loyalty of teenage smokers.

"They were amazing documents," recalled Walburn, who traveled twice to England to review material there and coordinated review back in the United States. "Some of them couldn't have been better if you'd written them yourself. We were struck by the breath and depth of industry deceit. It was almost mind numbing."

But as the Minnesota case began to take shape, Mississippi Attorney General Mike Moore wanted his pal, Skip Humphrey, to consider some other plans.

By March 1996, Moore had engaged in hushed conversations with the Liggett Group and its chairman, Bennett LeBow, about a possible out-of-court settlement. LeBow's small firm was now facing lawsuits filed by five states, including Minnesota. Each of those lawsuits represented a financial uncertainty to him. LeBow also was entertaining the takeover of RJR Nabisco, Inc. He was looking for an out-of-court settlement that would take away his legal problems and, if he successfully acquired RJR Nabisco, would end the lawsuits against its tobacco division as well.

Liggett was the smallest of the major U.S. tobacco companies with Lark, Eve, L&M, and Chesterfield as its principal products. It was barely profitable and could ill afford a court loss. So Moore, and his right-hand man for tobacco, Pascagoula, Mississippi, attorney Dick Scruggs, were intrigued when they were approached by LeBow through a third party.

Moore wanted to know if Humphrey was interested in negotiating with LeBow. Doug Blanke, Humphrey's consumer policy director, recalled that Moore contacted Humphrey and said, "Dick and I want to come up and share with you a settlement outline." Humphrey agreed to listen.

Moore and Scruggs flew to St. Paul on Scruggs' Lear jet to meet with Humphrey, Ciresi, and some of Humphrey's staff. The Minnesotans were surprised by Moore's proposed settlement for the states, and were unimpressed with the proposed terms.

"Where'd you get the authority to negotiate for us?" Ciresi pointedly asked Moore.

Humphrey asked to study the settlement and told Moore he'd get back to him. Humphrey's staff quickly determined the proposal was unacceptable and did not meet Humphrey's goals. As drafted, it did nothing in terms of document disclosure. It also contained little in the way of cash payments and would grant immunity to R. J. Reynolds Tobacco Company if LeBow's acquisition went through. Humphrey saw no upside for the state to go along. Moore argued that a settlement with Liggett would be a fulcrum against the other tobacco companies. Humphrey disagreed and was particularly disturbed by the provision granting immunity to industry giant RJR.

"We're not into that kind of a settlement," Humphrey told Moore several days later. "You've got to get at least *something* out of these guys."

LeBow reached agreements with Florida, Massachusetts, Mississippi, West Virginia, and a group of class-action lawyers known as the Castano group, who were involved in a New Orleans smoking case by that name. But the deal represented little more than a symbolic crack in tobacco's wall of invincibility.

Meanwhile, Minnesota's document depository was starting to fill up from a steady stream of damaging material. Teams of Robins' lawyers spent their daylight hours and most nights poring over the material.

The plaintiffs used some of their early discoveries to persuade Judge Fitzpatrick to order more disclosure. To obtain more information on research and development, the plaintiffs cited a Philip Morris memo about manipulating the level of nicotine in cigarettes to enhance the "kick" received by smokers. For further documents on youth marketing, the plaintiffs used an RJR document that reflected the company's interest in "younger adult smokers."

Cases were progressing in Florida and Texas as well. But as the litigation moved forward, Moore and Scruggs were laying groundwork for a national settlement with all of the cigarette manufacturers. With the blessing of Mississippi Senator Trent Lott, the Senate's top Republican as well as Scrugg's brother-in-law, Moore and Scruggs held indirect conversations with industry executives about possible terms of an agreement.

By August, Moore was ready to share an outline of a possible deal with his colleagues. He called 13 attorneys general—including Humphrey—who had filed or were about to file Medicaid lawsuits, to a meeting at the Democratic National Convention in Chicago.

"Now is our window of opportunity," Humphrey aide Eric Johnson recalled Moore saying. "We can do this before the election."

Humphrey disliked the proposal, which became public after it was leaked to the *Wall Street Journal*. It provided immunity to the industry from future lawsuits, which Humphrey opposed. It also would preempt the Medicaid lawsuits of Minnesota and other states, thus voiding Humphrey's goal of full disclosure of industry documents regarding smoking and health, as well as youth marketing. Comprehensive FDA regulation, another Humphrey standard, was not one of the terms, and the settlement cost, approximately $150 billion, was considered too low by Humphrey.

"It wasn't 'You have to do it Skip's way,'" Humphrey later said. "It was, 'If we're going to do this together, then we have to come to a common agreement before we go talking to the industry.'"

Moore hinted that the Clinton Administration looked favorably upon the proposal, which surprised Humphrey and his staff. "We've been talking to the White House too," Johnson told Moore, referring to recent conversations with Vice President Al Gore. "Who've you been talking to?"

Moore replied, "We've been talking to people well placed in the White House," Johnson recalled. When pushed, Moore revealed, "We're talking to the President's top adviser, Dick Morris."

Within 24 hours, Morris had lost his White House insider status with the disclosure of an affair with a Washington call girl. It was a huge embarrassment for the White House and it cost Moore an administration ally.

"We tried to stomp on the idea of Moore's settlement," Johnson said. "The Dick Morris escapade helped throw some cold water on it." Johnson said another attorney general later told Humphrey, "The damned hookers knew about this deal before I did."

The attorneys general formed a committee to work out a collective position on possible settlement terms. Humphrey was a participant.

After the Chicago meeting, the Moore-Scruggs proposal was sharply criticized by critics in the public health community and in Congress, where it was thought to be entirely too favorable to the tobacco industry. Nonetheless, negotiations with the industry, once viewed as impossible, continued.

At a December 1996 meeting of the National Association of Attorneys General in Florida, Humphrey called attention to the shortcomings of the proposed settlement. He urged alternatives that focused more on public health issues and that tightened the financial pain on the industry. His suggestions were greeted with displeasure by Moore and others. Grant Woods, the Arizona attorney general with whom Humphrey had a particularly close relationship, walked out, angered by Humphrey's criticism of settlement attempts. Humphrey's relationship with his colleagues was deteriorating.

"It was getting testy," said Humphrey. "They had a different perspective on how to approach this, but I wasn't going to give up."

Woods was leading an effort to strike a second, broader settlement with the Liggett Group. More than 20 states had filed Medicaid lawsuits by this time and LeBow was ready to deal again to save his company's financial skin.

On March 20, 1997, LeBow signed an agreement with 22 states, including Minnesota. Terms included an acknowledgment that smoking was addictive, a new warning on cigarette packs that said smoking caused cancer, a pledge to provide assistance in state Medicaid cases, and release of confidential documents, including files containing information from other cigarette manufacturers. Liggett also said it would stop any marketing techniques aimed at underage smokers. But Humphrey remained cautious. He was the last attorney general to sign the settlement papers.

"This is a one-time deal that absolutely will not be available to the other tobacco companies," Humphrey said from Washington, when the second Liggett agreement was announced.

But Humphrey was unaware of what was transpiring behind the scenes. By April 1997, talks between the attorneys general and the industry were serious again, although absent Humphrey's presence or, even, his knowledge. On Friday, April 11, Humphrey received a phone call from Christine Gregoire, attorney general for the state of Washington, inviting him to join the talks the following Monday. Gregoire was part of the core group who had kept the door open to the industry.

"We think we've got a major breakthrough here and we want you to be part of it," Humphrey remembered Gregoire saying. Humphrey asked who was involved in the talks and how long they had been going on.

"The tobacco executives are at the table," Gregoire replied. "Skip, you have to get out here. We need you in these meetings."

Humphrey acquiesced, concerned that this was something serious.

"Well, this is interesting," Humphrey thought. "Are we going down the same route? Is this something that's been pre-negotiated? Do they want to bring Humphrey in to seal the deal?

"Frankly, I was already anxious," he later confessed. "But you've got to remember, these were my colleagues professionally. They were my friends on top of that, both Republicans and Democrats. These were people I had great confidence in, even though we hadn't always agreed on all of this."

Humphrey and Ciresi flew to Washington, D.C., for the Monday meeting. But he immediately sensed that the real negotiations were being conducted privately.

"I remember walking into a room, sitting down, seeing some people I knew and a bunch of people I'd never seen before," recalled Humphrey. "I'm asking myself, 'Who are these people? Why are they sitting here? How come they seem to know things are going on? Who invited them?'"

About 20 people were seated at a table, including Humphrey, Ciresi, Moore, and Scruggs, who repeatedly excused himself for periods of time and left the room.

"There was an immediate attempt to isolate us," said Ciresi. "We were treated like pariahs."

"I said a few things. Mike said a few things. We kind of looked at each other and I finally decided I was out of there. I had to go back home," said Humphrey.

Humphrey returned to St. Paul that night to keep other scheduled commitments. Ciresi stayed at the talks and remained troubled by their direction.

Ciresi had spent the day shuttling between meetings at a Doubletree Hotel in suburban Washington, D.C. He sat in one room with the attorneys general and plaintiffs' attorneys. When the industry had an offer to make, the group would move to a larger room at the other end of the hall to hear the terms. Ciresi then noticed another small room where participants for both sides were meeting. It was clear to him that the settlement was being negotiated on the side.

Late Tuesday, Ciresi called Humphrey. "You've got to get out here. Things are moving fast."

At a Holiday Inn near National Airport that evening, Humphrey and Ciresi huddled with Humphrey's senior staff members and Ciresi's colleague Roberta Walburn.

"At that point we were very concerned," Eric Johnson recalled. "We knew—based on Skip's and Mike's earlier participation—that the attorneys general were on the verge of a very, very poor deal."

For Humphrey, the deal breakers were the absence of full FDA regulation on tobacco, an inadequate $300 billion settlement figure, and lack of full disclosure of corporate documents.

But any hopes for a neatly wrapped settlement fell apart Wednesday morning, when the *Wall Street Journal* disclosed the heretofore secret settlement talks. Because of Humphrey's opposition to the proposal, he was immediately suspected of being the story's source, which Humphrey denied.

"Skip was really persona non grata," aide Doug Blanke acknowledged.

News of the talks was a big story in Washington. The media had discovered the location for the settlement talks and ringed the Doubletree Hotel. When Humphrey pulled up in front in a cab, he found a circus and the Minnesota attorney general had to decide what course to follow: to participate, or walk away and—

for the first time—go public with his opposition to the settlement.

He turned to Ciresi. "Mike, you do what you have to do. Mr. Johnson and I are going to Capitol Hill. We've got some folks to talk to, to say we're not in on this."

It was a tough decision for the attorney general to reach. "I'd enjoyed my friendship and professional relationship with these folks. Many had supported me as president of the attorneys general association. But they were obviously resolving matters without our participation."

The Humphrey entourage of six split up. Ciresi, Walburn, and Deputy Attorney General Lee Sheehy went to the Washington law offices of Verner, Lipfert, Bernhard, McPherson & Hand, where the negotiations had been moved, out of the media's spotlight. Johnson, Blanke, and Humphrey headed to Capitol Hill, where Humphrey eventually attended a press conference with Senator Paul Wellstone, a Minnesota Democrat, and several other senators, who also were concerned by the direction of the negotiations. Because of Senate rules, Humphrey could not speak during the press conference, but reporters mobbed him in the Senate press gallery afterward to record his objections to the deal.

It was Humphrey's first public break with his colleagues, and it was ugly. He made one more stab at convincing his colleagues to go slow. At a meeting later that month in Chicago, attended by 24 attorneys general, he argued it was too early to settle. But when Moore asked the group if the talks should proceed, 23 voted yes.

The only negative vote was Humphrey's. He now was viewed as an impediment, willing to squander a potential landmark deal with the industry because its terms weren't to his liking.

Humphrey was on his own. The settlement talks continued.

However, so did Humphrey's warnings. On May 17, Humphrey blasted the settlement during a keynote address before a national conference of the American Lung Association in San Francisco.

"We find ourselves today at a historic moment, perhaps the defining moment for the number-one health issue of our time," Humphrey said. "You are well aware of the ravages of tobacco. Many of you have devoted your lives to changing the way society views this deadly product. You know that tobacco kills more victims than homicides, alcohol, illegal drugs, AIDS, suicides, highway accidents, and fires combined. Today we find ourselves at a critical juncture for deciding whether we defeat this epidemic, or whether we squander the opportunity of our generation, by settling for a false solution."

He told the audience that the rumble they heard rising was that of "the Settlement Train." Humphrey asked, "Is it on the right track? Will it take us to a healthier, smoke-free society? Or will it carry us, once more, to a false solution that guarantees the merchants of death another 25 years of uninterrupted prosperity?

"Make no mistake about it. The answers to those questions depend on people just like you, all over this country. Unless you, and organizations like the American Lung Association, are vigilant and vocal, we may all be run over. With your help, we can ensure that a train of settlement does not become a train of capitulation. If we stand firm, and stand together, we can slow the train down enough to keep it on the right track."

Humphrey had hit his stride. At the conclusion, the audience rose for a standing ovation.

But his harsh comments came with a price. Mike Moore stopped returning phone calls. Other attorneys general and their staffs scoffed, saying Humphrey was crazy to think the states could get more money from the industry.

"There were some real nasty personal shots, and lectures," Eric Johnson recalled. "Occasionally we would get AGs (attorneys general) calling us back after the conference call, not the offending AG, but the other AGs calling to stress how disappointed they were about the personal attacks. But it got pretty ugly. And when that was happening, we just decided to keep Skip off the calls and keep him focused on the message."

Humphrey's staff saw the personal pain Humphrey was feeling from the continued jabs at his opposition to the settlement.

"Although it caused him a great deal of anguish, he just said, 'You know, we're right on this, and we're going to fight until we win,'" Johnson said.

Despite Humphrey's protestations, however, the Settlement Train continued on its way, culminating on June 20, 1997, when a heralded $360 billion tentative agreement was announced in Washington, D.C. (The settlement would eventually grow to

$368.5 billion.) A disappointed Humphrey and his staff watched the press conference announcement on CNN from their offices.

The agreement contained significant concessions by the tobacco industry, including the elimination of outdoor advertising, stronger health warnings on cigarette packs, and additional fines if youth smoking didn't decline over the next 10 years. "In essence, the Marlboro Man will be riding into the sunset on Joe Camel," declared Florida Attorney General Bob Butterworth.

A few hours after the Washington announcement, Humphrey conducted his own press conference. He voiced his ongoing concern that the proposed agreement contained inadequate FDA regulation, limited punitive damage awards, restricted disclosure of industry knowledge of the connection between smoking and health, and had an inadequate cash settlement.

"This fight was supposed to be about lies and cover-ups, but this deal allows lies and cover-ups to live on," said Humphrey. "No other business in America gets that kind of special treatment, and that's outrageous."

Humphrey's adamant position did not sit well with those who negotiated the agreement. During an edition of ABC's *Nightline* later that summer, Arizona Attorney General Grant Woods and Humphrey sparred over the settlement terms. At one point, Woods asked moderator Ted Koppel, "Do we want to do what Attorney General Humphrey wants to do? Do we want to just wait? Do we want to spend years and years in continued litigation while lawyers fight this out? Or do we want to resolve this now?

Nobody else thinks we should wait to try to resolve this matter."

Skip Humphrey, long the consensual politician, found himself out on a limb.

"He was enormously courageous," said Congressman Waxman, whose congressional hearings three years earlier helped frame and define the tobacco industry debate. "I know the other attorneys general were putting a lot of pressure on him to just go along. There was a lot of money at stake. I can imagine that, with his political prospects as governor, it would have been as appealing as it was to these other attorneys general to bring home a lot of money and not have to go to court to get it."

With the support of the likes of Waxman, former Surgeon General C. Everett Koop, and former FDA Commissioner David Kessler, Humphrey and his staff began to light backfires in Washington in the hope of bringing attention to their perceived shortcomings of the agreement.

Humphrey got support from Democratic Senator Edward Kennedy, a strong antismoking voice in the Senate. He retained the lobbying services of Tom Downey, a former congressman from New York who had close ties to Vice President Gore. He consulted with Donna Shalala, head of the Department of Health and Human Services.

By September, Humphrey sensed progress when the Clinton Administration urged that more work be done to fine-tune the proposed settlement, including the granting of full authority for the FDA to regulate cigarettes and other tobacco products.

Clinton also asked for a $1.50 per pack increase in the federal excise tax over the next 10 years.

The tobacco deal wasn't quite dead, but it did become mired in the political backwaters of Congress and failed to gather sufficient support for passage the remainder of the year. Republican-backed attempts to add provisions such as a $50 billion tax credit for the industry to moderate the financial impact of the settlement didn't help either.

As settlement talks rumbled across the landscape, Blue Cross had more than passing interest in Humphrey's role in the negotiations, or lack thereof. Because it was a private company, Blue Cross would not be a party to any settlement ironed out by the attorneys general and sent to Congress for passage.

"We had concerns about how all that would play out," Czajkowski said. "We were comforted by the fact that Skip was staying the line. We would have gone it alone. Having the state with us was very helpful, but we were prepared to go it alone."

But the state and Blue Cross continued to move forward as a team in court, amassing nearly 30 million pages of documents in their search for damning evidence of industry misconduct.

The only diversion of interests between the two plaintiffs was over the issue of settlement with the Liggett Group. Blue Cross, as a private company, was not a party to the agreement between Liggett's LeBow and 20 states. Liggett remained a defendant in the insurer's lawsuit.

Throughout 1997, Congress failed to get its hands around

tobacco legislation that was acceptable to the states, the industry, and the public health community. The euphoria from the June 20 announcement began to fade.

Humphrey's standing among health groups was growing. Privately, some attorneys general were voicing support for his position that the proposed settlement was inadequate. Wisconsin's Jim Doyle was offering Humphrey moral support and Maryland's Joe Curren was raising questions about the national agreement as well. And other health insurers began to examine Blue Cross's participation in the litigation as a potential model, should they ever decide to sue.

Back in Judge Kenneth Fitzpatrick's St. Paul courtroom, tensions were rising. The defense team kept changing faces. Although each defendant had retained a Twin Cities law firm, the national counsel of each remained in actual control. Three different national attorneys appeared at various times before Fitzpatrick representing themselves as lead counsel for the defendants (the first two retired from practice). The last was Peter Bleakley, a Washington, D.C.–based attorney who'd represented Philip Morris for more than a decade. His first appearance before Fitzpatrick came only two months before the scheduled start of trial. The lack of continuity within the defense ranks would affect their performance and relationship with the judge at the most critical stage of the case, the looming trial.

Earlier in the year, Fitzpatrick appointed St. Paul attorney Mark Gehan to act as a special master in the case. As such, Gehan was a officer of the court. His duty was to review industry documents for which attorney-client privilege was claimed, which Fitzpatrick couldn't do because of the workload the case already carried. It was a full-time job for Gehan, and would generate controversy well into the trial. It would also result in landmark decisions regarding exceptions to the privilege claim, when evidence of crime or fraud is found (known as the crime-fraud exemption).

In September, Gehan reported to Fitzpatrick that some 800 Liggett documents should be given to the plaintiffs because the claim of attorney-client privilege was improperly applied. Gehan's detailed findings, however, remained under seal while Fitzpatrick studied the report and recommendation. Gehan, meanwhile, began to review 240,000 additional industry documents for which privilege had been claimed.

As the case passed its third birthday, it was becoming evident that Fitzpatrick's patience with the defense was wearing thin. In November, Fitzpatrick conducted three days of summary judgment hearings where the industry attempted to have the lawsuit dismissed. The judge made it clear that he would not be sympathetic to one of the claims the defense considered critical to its case—that the state benefited financially from the excise taxes it collects on each pack of cigarettes.

The defense contended the excise tax, amounting to $175 million a year in Minnesota, should be used to offset medical costs associated with sick smokers. The plaintiffs maintained that smokers actually paid the tax and that fraudulent conduct by the industry's liability should not be offset by taxes, no matter who paid them.

The trial clock was ticking.

On December 16, 1997, one month before it was scheduled to begin, Fitzpatrick unsealed the September report of Special Master Gehan in which Gehan concluded that tobacco companies used the shield of attorney-client privilege to hide potentially incriminating material from public discovery. Accompanying the report was a scathing rebuke of the industry written by Fitzpatrick.

He accused cigarette manufacturers of "a conspiracy of silence and suppression of scientific research." In an order that would be a foreboding to the industry for the months to come, Fitzpatrick concluded, "The facts and application of the law demand that the light of discovery penetrate to some of the darkest bowels of the tobacco industry, revealing what the industry knew, when it knew it, and if the information was disseminated."

Attention in the tobacco debate was shifting from the nation's Capitol to the heartland. Minnesota was headed to a courthouse showdown with Big Tobacco.

Chapter Two

Jury Selection

lthough Minnesota's tobacco trial wasn't scheduled to begin until late January, 180 Ramsey County residents got a taste of what lay ahead on January 6, 1998, when—responding to the jury summons they'd received in early December—they gathered in a large windowless basement room of the Ramsey County Courthouse. The group had been randomly selected, as all Ramsey County jurors were, from voter registration rosters, Minnesota Department of Motor Vehicles records, and property tax rolls.

Dorothy Hallen,* a 44-year-old cosmetologist, was among them. Hallen was excited at the prospect. She'd always wanted to be on a jury, and her life contained few obstacles at present. Her only concern was social—she was shy around large groups of people she didn't know. She'd expected to be in a room with about 40 to 50 other people, doing a lot of waiting. She wondered

*Hallen and five other jurors agreed, after the trial, to allow their names to be used in this book. The other six jurors remain anonymous.

how many books to bring to pass the time. She wondered if she'd get a case.

On the appointed day, her husband, Chris, dropped her off on Kellogg Boulevard in front of the Ramsey County Courthouse. Once inside the beautiful, art deco–styled building, she was directed downstairs, to the courthouse basement. Hallen was completely unprepared for the sheer numbers of people she found gathered there. Was this normal? Perhaps it was just larger than usual because of the recent New Year's holiday.

"It might have to do with that big tobacco trial that's coming," one man speculated. Hallen was surprised. She knew that the tobacco companies were being sued quite regularly, but she was unaware of a Minnesota lawsuit.

Guards carefully checked people in at the door, directing them to sit at one of 20 cafeteria-style tables that had been set up, facing a podium at the front of the room.

Initially, the subject matter of the trial went unaddressed. As they were checked in, the prospective jurors' identities were stripped away and replaced by numbers. From now on, only a judge and his clerk would know how the names and numbers matched up. Hallen sat down, and read a two-page questionnaire she had been given. Would serving on a trial cause any financial hardship? Did the prospective juror suffer from any mental incapacity that would hamper the ability to make a fair and rational decision after hearing all the evidence?

Hallen pondered each briefly, before answering "no." She was self-employed and worked only two days a week at nursing homes, so there were no employers with whom to contend. She was married, but her stepdaughter was away at school in Michigan, so child care wasn't a factor. Her life was busy, but quiet.

Across the room, Jill Burton also wrote "no" in the boxes indicated. The 37-year-old legal secretary wouldn't face financial hardship—her part time job at the Fredrikson & Byron law firm included reimbursement for jury duty. Her husband worked full time; Burton's four-member family lived comfortably in the St. Paul suburb of Mounds View.

The questionnaires were collected. The jurors waited while they were reviewed.

The court officer came back and dismissed some 30 people.

Presently, Judge Kenneth Fitzpatrick arrived in the jury room in his black-robed judicial garb. He informed the crowd that they had been selected for a trial of great importance, a case brought by the State of Minnesota and Blue Cross and Blue Shield of Minnesota against the nation's tobacco manufacturers. It was a case that might run for three or four months, he said. For their safety, Fitzpatrick told them ominously, they would remain anonymous to everyone involved in the trial—from lawyers, court personnel, and, particularly, the media.

That suited Dorothy Hallen just fine. She didn't know how unusual this procedure was; she'd never really been to court before.

The procedure, in fact, *was* highly unusual, rarely seen outside of Hollywood movies, John Grisham novels, or high-profile criminal trials, like those for O. J. Simpson or Oklahoma bomber Timothy McVeigh. The practice was almost unheard of in civil litigation.

However, Fitzpatrick was adamant about keeping his prospective jurors protected. Some court observers speculated that his decision to keep them anonymous had been inspired by reports that the American Tobacco Company had hired investigators to scour the private lives of prospective jurors in a 1987 Mississippi tobacco trial. However, attorneys involved in the Minnesota trial were told by Fitzpatrick that it stemmed from media conduct during the more recent tobacco trial in Florida, where prospective jurors, before they'd even appeared in court, had been contacted at home by reporters.

Fitzpatrick had the crowd rise, swore them in, and left. Court personnel then distributed a second questionnaire—a 26-page survey that sought information on everything from personal employment history to attitudes toward big business and, in particular, the tobacco industry.

As they turned in the completed forms, each jury candidate was handed a new summons to report back to court on January 20. Until then, they were not to discuss the tobacco trial. They were to avoid all tobacco-related stories in the newspapers, on television or radio. As she waited to catch a bus, Dorothy Hallen, now known only as prospective juror 34, had a feeling that she would be picked. "I think it was just one of those 'this-is-what-is-supposed-to-happen-to-your-life things.'"

She shared that feeling and the day's events with her husband that night. "Well, I suppose I'll have to quit smoking," he joked. He thought her chances of being selected were slim.

Jill Burton wasn't terribly concerned either. Although her prospective juror number—12—was low, she figured no one would want a law firm employee on a jury.

According to Judge Fitzpatrick's strict instructions, the 26-page questionnaires were provided to attorneys for each side with stringent restrictions. Initially, each side was provided with only one copy of each juror's questionnaire, each carefully coded so that they could be easily tracked. The plaintiffs' questionnaires were printed on yellow paper, the defendants' on pink. Under no circumstances could the questionnaires be copied. Nor could they be made available to clients. If Attorney General Hubert H. Humphrey III or Philip Morris' general counsel wanted to peruse them, they were simply out of luck.

When the defense team protested that its 11 parties needed more than just one questionnaire per prospective juror, Fitzpatrick grudgingly provided additional pink copies. The judge ordered the questionnaires kept in a locked office at each party's respective local law firm. Once the final jury was selected, all the other questionnaires were to be returned to the judge. "You'd think we were dealing with original sets of the Constitution," one attorney grumbled.

While attorneys poured over the jury questionnaires, the subjects of their attention would have plenty of trial-related news to avoid during the next two weeks. The media were full of news about the upcoming trial, although few believed it would actually start. After all, lawsuits in Mississippi, Florida, and Texas all had settled—Florida's in the midst of jury selection. But Skip Humphrey was used to standing alone by now—settlement seemed remote.

Appearing before reporters on January 16, Humphrey brushed aside questions regarding settlement. "Our goals are clear and I do not intend to compromise," he said. "The ground rules are different here." He addressed the coming trial in fighting terms. "The line in the snow has been drawn," he declared. "Our case against the tobacco cartel has been called the most powerful case in the country." His "line in the snow" proclamation would be reproduced in headlines across the country.

When the defense team convened its own press briefing three days later, they first had to contend with the unexpected appearance of plaintiffs' attorney Mike Ciresi—who arrived dressed like a fighter pilot in a leather bomber jacket, plaid scarf, and tan pants.

As Philip Morris spokesman Michael York attempted to explain to the attorney that this particular event did not include him, Ciresi sparred: "Don't you want to pick an impartial jury? This is inappropriate the night before the trial." Heads turned, cameras swung around, and reporters grabbed their notebooks and tape recorders and headed toward the confrontation—their original reason for being there all but forgotten.

"You're trying to precondition the press," Ciresi accused. He exited into the hall, with most of the media following in his wake.

Eventually, the briefing resumed and the defense team presented their theory of the case.

"This case is about money," said Philip Morris Associate General Counsel Greg Little. "It's about politics. It's an attempt to use the court system to enter a new era of prohibition. Humphrey's trying to legislate public behavior through the court system. Individuals choose to smoke with an awareness of the health risks involved. Mr. Humphrey is terrified of choice and responsibility. It's an illegal attack on a legal product."

"What's next?" Little asked. "Skiing? Snowmobiles?"

He called the statistical model that the plaintiffs had constructed to calculate actual damages "junk science."

R. J. Reynolds (RJR) Assistant General Counsel Thomas F. McKim noted that the state had collected "more than $2 billion in cigarette excise taxes since 1978." He added that the state had even banned cigarettes at one time, prohibiting their sale for six years in the early 1900s.

They delivered great quotes and sound bites, which under normal circumstances would have been reconstituted into focused stories about the defense's viewpoint. But Ciresi's ambush captured the news coverage.

Ciresi, the bulldog, had set the agenda, keeping his opponents off balance and defensive. The trial was shaping up to be a first-rate legal brawl.

If there was any question that the matter of the *State of Minnesota, et al. v. Philip Morris, et al.* was going to proceed in standard fashion through Ramsey Country's trial courts, it vanished on Tuesday, January 20, the first day of jury selection. In order to accommodate the sheer number of attorneys involved in the case, the proceedings had been moved from Judge Fitzpatrick's small Ramsey County Courthouse venue to a large courtroom on the seventh floor of the Warren E. Burger Federal Courthouse, several blocks away at 300 Robert Street. Inside, visitors had to first pass through metal detectors and endure scrutiny by a crew of federal security guards, many of them retired police officers. Anybody entering the seventh floor courtroom, attorneys included, had to show court-issued credentials.

The media had rented a conference room on the first floor of the courthouse, where a closed-circuit television set would broadcast the trial's proceedings. The defense team had rented a similar venue just down the hall. The plaintiffs' legal team had its trial room on the seventh floor. Uniformed private security guards patrolled the halls, hired specifically for the trial. Fitzpatrick had mentioned several times that those gathered for the trial would be "guests" at the borrowed courthouse. And this affair would be tightly chaperoned.

One reporter, on her way to the seventh floor one morning, found an elevator closer to the media room than the ones in the courthouse lobby, and took it. When she exited, she found her-self in the seventh floor corridor where the judges' chambers were located. She immediately was accosted by a security guard who confiscated her driver's license, despite her attempts to explain an honest mistake. When Fitzpatrick heard of the mishap, he told guards to yank her credentials. A security guard followed her around the courthouse for the better part of a morning until a judicial press liaison officer interceded on her behalf. Paranoia ran rampant.

Once the courtroom was filled, a private security guard laid down the court's rules, which would be repeated almost daily. During proceedings, the doors to the courtroom would be locked; no one would be allowed to enter or exit. There would be no reading of any kind allowed—even while waiting for court to begin. Cell phones were to be turned off; pagers had to be put on vibrate mode. If they weren't, they would be confiscated on the first interruption. A second interruption would result in the owner's expulsion from court. There would be no talking, no whispering, no facial expressions, no paper shuffling, and no sleeping.

The courtroom's "well," in front of the bar, was packed with some 20 attorneys, who filled three conference tables brought in for the trial. A row of seats had also been set up in front of the bar to accommodate so-called "VIPs;" that is, those invited to sit there by the judge himself. It was a highly unusual addition.

While defense attorneys were setting up for the proceedings the day before, Judge Fitzpatrick's law clerk, Michelle Jones, had specifically prohibited them from placing a flip chart on an easel next to the attorney's podium. It was the most logical position, easy for the attorney to write on, and easy for the judge and jury to see. But Jones informed them that it would "block the view of the dignitaries," defense attorney Jack Fribley recalled. "We had no idea who they would be."

The first two rows of benches behind the bar—each row seating 12 to 15 people—were reserved for extra attorneys and other observers from the plaintiffs' and defense teams. The next row was reserved for the media, and the last two rows were set aside for the public.

The 150-person jury *venire*—as it was called—congregated in a courtroom next door. Twenty-five prospective jurors would be brought into Fitzpatrick's courtroom as a group and asked general questions by the judge. Then they would leave, and return individually to answer attorneys' questions, a process known as *voir dire*, the literal French translation being "to see, to say." In this fashion, attorneys hoped to select a panel that could be fair and impartial as it listened to the evidence presented in the case. Whatever other qualities they were looking for in an "ideal" juror would be kept a closely held secret by attorneys and jury consultants for both sides, although Ciresi acknowledged that attorneys would have trouble finding potential jurors who didn't hold any opinions about smoking, pro or con.

For this trial, a jury of 12 would be selected. If any juror dropped out during the course of the trial, the case would be decided by the first six enpaneled. The remaining jurors would then be considered alternates.

At 9:59 A.M., court was gaveled to order and jury selection began. The first group of 25 prospective jurors was led into a courtroom filled with attorneys, jury consultants, reporters, and a few curious members of the public.

Jill Burton, a member of the first group, scanned the room and thought, "Man, there's a lot of attorneys out there." Looking over the tables packed with attorneys, the legal secretary saw not faces, but "a sea of billable hours."

That sea was already a bit stormy. Although defense attorneys had intended to question the panel en masse, they were informed that morning by law clerk Michelle Jones that they could not do so.

"The court changed course without any prior notice," RJR's attorney Robert Weber recalled. "We wanted to see the interaction among the jury, to see what people brought up on their own, and how they reacted to the statements of other jurors. This changed the dynamic."

It wouldn't be the last thing Fitzpatrick would do that week to upset the defense team.

After briefly explaining the issues in the case to the first group, Fitzpatrick asked a few general questions. Did any of the potential jurors know any of the individuals in the case? Did they ever work for the attorney general? Had they ever worked on behalf of any tobacco companies? Did they know any of the attorneys? To make sure, Fitzpatrick recited a list of the law firms and lawyers involved in the case. It included 36 lawyers and 27 firms—12 were local, the rest spanned the country: New York, Cleveland, Los Angeles, Atlanta, Kansas City, Chicago, Washington, D.C., and San Francisco.

"This is a somewhat painful process," Fitzpatrick warned, as he next read the names of some 200 potential witnesses. None appeared to mean anything to the jury panel.

To accommodate the agreed-upon six preemptory strikes for each side, the 12 final jurors would be selected from a field of 24. Defense attorneys Peter Bleakley, David Bernick, and Robert Weber—the lead attorneys for, respectively, Philip Morris, Brown & Williamson (B&W) and RJR—would question jurors for the defense. Ciresi would handle plaintiffs' questions.

They immediately discovered that antismoking sentiment was strong among the prospective jurors.

"Me and my wife both smoke," said the second pool member to be interviewed. "It's just so hard to quit. I would have difficulty putting that aside. I would have difficulty accepting evidence that it is not addictive. It's got me hooked. I mean, I can't get off it. I don't know if I could be fair. I would try and keep an open mind, but I wouldn't want someone like me on the jury." He was excused on the spot.

Jury candidate three voiced similar beliefs. "Anybody that promotes tobacco smoking doesn't rank high on my scale," he said.

He expressed other concerns, including a 15 percent cut in pay (from loss of sales commissions) if he was selected as a juror on such a lengthy trial.

He had three children in college. His wife had just taken a cut in pay. "That's not your problem, it's mine," he acknowledged, "but it is a substantial hardship. It hasn't been a great year for me moneywise. . . . I'm already on the verge of losing one of the vehicles in our household, so it will affect us." However, he promised, "If I'm called, I'll come." By week's end, juror candidate three would be the first juror officially impaneled.

James Livingston, a 25-year-old welder from St. Paul, was also concerned about financial hardship. Although he hadn't indicated a hardship claim on his January 6th questionnaire, he'd since discovered that he would only be paid for two weeks of his jury stint, the amount required by law. After that, he'd be on his own. As it was, he said, he already worked 50 hours a week to make ends meet.

"Would that be a severe hardship for you?" Bleakley asked.

"Yes. I work a lot of overtime," Livingston replied, adding that, even though his wife worked as well, "We have a lot of expenses. We got a new car, you know, car payment and all that, house payment."

"Would you be able to meet your financial obligations?"

"No."

Ciresi's also addressed the hardship question with Livingston.

"After the two weeks, they're not paying anything?"

"That's correct."

"So it's not just the overtime you would lose, but it would be other wages?"

"It would be everything."

Ciresi moved on. Other than the hardship, he appeared to be a good candidate. James Livingston had no preconceived notions about the trial and thought he could be a fair juror. However, while Fitzpatrick considered the hardship issue, Livingston would remain in limbo, neither accepted nor rejected from the panel.

Prospective juror number eight, Terry Zaspel, drew laughs from the courtroom when she confessed to Bleakley that she'd read a newspaper article about the case. "It was a profile of the two main attorneys. You two," she said, indicating Bleakley and Ciresi.

"I hate to ask the next question," Bleakley began.

"Then don't," Ciresi said, chuckling.

"Did anything you read in that article affect your ability to be fair and impartial to the parties in this case?

"No," Zaspel replied.

"Made you like us even better?" Bleakley teased.

"You don't have to answer that," Fitzpatrick said, smiling.

Zaspel, a 52-year-old secretary at 3M, smoked six or seven cigarettes a day. She believed she was addicted, but didn't hold the tobacco companies responsible for her smoking. Nor did she blame them for the death of her father from lung cancer. She believed she could be a fair and impartial juror. To her, jury duty was "an honor."

Jury candidate number nine, David Olson, having talked with his employer after he discovered the potential length of the trial, also faced a hardship issue. The 47-year-old White Bear Lake resident was a single father raising two daughters. A long trial for him would spell financial disaster. Olson's employment contract would only pay him for two weeks of jury duty. He knew that his bank account wasn't deep enough to sustain such a blow to the family's finances.

Curiously, Olson didn't reveal many of those details during questioning. When Bleakley asked him about hardship, he explained that he would have no other income, but let the matter rest there. When Ciresi followed up on the hardship issue, he asked, "Did your employer tell you that he wasn't going to be able to pay you during this period of time."

Said Olson, "He more or less said 'You better get out of it.'"

Like Livingston, Olson's status would remain unclear until the judge decided what to do with him.

There were few other hardships among the remaining jury candidates. For most of four days the jurors were questioned, they responded mainly with concerns about smoking and addiction, teen usage, sick friends, and relatives who smoked. Not all were antitobacco. Some stated that smoking was a matter of personal choice. One candidate said the warning label on each cigarette pack covered it all.

Jill Burton felt her chances of being selected for the jury were slim, following her questioning. "They only asked me a few questions. I was surprised." She told Bleakley that, although both her grandparents had been heavy smokers who'd died of lung cancer, it wouldn't affect her ability to be fair. Ciresi only wanted to know whether her law firm work would hurt her ability to keep an open mind. Burton said it would not.

Other candidates weren't as neutral; although, as *voir dire* progressed, dismissing them became a problem for the defense. James Otis, an assistant grocery store manager, told Bleakley he was "a little prejudiced" against tobacco. "Maybe being a non-smoker, I couldn't keep it equal at the beginning."

Otis disliked the idea of chemicals being added to cigarettes. He told Bleakley he didn't think he could give defendants a fair shake at trial.

"You think. . . . it would be difficult to be fair and impartial to the tobacco companies?" Bleakley asked.

"Yeah," Otis answered.

"And so we don't start out even."

"Correct," said Otis.

Otis repeated those assertions to Ciresi in more detail.

"I have some past family members that have, you know, passed away from lung cancer. . . . it's one of the reasons I quit myself, and I feel pretty strongly against smoking. . . . I feel it would affect my decision."

Ciresi wasn't going to let him go. "Could you put aside those feelings about people who have been smoking, and just deal with the issues as you're instructed to by the court, and the evidence that you hear on those issues, and decide it on that? Could you do that?"

"I think I could be fair in that way," Otis allowed.

Bleakley moved to excuse Otis for cause. Ciresi objected. Fitzpatrick sided with the plaintiffs. Otis would remain a candidate.

Otis was amazed. "I didn't think I could be a fair judge," he said after the trial. "But Ciresi got me to say what he wanted me to say. I was pretty much set against [the tobacco companies] from the start."

Another juror candidate, an associate professor at the University of Minnesota, acknowledged that he'd donated money to antismoking groups for the past decade. He believed cigarette companies marketed cigarettes to children. He told B & W's David Bernick that he believed that smoking was addictive and caused cancer. He would try to be impartial, but couldn't guarantee it.

Bernick moved that the candidate be excused. Ciresi objected. Fitzpatrick kept the juror on the panel. RJR's Weber grew frustrated. "No matter what the jurors said, if the plaintiffs opposed our motions to exclude for cause, we wouldn't win."

Prospective juror 20 was a good example. She had seen a lot of news stories on smoking and was sure tobacco companies believed it was addictive. She'd come from a family of smokers, though six of her eight brothers had since quit. She believed that cigarette advertising should be banned. She didn't think she could be impartial.

Ciresi sought to rehabilitate her, asking, "You can be fair to both parties. . . . can't you?"

"I might be impartial—or biased," she answered, perplexingly.

"Don't you think you can put that aside?"

"I would try to."

"Well," said Ciresi, "we're not asking for a guarantee here, ma'am."

Attorney Bernick moved to excuse the juror for cause. "I think she was very clear in saying she would be biased," he told Fitzpatrick.

Ciresi disagreed. So did Fitzpatrick. Prospective juror 20 stayed on the panel.

Candidate 33, a part-time receptionist at the Minnesota Club, quit smoking 33 years ago and said she had a "somewhat unfavorable" view of the industry. However, she told both Weber and Ciresi, she could be open-minded and impartial. But she did voice a concern: "I'm questioning my ability to adapt to being so confined."

"What, is there some medical problem?" the judge asked.

"It will infringe on my free spirit."

The courtroom broke up, but Weber had missed the response and asked the judge about it after the juror had left the courtroom.

"She's a free spirit," Fitzpatrick replied, dryly.

When that juror ended up among the final 12, Fitzpatrick's

nickname stuck, and she would be referred to as "Free Spirit" for the remainder of the trial.

By the time Dorothy Hallen was called in, she'd been waiting for three stressful days. Not a big fan of the unknown, she worried about being alone on the witness stand. Finally, her number, 34, was called.

"I was so nervous," Dorothy Hallen recalled. "I never expected that many people." Under Weber's careful questioning, Hallen's views unfolded. She acknowledged that she started smoking at 18 and quit about 17 years later. "I quit cold turkey," she said. "It was pretty difficult. It was painful. I won't have a cigarette now because I believe I'd start smoking again. My brother and husband are addicted. It's stronger than a habit."

Nonetheless, she told Weber she would have the patience to hear all the evidence before making a decision in the case. "I've always wanted to serve on a jury," she said. "But it would be a change of my lifestyle. It would be different."

"This has changed all our lifestyles," Fitzpatrick chipped in.

Weber laughed. "It's like that old saying, 'Be careful what you wish for.'"

By noon on Friday, January 23, after 38 interviews, the case had its 24 juror finalists. But as the two sides gathered to select the final 12, the defense team wasn't at all pleased. For one thing, four of the jurors who claimed financial hardship had not been dismissed by Fitzpatrick. He told attorneys in his chambers that he rarely granted hardship exemptions, even if both sides agreed to the dismissal. Although the Minnesota Rules of Court stipulated that jurors could be excused because "their service would be a continuing hardship to them," the decision was ultimately left to the judge. And this judge, for reasons known only to him, didn't see financial hardship as a problem on a case that was expected to last some four to five months.

Bleakley was furious. "The fact that he didn't excuse those people with hardships was outrageous."

The defense filed a motion challenging his hardship standard, but it was ignored. "We deserved a jury that wouldn't be sitting there worrying about paying their bills each day," said Weber. "We could have found a wealth of people who would have been paid or who didn't care."

Even more irritating to the defense team was their perception that Fitzpatrick had declined to excuse prospective jurors who, they felt, had clearly stated that they were biased against the tobacco industry.

Said Bleakley, "It isn't like excusing the ones who'd expressed bias was going to result in delay. We had enough jurors there. In my view, he decided to put biased people on that jury. That was not a good sign."

When the attorneys for both sides exercised their preemptory strikes later that afternoon, their choices weren't particularly surprising. However, by the defense's reckoning, there were more who needed to go.

The jury was set. Six men. Six women. Three smokers. Six ex-smokers plus one who experimented in college. Average citizens. No professionals. No neckties. No suits. No business owners. The once prospective juror numbers were now replaced with new ones.

Juror One had declared that he'd suffer a 15 percent cut in pay, if selected.

Juror Two was James Livingston.

Juror Three was Terry Zaspel.

Juror Four was David Olson

Juror Five was Jill Burton.

Juror Six was Jim Otis. The defense hadn't been able to get rid of him—they'd used up their six strikes on jurors they considered to be worse.

Juror Seven was the nonsmoking sister with the eight brothers, who thought cigarette advertising should be banned. The defense hadn't been able to convince the judge to excuse her either.

Juror Eight was a security guard at Honeywell who'd quit smoking for eight years, but resumed in 1997.

Juror Nine: Free Spirit.

Juror 10 was Dorothy Hallen.

Juror 11, a Hungarian immigrant who worked as an outdoor painter at West Publishing, had no preconceived notions against cigarette manufacturers nor people who smoke. He was a former smoker himself. He could "absolutely" be fair, he told both Ciresi and Weber.

Juror 12 worked for the U.S. government as a lockman, tending boats through river gates. He told Weber that he thought big cor-porations were more deceptive than other businesses, and said he had doubts about his ability to be fair. Weber had moved to dis-miss him as a juror. Ciresi—who had extracted a promise that he would just listen to the evidence with an open mind—objected. The judge had allowed him to remain.

Later that day, the defense made its first direct challenge to Fitzpatrick's stewardship over the trial. Claiming the jury pool was "infected with bias," the defense asked Fitzpatrick to dismiss the entire pool and start the jury selection process over again. Fitzpatrick made no reference to the filing at the end of the day's session, and instead announced that opening arguments would begin the following Monday.

Ciresi and his team had no objections whatsoever to the 12 seated jurors.

Tobacco's jury of its peers was ready to begin its duty at the Ramsey County rate of $30 a day. For the next four months, Dorothy Hallen would have a front-row seat to watch a historic legal battle played out on behalf of her and her 11 new friends. She worried about having enough good clothes to wear to court.

David Olson and James Livingston worried about where their next paychecks would come from.

Life would be different.

Chapter Three

Team Ciresi

When the *National Law Journal* named Michael Vincent Ciresi one of the "100 Most Influential Lawyers in America" in 1997, the magazine hailed him as "one of the most feared and successful trial attorneys in the United States." The Minnesota Tobacco Trial, the biggest in his career, gave Ciresi four months to live up to that billing.

At age 51, Ciresi showed no signs of resting on his press clippings. For nearly four years, he'd been laying the groundwork for this trial, battling more than two dozen law firms hired by the tobacco industry to fight the fraud and antitrust allegations brought on behalf of the state of Minnesota and Blue Cross and Blue Shield of Minnesota.

His trial strategy was to overwhelm the tobacco industry with its own documents that demonstrated what executives, lawyers, and scientists knew about addiction and disease—but failed to tell the public. It wouldn't be the first time Ciresi employed such an approach. He'd perfected the document case against other corporations in other industries over the last 15 years.

Cocksure and nimble-footed, Ciresi was not one to back down from a fight. His instincts told him the tobacco industry was vulnerable, weakened by disclosure of long-held secrets, by inconsistencies in public comments versus private knowledge.

At Ciresi's side was law partner Roberta Walburn, his teammate on large, complex cases since 1985, when she first joined Robins, Kaplan, Miller, & Ciresi. Though of like minds, the two were a contrasting duo. Walburn was tall and lean; Ciresi was short and stocky. Walburn's hair was spiked; Ciresi was balding. She was stoic; he was theatrical. But Walburn was equally convinced in her understated manner that the case against the tobacco industry was strong. Ciresi and Walburn made a formidable team.

Ciresi came from blue-collar roots, growing up near St. Paul's Como Park. The youngest of three children, he learned about self-reliance early on. His mother, Selena, died after a long illness while Ciresi was in junior high school. His father, Sam, owned a neighborhood grocery store, and later ran a White Bear Lake liquor store, where Ciresi worked weekends and summers while in college and law school. Ciresi called his father, "tough, but encouraging." Ciresi said his father, who left school in seventh grade to peddle fruit door to door, was a strong family man and believed firmly in the value of education.

As he grew older, Ciresi seldom played by the conventional rules. At 5 feet, 8 inches, and 200 pounds, Ciresi didn't fit the image of a linebacker, even at a small college like the University of St. Thomas, which he attended. But Ciresi was too tough to quit and was starting linebacker his senior year.

He glided through his first year at the University of Minnesota Law School, then realized he needed to buckle down. After his second year, he obtained a summer clerk job at the Robins firm and learned the risk-reward for hard work. Firm founder Solly Robins hired Ciresi right out of law school in 1971. But not everyone in the then-30 lawyer firm took a shine to the self-confident young attorney. He didn't make partner the first year he was eligible for it because of a feud with a senior partner. Ciresi nearly quit the firm but was persuaded to stay by his mentor, Robins, and he became a partner the next year.

The Robins firm seemed to fit Ciresi's scrappy and independent personality. It was founded in 1938 by Solly Robins, who liked the notion of representing the little client against big business. He specialized in personal-injury lawsuits, including workers' compensation claims, and represented unions.

As the firm grew, it was more entrepreneurial and less adverse to risk than the large, white-shoe firms that dominated the Twin Cities legal scene. At any given time, 30 percent of its cases involved contingency-fee arrangements.

Both Ciresi and the firm prospered as high-profile clients acquired headline status. Armed with its own team of investigators and a sophisticated software system to organize thousands of pieces of evidence, the Robins firm exploded onto the national legal landscape.

In 1985, *Time* magazine called the firm and its lawyers the "Kings of Catastrophe," recounting its involvement in the 1976 collapse of the Teton Dam in Idaho, the MGM Grand Hotel fire in Las Vegas in 1980, the skyway collapse at the Kansas City Hyatt Regency Hotel in 1981, and a $38 million settlement for 198 users of the Dalkon Shield IUD in 1984.

By the start of the tobacco trial, the Robins firm numbered 230 attorneys and Ciresi was chairman of its executive committee.

"It's not a country club," Ciresi told the Minneapolis *Star Tribune* in 1997. "People will tell you what they think. Not everybody likes that and some will decide this is not for me."

Ciresi's rise to national prominence began in the early 1980s with the Dalkon Shield case. Working with Dale Larson, then a name partner, Ciresi doggedly pursued the A. H. Robins Company with claims that company officials knew of defects in the product and hid that knowledge.

One of their bigger breaks in the case came when Ciresi deposed a former A. H. Robins attorney who had been in charge of the Dalkon Shield litigation. Under routine questioning, the attorney admitted that he had destroyed incriminating corporate documents under directions by a top executive, except for one set —his own—which he then produced. And in that set was a memo showing that A. H. Robins concealed vital information from the Food and Drug Administration that would have resulted in greater testing of the IUD before it entered the marketplace.

Within two months of that July 1984 deposition, A. H. Robins agreed to the $38 million settlement.

In 1985, Ciresi and his firm represented the government of India's claims against Union Carbide Corporation following the deadly gas leak in Bhopal, which killed 2,000 and injured 200,000 more. Ciresi battled against dozens of plaintiffs' attorneys in the United States, including the likes of Melvin Belli and F. Lee Bailey, scurrying at the same time to file claims for individual victims of the disaster.

The case eventually was transferred to India. But, partly as a result of a battle over representation, the stalemate between Union Carbide and the Indian government lingered for more than two years before Union Carbide agreed in early 1988 to pay $470 million to the government for victims and survivors of the gas leak. Ciresi called the delay in resolution of the case one of his career disappointments.

Ciresi's experience with high-profile cases gave Ciresi time and opportunity to hone his courtroom demeanor. He had the ability to dominate a courtroom, alternately coaxing a friendly witness and badgering a hostile one. Peering over his half glasses, Ciresi's withering cross-examination could intimidate even the strongest defense witnesses. He could take his questioning down several different routes and then tie it all up in one complete package for the jury's understanding.

But, without question, his favorite tactic consisted of confronting a witness with a memo or document that flatly contradicted, or raised strong doubts, about public positions taken by an opponent. In the tobacco case, the tobacco industry had been forced by Ciresi and his team to produce nearly 30 million pages of documents for review.

Ciresi was prepared to go toe-to-toe with the industry's best scientists, experts, and executives in a trial expected to last all winter and probably drag into the Minnesota spring. His stamina and concentration were unmatched in a courtroom full of top-line litigators.

But, above all else, Ciresi was not in court to make friends. "Come and get me," Ciresi seemed to say to the tobacco industry's best and brightest attorneys during three-and-one-half years of pretrial jousting. "Give me your best shot."

In a 1988 story in the *New York Times*, Minneapolis attorney Michael Berens complained about Ciresi's aggressive courtroom behavior. Berens had been opposite Ciresi on several Dalkon Shield and Copper 7 IUD cases.

"Smirks, histrionics, visible demonstrations of incredulity at what an opposing witness might be saying and apparent disrespect for opposing attorneys—as well as his ability to browbeat and intimidate witnesses—are all part of his strategy to create an atmosphere of tension and combativeness in a courtroom," Berens said at the time.

Ten years later, Beren's assessment of Ciresi was more reflective.

"The thing with Mike is he always beats the guy who gets annoyed by all of this. He gets them off their game."

Once Ciresi put on his game face, there was no crack to be found. His demeanor was singularly focused. His confidence was gut sure. If he ever had misgivings, they were not publicly shared.

For the 46-year-old Walburn, the tobacco case was a paramount trial of her already bright career. The daughter of a high school teacher and an accountant in Buffalo, New York, Walburn was a late-blooming attorney. She spent the first nine years of her professional life as a newspaper reporter, working first in her hometown of Buffalo, New York, before moving to Minnesota in 1977 as a reporter for the then-*Minneapolis Tribune*. She entered the University of Minnesota Law School in the fall of 1980, still working part time at the newspaper, and graduated in the spring of 1983.

From law school, Walburn took a clerk's position with U.S. District Court Judge Miles Lord where she learned from a master about the misdeeds of corporate America. Lord was a rebel judge and was handling Dalkon Shield cases when Walburn reported to his chambers. Ciresi was representing Dalkon Shield plaintiffs at the time and appeared frequently before Lord.

With Walburn in tow, Lord traveled to the headquarters of IUD manufacturer A. H. Robins in Richmond, Virginia, to supervise document discovery and oversee the depositions of top corporate executives. Walburn learned firsthand about the ways in which product defects could be hidden from an unsuspecting public.

Walburn joined Robins, Kaplan, Miller & Ciresi in January

1985, impressed with what she saw of Ciresi during the Dalkon Shield cases in Lord's courtroom. "It was a larger firm and could bring more resources on behalf of the plaintiff," Walburn said. "I liked the sheer talent and approach to litigation, which I would characterize as aggressive." Ciresi similarily had been impressed by Walburn's handling of the Dalkon Shield case for Lord.

Walburn almost immediately became attached to Ciresi as their courtroom successes started to assume parallel paths. One month after she started as a $35,000-a-year rookie attorney, Walburn was on her way to India with Ciresi and Bruce Finzen, to represent the government of India on behalf of the Bhopal victims. Walburn went directly to the big leagues.

By 1988, the India case wound down, and Walburn and Ciresi turned to another defective interuterine device, the Copper 7 IUD. They won an $8.75 million jury award for a Minnesota woman from G. D. Searle & Company and enhanced their credentials as corporate dragonslayers. When another Copper 7 case settled on the eve of trial in 1989, Walburn and Ciresi started eyeing the tobacco industry, which had nearly lost its first case a year earlier in New Jersey.

Their vision came while on a hillside in the heart of California wine country. Ciresi, Walburn, and Ciresi's wife and legal assistant, Ann, had just finished a West Coast visit to wrap up Copper 7–related matters.

"We were just sitting on a hill in the Napa Valley contemplating our future," recalled Ciresi. There, they concluded, the tobacco industry's conduct represented the "greatest abuse of power in the legal world."

"We wanted to go where no one had ever gone before," said Walburn.

The two lawyers contemplated how they could effectively take on the tobacco industry. Ciresi recalled of their early discussions on the issue: "You weren't going to do it with individual smokers. It had to be a company. It had to be a state. We started looking at health care costs."

But they put the issue aside for a few years, as other cases came before them, and Walburn took a leave of absence from the firm to work on Capitol Hill drafting legislation for Minnesota Senator Paul Wellstone.

Ciresi, meanwhile successfully represented Minneapolis-based Honeywell in a patent infringement case against Japanese camera maker Minolta over rights to an auto-focus lens. A jury awarded Honeywell $96.3 million in February 1992, and Minolta eventually agreed to pay Honeywell $127.5 million. Ciresi pursued other auto-focus camera manufacturers on behalf of Honeywell and negotiated for an additional $370 million by August 1993.

By then, Walburn was back in Minneapolis working for Robins. She and Ciresi began researching possible strategies for taking on the tobacco industry.

They surveyed consumer fraud and antitrust laws and took their theories to the attorney general's office, which had similar interests. By the spring of 1994, the outline of a possible lawsuit began to take shape.

Ciresi and Walburn knew the case would be a flat-out war with the potential for plenty of casualties and tons of expenses. They knew Big Tobacco would fight tenaciously to protect its business. They also knew that Robins, Kaplan, Miller & Ciresi relished high-stakes litigation if the risk-reward ratio made sense. Ciresi's partners felt it made sense in this case. Big sense.

Ciresi began recruiting his tobacco team in the spring and summer of 1994.

"This will be very, very intense. This will be beyond anything we've done in the past," Ciresi told the team. But Ciresi's flair for the dramatic also revealed a shade of unnecessary paranoia. "They'll stop at nothing," he said of the industry's conduct. "If there is anything in your background that you don't want published, then don't get involved." Ciresi later acknowledged that he never saw any evidence that the personal lives of any of the tobacco team were investigated.

Thomas Hamlin was on the team from the start. He was trained in the intricacies of complex litigation and was considered thorough and cerebral by Ciresi. Hamlin and Ciresi had worked together on the Honeywell-Minolta patent infringement. For the tobacco case, Hamlin was assigned to help build the financial damage model for the state and Blue Cross, one of the most detailed and essential elements of the case. The model was intended to be the most sophisticated of its type used in tobacco litigation to date.

Hamlin, 51, had the compact, trim look of an athlete. He received his law degree from the University of North Dakota, where he graduated with honors. Hamlin had extensive experience in patent infringement litigation, beyond the Honeywell case. With a full head of distinctive silver-gray hair and wire-rim glasses, Hamlin also had an academic's presence, reflecting his prior position on the faculty of the University of Minnesota Law School.

Susan Richard Nelson, 45, was recruited to assist the state and Blue Cross with discovery requests from the defendants. Her practice was in automotive and pharmaceutical product liability. She also helped develop medical testimony for the case. Nelson was another highly motivated Robins, Kaplan attorney, graduating with honors from both Oberlin College and the University of Pittsburgh Law School.

Tara Sutton, at 30, was the youngest member of the team. Tall and soft-spoken, Sutton specialized in civil litigation and had joined the firm right out of the University of Iowa Law School in 1992. Sutton was on the tobacco team from the start as well and wrote pretrial briefs. She was Ciresi's in-court document coordinator for the trial.

Walburn, who received her undergraduate degree at the University of Michigan, was intimately involved with nearly all aspects of the case. For the trial she also focused on child-marketing issues.

"I wanted to make sure all the lawyers went into this with their eyes open," said Ciresi. "I knew what would be required to beat these people. I told them to expect to work seven days a week, 18 hours a day. I said there won't be many vacations and the industry will come at us with a lot of money."

Richard Gill was the last Robins attorney to join the trial team. "I wanted Dick in the courtroom with me," Ciresi said.

Ciresi had asked Gill if he was interested in the case during a round of golf in 1996. "Yeah, sure. It's a landmark case," Gill replied. But first Gill had to pare down his product-liability, personal-injury and insurance caseload. By Labor Day of 1997, Gill was one of the group, focusing on the antitrust aspects of the case.

Gill and Ciresi had a long professional and personal relationship dating back to their days as classmates and football teammates at St. Thomas. The six-foot Gill played in both the offensive and defensive backfield; Ciresi was a linebacker.

"Ciresi was an extremely intuitive, aggressive, combative player," said Gill, using terms that described his partner's courtroom approach. "He played well beyond his size."

The son of a Illinois state court judge in Chicago, Gill also attended law school with Ciresi at Minnesota. After graduation in 1971, Gill went to work for Attorney General Warren Spannaus while Ciresi joined the Robins firm. Gill was in private practice in 1984 when Ciresi persuaded him to move over to Robins.

"You're working at the MIAC level," said Ciresi, referring to the athletic conference of which St. Thomas was a member. "You're not going to be in a situation where there are huge chips on the line."

Gill, like Ciresi, was a litigator and lead counsel in more than 250 cases that he had tried or settled. He was assigned to cover the antitrust aspects of the tobacco case. The tobacco trial would be a new experience for Gill because he wouldn't be in the first chair when testimony began. But, Gill said, the demands of the case required one lead attorney with nearly "dictatorial authority" to make the strategic decisions. That was Ciresi.

The adjunct member of the tobacco team was Bruce Finzen. A member of the Robins firm since 1974, Finzen and Ciresi had two decades of work experience together, including the Bhopal case.

Finzen, 50, specialized in mass tort litigation, personal-injury cases, and product-liability law. Like most of the trial team, Finzen had strong Midwestern roots. A graduate of Mankato High School in southern Minnesota, Finzen majored in history and psychology at the University of Minnesota and earned a law degree from the University of Kansas School of Law, where he was editor of the *Kansas Law Review*.

"Mike's a tremendous visionary," Finzen said of his years with Ciresi. "He has the ability to see well into the future and set courses and decide what to do at each turn."

In the months before the trial, Finzen worked with jury consultants to draft the questionnaire filled out by 180 potential jurors to weigh their attitudes on a broad range of topics, including their feelings about punitive damages, the legal system, and the cigarette industry.

During jury selection, Finzen sat with Ciresi at the plaintiffs' table and offered background and ranked the individual candidates during their interviews. Then Finzen departed the courtroom. But his role in the case was far from finished.

Like Ciresi and Walburn, the hand-picked trial team was driven, focused, and disciplined. Another half-dozen attorneys from the Robins firm worked behind the scenes, writing briefs, reviewing testimony, sorting documents, traveling across the country to conduct depositions, and helping prepare witnesses for the plaintiffs. They included Corey Gordon, Gary Wilson, Martha Wivell, Howard Orenstein, Dan O'Fallon, and Vince Moccio.

Ciresi's team wasn't shy in the courtroom. It was relentless and direct, which frustrated defense attorneys not used to fighting with plaintiffs' attorneys who had the resources and depth of experience as this group.

In the three-and-one-half years leading up to the trial, Walburn, Ciresi, and the rest of the tobacco team engaged in one of the broadest discovery efforts in the history of corporate litigation. When the industry argued and appealed decisions to produce more documents, the Ciresi team was unyielding in its demands.

To avoid distractions during the coming months, Ciresi had the trial team sequestered, in a fashion, at the St. Paul Hotel, a downtown landmark and elegant old hotel with a chandeliered lobby, wood-paneled bar, and an acclaimed restaurant, The St. Paul

Grille. Their home was the 11th floor, which also doubled as their trial headquarters. Ciresi had booked the rooms a year in advance to avoid any last minute scrambling for space. Planning and details were Ciresi hallmarks.

Off-duty St. Paul police officers provided around-the-clock security for the floor on which Ciresi had set up the firm's top-secret trial management system. Outsiders were not allowed to visit.

"It was like being in a plush bunker where there was a great restaurant," said Gill. It was a singular existence, but one Ciresi felt necessary because of the stakes at play. "You've got to be totally focused in a case like this," he said.

Ciresi's strategy going into the trial was simple: Present a forceful outline of the case for the jury in his opening statement, present the evidence, and bring it full circle in the end with the closing argument.

"Here's what we're going to show you. This is what the evidence is going to be," Ciresi said of his game plan. "During the process of the case, you show them the evidence and then at the end you remind them that you told them what you were going to show them.

"A trial is a series of impressions."

By the time of the trial, Ciresi's law firm, Robins, Kaplan, Miller & Ciresi had committed well in excess of $10 million in out-of-pocket costs for the case. If Ciresi lost, the firm would get none of it back.

Ciresi and his team were eager to get started. Rarely prone to understatement, the feisty son of a St. Paul grocer was ready to step in the ring. The Minnesota tobacco case was not merely a potentially historic trial; to Ciresi it was "one of the most important civil cases ever tried."

Chapter Four

Opening Arguments, Leadoff Witnesses

On the morning of Monday, January 26, Minnesota Attorney General Hubert H. Humphrey III walked briskly up to St. Paul's Warren E. Burger Federal Courthouse where the stage was set for opening arguments in the Minnesota Tobacco Trial. Dressed in a heavy black topcoat and black Borsalino hat, he looked like a diminutive Clint Eastwood arriving to do battle with bad guys.

Television camera crews surrounded Humphrey and Andy Czajkowski, the neatly dressed chief executive of Blue Cross and Blue Shield of Minnesota. The attorney general declared that Minnesota, unlike states that had settled with Big Tobacco, would not be bought off. Minnesota was ready to fight. Settlement would only be possible, Humphrey said, if the industry made some serious concessions.

Seven floors above the Robert Street entrance to the courthouse, in his rented "war-room," Michael Ciresi made final preparations for his opening statement. Outside, the halls were filled with wandering attorneys, reporters, and stock analysts making one last cell phone check-in with their respective offices before they were locked into Judge Fitzpatrick's courtroom.

By 9:00 A.M., the courtroom was filled. Of special interest were the two female occupants of the unusual VIP section the judge had established in front of the bar. They turned out to be his wife, Mary Ann, and his sister. Humphrey, Czajkowski, and U.S. Attorney David Lillehaug sat in the front row of the section reserved for the plaintiffs' observers. The defense team's rows were packed with attorneys from tobacco companies and their law firms, as well as several jury consultants. Filling the media rows were reporters from the *Washington Post*, *Los Angeles Times*, *Wall Street Journal*, *USA Today*, CNN, and a full complement of local Twin Cities media.

Sprinkled through the rows reserved for the public were several high-profile Wall Street tobacco analysts, including Sanford C. Bernstein & Company's Gary Black and Martin Feldman from Salomon Smith Barney. Black, a tall man who dressed more like a cowboy than a stock analyst, tried to dodge reporters' questions that day. He'd be less reticent in the future, and would assume a major role in leaking settlement information to the media as the trial progressed.

The courtroom was hot-wired with high-end technology: real-time transcripts that appeared on laptop computers on the attorneys' tables, computerized document-retrieval systems, electronic highlighters, sophisticated projection equipment, and closed circuit television cameras to transmit the proceedings into the media and defense conference rooms on the first floor.

Over the weekend, Fitzpatrick had ruled that the defense could not argue that the early death of a smoker from a smoking-related disease saved money for society in terms of such expenditures as nursing home costs and retirement benefits. He called this so-called "death benefit" theory (as the plaintiffs had quickly dubbed it) "abhorrent and horrendously contrary to public policy that a party should, in whatever guise, claim that the killing of individuals should be used as a defense or as a factor in mitigating damages."

If tobacco attorneys had any doubts about the battle before them or the mindset of the judge in front of the courtroom, they were quickly being erased.

Before opening statements began, Fitzpatrick had a few particularly unpleasant words for the defendants. Fitzpatrick informed the courtroom that the defendants—with the exception of Liggett—had filed a motion to strike the jury panel. The judge reiterated that each juror had promised to be fair and open-minded about the evidence presented.

"Now the fact that some of the jurors viewed with some skepticism the defendants' position that cigarettes are not addictive and that smoking does not cause disease is not a sufficient basis to strike the . . . . jurors for cause," Judge Fitzpatrick continued. "It would certainly not be grounds for removal of a juror if a juror were skeptical when a litigant in a proceeding argued a position that the sun sets in the east."

Members of the defense team looked at each other with concern. Comparing their case to the sun setting in the east left little doubt about how the judge felt about their arguments.

Lorillard Tobacco's local defense counsel David Martin was so stunned that he checked his real-time transcript monitor to reread the remarks. "Even then, I thought the court reporter had put it down wrong. It was absolutely gratuitous."

Fitzpatrick went on to scold defense attorneys for not using their preemptory strikes to remove some of the allegedly biased jurors (which they had), then ruled tersely, "The motion. . . to strike the jury is denied."

The jurors themselves sat in a cramped, stuffy room just behind the courtroom. "If that wasn't the kick," Jill Burton recalled thinking when she saw the room. The tiny quarters featured a table crammed with 10 chairs, and a couch to hold the overflow. "There were women's and men's bathrooms, a microwave, a coffeemaker and a little refrigerator. The end. Two people couldn't go sideways," Burton said.

Presently, law clerk Michelle Jones arrived and laid down some rules for the jury. At first the instructions were familiar: don't talk about the case; don't read, listen, or watch any media reports of the case. Then the instructions got curious. Jurors couldn't address each other by name, only by juror number. "What if we get sick?" Burton asked. She recalled Jones replying, "Well, you'd better be in the hospital or in the emergency room. If you're not in the hospital or the emergency room, you're in the jury chair." Burton said Jones also told them, "If you don't show up [for jury duty], we'll send sheriffs out to arrest you."

Jurors were also told that they couldn't make or receive phone calls during their days in court. The only way they could be reached in case of an emergency was through Jones' pager.

The jurors filed in, some warily eyeing the capacity crowd that awaited them in the courtroom.

"It was fun to see all those faces—Humphrey was there that day," Dorothy Hallen recalled, "but it was hard to have everyone just staring at us. I didn't know if I should even scratch my nose."

Physically, Hallen noted, many of the attorneys were pretty small: "I wondered if that was a lawyer thing."

The setup had changed dramatically since their appearance a week earlier. A large projection screen had been set up in a corner, angled to allow viewing by both the jury and the court gallery. In addition, two large television monitors had been placed on either side of the jury box. Clearly, during this trial, there would be more to watch than attorneys or live witnesses.

It was finally Michael Ciresi's moment to begin the most intense case of his life. Dressed in a dark blue, pinstriped suit, he approached the podium to begin his opening statement—to present an overview of the case to jurors. He began his presentation in deliberate, measured sentences, reading from a notebook in front of him. Usually a tenacious and spirited litigator, Ciresi chose this day to forego theatrics or emotion.

"This case began in August 1994, shortly after the chief executive officers of the major U.S. tobacco companies testified under oath in Congress that cigarette smoking was not addictive," Ciresi began. "To this day all of the defendants, save one—Liggett—still publicly deny that cigarette smoking is addictive and causes disease. These public statements were and are false, and the evidence in this case will prove that.

"Over the last three-and-one-half years we have obtained, through the legal process, millions of the defendants' secret documents which had never before seen the light of day. These documents will bring to life the decades-long illegal conduct of the defendants through their own written words; yet in this courtroom you will see these defendants deny and try to explain away those words."

Warming up to his subject, Ciresi next turned to some statistics.

"Every year, 3,000 of our youth start smoking. Every year over 400,000 individuals die from smoking-related diseases—a staggering number—that is, one out of every six deaths in the United States. In Minnesota alone, smoking causes more than 6,000 deaths a year from diseases, including lung cancer, heart disease, emphysema, and bronchitis. This human carnage, of which only the dead, the afflicted, and their families feel the full personal consequences, inflicts an enormous economic burden of health care costs on the state of Minnesota and Blue Cross and Blue Shield.

"The defendants in this case ensured a captive market for this inevitable march of death and disease by intentionally attracting children and adolescents and addicting them to a product which kills and causes disease when used as intended. The defendants have long known the addictive nature of nicotine which thwarts and compromises the smoker's abilities to exercise his or her desire and choice to quit."

Ciresi's next statement would be embedded in the lead paragraph of almost every news story filed about his opening arguments: "The evidence will show that three starkly descriptive words—deceit, exploitation, and greed—have been and are indeed today the guiding beacons which have directed the cigarette industry in over four decades of intentional conspiratorial and unlawful conduct. The exposure of that conduct in this trial will be based not on speculation, conjecture, or opinion by outsiders, but will be disclosed through the defendants' own documents which they have been forced to produce in this litigation.

"The purpose of this lawsuit is to hold the industry accountable, accountable for its own illegal actions. This, the evidence will show, is a case of corporate irresponsibility in which an entire industry, in a half-century-long combination of conspiracy, of willful and intentional wrongdoing, violated the consumer protection and antitrust statutes of the state of Minnesota.

"These defendants," Ciresi said, "falsely promised the American people that they would undertake a special duty to protect the public health and to conduct research and disclose complete information about smoking and health. They further promised America and its public health authorities that they considered this a basic and paramount responsibility of conducting their business, and they asked the public to rely on their integrity and truthfulness. Yet, these same defendants over that half century intentionally chose to engage in a unified campaign of deceit and misrepresentation by suppressing their own knowledge concerning the addictive nature of nicotine and the severe health risks tobacco presents to smokers. They chose to do all that in the name of profit and to preserve their way of doing business."

As Ciresi spoke, the only sound discernible in the silent courtroom was the faint scribbling from reporters rapidly recording his words into their open notepads.

"In short, ladies and gentlemen, the evidence will show that this was an industry which conceived of a strategy of deceit and, through an arrogance of power, promoted and fortified that sanctuary of deceit for the sole purpose of achieving their objective of the continuous recruitment of teenagers to a product which they knew was addictive and fatal. Indeed, you will learn that the industry did not consider its product to be tobacco at all, but rather nicotine, which they intentionally and internally not only called an addictive drug, but secretly manipulated to maintain its addictive power. Yet, except for Liggett, which has finally admitted the addictive nature of nicotine, not one of the defendants, the other defendants in this case, have to this day disclosed all that they know about that drug."

Borrowing the words made famous during Watergate, Ciresi told jurors to focus on "What these defendants knew about the hazards of smoking, when they knew it, and what they did with that information."

With the central premise of his case laid out, Ciresi took the jury back in time, to a meeting in 1953 that ultimately resulted in a document his team planned to use as the cornerstone of their case. The meeting took place on December 15, 1953, at the Plaza Hotel in New York. There, the chief executive officers of five major tobacco manufacturers—Philip Morris, R. J. Reynolds (RJR), The American Tobacco Company, Brown & Williamson (B&W), and Lorillard—met with representatives from Hill & Knowlton, the industry's public relations firm.

"The meeting was called as a result of recently published medical studies linking cigarette smoking with cancer, specifically lung cancer," Ciresi said. "The stock prices of the companies had declined and the chief executive officers wanted to sponsor a public relations campaign which was entirely pro-cigarette and positive in nature."

After listening to the CEOs, Ciresi said, Hill & Knowlton personnel drafted a memorandum about that meeting. "And this is [sic] Hill & Knowlton's words, not mine," Ciresi emphasized, before reading: "'There is only one problem—confidence and how to establish it, public assurance and how to create it, and perhaps a long interim when scientific doubts must remain.'"

"That long interim, ladies and gentlemen, during which the

industry has steadfastly tried to create doubts, has lasted to this day."

The Hill & Knowlton memorandum of that meeting listed some objectives, Ciresi said, ". . . . and I quote: 'The very first problem is to establish some public confidence in the industry's leaders themselves so that the public will believe their assertions of their own interest in the public health . . . . to reassure the public and quiet instinctive fears in this interim when definitive facts for giving complete assurance are still lacking, when scientific doubts must remain, and when new unfavorable information can emerge from some laboratory at any time to act as a bombshell on the whole tobacco industry.'"

The memo continued, dissecting Big Tobacco's problems in coldly dispassionate terms. "In the past, industry has given little twists to the facts of science, to convert them into sales propaganda, without much risk," it stated. "The cigarette industry has indeed been doing this for years. We can therefore readily understand its assumptions that the same techniques will work now in devising propaganda. But it is highly important to note that the deep issues of life and death that are now involved make highly doubtful the question as to whether the familiar techniques can be relied on. The stakes are too large; the penalties for losing could be too great."

The memo explained that cigarette CEOs tended "to assume that agents, like science writers, can be guided and encouraged to disseminate special interpretations of current findings, in ways

that would blame lung cancer on everything else but cigarettes—
or (even better) in ways that would throw doubt on the validity
of statistics showing great increases in lung cancer. If the issue
were merely coughs or sore throats or worse, this might work.
There is serious question as to whether anyone—after due reflection— would consider such a course useful for long-term purpos-
es in the present circumstances."

Hill & Knowlton's solution to these problems was unveiled on
January 4, 1954, Ciresi said, in the form of a full-page newspaper
advertisement that ran in every U.S. city with a population over
50,000. Ciresi nodded to attorney Tara Sutton, and a copy of the
statement was thrown up on the courtroom projection screens
and television monitors, while a large poster-board reproduction
was placed directly in front of the jury box.

"In this Frank Statement. . . .the industry voluntarily undertook a special responsibility and duty to the people of America."
Ciresi then read from the document itself: "We accept an interest in people's health as a basic responsibility, paramount to every
other consideration in our business. Two: We believe the products
we make are not injurious to health. Three: We are pledging aid
and assistance to the research effort in all phases," and he emphasized, "all phases—of tobacco use and health. This joint financial
aid will of course be in addition to what is already being contributed by individual companies."

In silence, the courtroom audience read along with Ciresi the
artfully constructed piece of public relations prose released more

than 40 years earlier. Although the statement had been used by other plaintiffs' attorneys in other venues, it was the first time many in the St. Paul courtroom had ever seen the statement. It would, by no means, be the last. In the weeks to come, Ciresi and his team would hang this albatross around the neck of nearly every tobacco industry–related witness who would take the stand. Its weight would drag many of them down.

For Ciresi, it was the key: "As the trial unfolds, ladies and gentlemen, you will see these defendants, through deceit, exploitation, and greed, did deliberately embark on the course of conduct that was set by Hill & Knowlton, the one that they should not have followed. The industry blamed lung cancer and other fatal diseases on alternative causes. They twisted the facts, and while doing so, steadfastly refused to conduct the type of biological research within their own laboratories which would enable them to answer the life-and-death questions raised by the selling of their product.

"You will see, over the course of years this twisting of the facts led to complete denials until they started talking about 'risk factors'—you'll hear about that during the course of this litigation—but the evidence will show that, constantly, they attempted to undermine the scientific validation that smoking causes serious diseases, and they did it in concert and they did it intentionally. They took this action, this course of action, although they knew it was their legal duty to know what could be known about their product. As an excuse for failing to conduct research, they claimed they had financed those who were competent to conduct such research, claiming that they themselves internally were not competent. You will see from the defendants' own documents that these representations are false and the real reason they didn't undertake appropriate internal research was to preserve their freedom to criticize, undermine, and twist the facts of those who did.

"The publication of the medical studies in the early 1950s concerning cancer and smoking presented a choice to the industry. They had a choice: Should they take the high road and disclose the information they already knew and had proof of in their files, and conduct appropriate biological scientific studies into whether cigarette smoking caused disease, or should they provide a sanctuary for smokers by implying that the charges were not scientifically valid?"

Ciresi said of their decision, "The industry chose darkness while publicly claiming they were pursuing the truth."

As his opening arguments continued, Ciresi unveiled some of the so-called "smoking howitzer" documents culled from the millions of pages of material his team wrested from the tobacco companies in the three-and-a-half years of discovery that preceded the trial.

In 1958, Ciresi said, quoting from an internal British-American Tobacco Company memo, BAT scientists from Great Britain concluded, after a visit to counterparts in the United States, that there was virtual unanimity about the connection between smoking and lung cancer.

"Their words, ladies and gentlemen, not mine," Ciresi noted, as the theme in his presentation emerged. "This is a renegade industry that has placed profits above the health and well-being of its customers. It turned its back on its customers in order to preserve its way of doing business."

Ciresi referred to a "gentleman's agreement" among tobacco company executives not to conduct in-house biological research on animals on the grounds that the results might be incriminating and could undermine their public position on the issue of smoking and disease. He claimed that research was placed under the direction of attorneys so it would remain confidential under the guise of attorney-client privilege. In a 1978 memo cited by Ciresi, the president of Lorillard Tobacco complained that the industry had "abdicated research to the lawyers."

As an example of "the lengths that these defendants will go to, to keep their dark secrets locked within the bowels of the industry," Ciresi put up on courtroom monitors a Philip Morris memorandum his team unearthed in their search for documents.

"At the top you'll see it says, 'Ship all documents to Cologne. Keep in Cologne . . . . These will be destroyed . . . .If important letters and documents have to be sent, please send to home—I will act on them and destroy.'

"This is by a Mr. Osdene, who is the director of research at Philip Morris," Ciresi explained, adding, "And what was going on is that Philip Morris was conducting research in a facility over in

Cologne, Germany, but of course they didn't want any of this information in their files here. It might be subject to discovery in a lawsuit and then people would find out what the companies knew, when they knew it, and what they were doing about it."

With the appropriate combination of glee and disgust, Ciresi unveiled piece after piece of dirty tobacco laundry on the courtroom projection screen, all the while intoning, "Their words, ladies and gentlemen, not mine."

Flushed with luck that the tobacco industry was filled with prolific memo writers, Ciresi quoted Philip Morris scientist William Dunn, also known around the company as "The Nicotine Kid," on his analysis of nicotine's affect on the body. "As with eating and copulation, so it is with smoking," Dunn wrote. "Without nicotine, there would be no smoking." Dunn called the cigarette "among the most awe-inspiring examples of the ingenuity of man."

A 1980 memorandum prepared by an official at the Tobacco Institute, the industry's public relations arm, referred to one of the defense law firms, stating, "Shook, Hardy & Bacon reminds us, I'm told, that the entire matter of addiction is the most potent weapon a prosecuting attorney can have in a lung cancer/cigarette case. We can't defend smoking as 'free choice' if the person was 'addicted.'" Their words, not mine, Ciresi intoned.

As powerful as Ciresi's statement had been to this point, he fired on all cylinders when he came to the subject of youth marketing. "It's no coincidence that Philip Morris is the largest tobacco company in the United States and Marlboro is the number-one cigarette. It rode to that position on the backs of youth," Ciresi said.

He told of internal studies by all the major manufacturers about the smoking habits of teenagers and their brand choices. "Today's teen is tomorrow's potential regular customer," said a 1981 Philip Morris memo cited by Ciresi.

Philip Morris' success in wooing teen smokers was the topic of a 1980 RJR document that stated, "Philip Morris has a total share of 59 percent among 14 to 17 year-old smokers, and . . . .Marlboro has a 52 percent share." Discussing RJR's own efforts, the memo continued, "Hopefully our various planned activities that will be implemented this fall will aid in some way, reducing or correcting these trends."

In a 1973 document, B&W reported that "a smoker in the 16- to 23-year-old age group will soon be three times as important to Kool as a prospect in any other age category."

And Lorillard said of its Newport brand, "The base of our business is the high school student."

Ciresi charged, "They treated America's youth as a commodity who were the source of replacement smokers for those who were able to beat the addiction and quit, and for those who died from diseases caused by smoking."

"This has been a total, deliberate, and sustained course of conduct that has caused damages to the state and Blue Cross and Blue Shield of Minnesota," the attorney said, as he wrapped up.

"It's a case of deceit and exploitation guided by their allegiance to the bottom line. It's not about free choice; it's about the illegal conduct of these defendants."

In two hours Ciresi outlined a dramatic indictment of the industry, the most exhaustive of its kind ever to go to trial. This case would feature no smoking victims taking the witness stand. No grieving relatives of deceased smokers would sit with the plaintiffs' attorneys. This was a case about consumer fraud and conspiracy—and Ciresi believed he had the documents to prove it.

However, something was missing from Ciresi's dramatic opening statement—the specific rationale for asking for $1.77 billion in actual damages to the State of Minnesota and Blue Cross and Blue Shield of Minnesota. Of that, Ciresi had but one sentence, "Those damages will be established through the introduction of a sophisticated and scientifically valid statistical model based upon detailed and extensive health care cost records of the state and Blue Cross."

The defense would seize on that omission during its presentations.

During the 90-minute lunch break, defense attorneys retired to their ground floor conference room where a catered lunch awaited. Team Ciresi got their lunch from Amanda's, across the street from the courthouse, and ate it in the banker's box–laden warroom on the seventh floor.

In the jury room, 12 men and women ate the box lunches that

had been brought in and slowly got to know each other. It didn't take long to break the ice. Seeking some common ground, they quickly found it with Ciresi associate Roberta Walburn.

"Is Marcia Clark driving you crazy?" one of the jurors asked the group. Laughter erupted. Everyone knew what he was talking about, as Walburn, with her hip brunette standup shag haircut, was the only attorney in the courtroom to bear faint resemblance to the O. J. Simpson prosecutor.

"Roberta would turn her chair, fold her arms, and just stare at us, one after another," Hallen explained. "I thought her job was just to sit there and 'read' us."

Thus, the first juror nickname of the trial was coined. More would follow. The jurors also informed law clerk Jones that they were going to be together for too long to refer to each other by number, and quickly introduced themselves by name.

Firing the first defense volley that afternoon would be Peter Bleakley, on behalf of Philip Morris. Bleakley, 61, was almost a decade older than Ciresi—though he hardly looked it—and presented a lean and stylish physical contrast to the plaintiffs' lead attorney. A top product-liability attorney at the prestigious Washington, D.C.–based firm of Arnold & Porter, Bleakley was no stranger to tobacco litigation. In 1989 he had successfully represented Philip Morris in a New Jersey lawsuit brought by the family of deceased smoker Rose Cipollone, a case that gained brief eminence at the time as the first chink in the industry's litigation-proof armor. Cipollone's family won a $400,000 judgment from Liggett & Meyers, but it was overturned on appeal. Philip Morris walked away clean, thanks to Bleakley, who was regarded as one of the company's top outside litigators.

Bleakley, an attractive man with curly salt-and-pepper hair, didn't bother to reintroduce himself before getting straight to his point. "This case before you is about money," he told the Minnesota jurors, just as he had at the Cipollone trial. "What Mr. Ciresi and his clients want you to do at the end of this case is to award money, money for injuries they claim were caused by the defendants' wrongful conduct. What I'm going to tell you this afternoon is that the state and Blue Cross are not going to prove that they suffered any of the injuries they claim they suffered because of the defendants' wrongful conduct.

"Let me make very clear right at the beginning what I am talking about," Bleakley said, as he walked to a large pad of paper sitting on an easel in front of the jurors.

"There are three very specific health care programs involved in this case. The first of those is Medicaid, the second is General Assistance Medical Care, and the third is Blue Cross insurance. And the reason why I'm writing this up here—and I'm going to leave it up here through the opening arguments in this case—is that we're not talking about healthcare costs in general. The state and Blue Cross are seeking recovery under these three very specific programs. . . . and they are not going to prove that they have suffered any increased healthcare costs because of the defendants' conduct."

First, Bleakley had some concessions to make. "The defendants understand that many of you, maybe even most of you, don't like smoking very much, and some of you don't even like cigarette companies very much. We know that some of you may think that cigarette advertising should be banned. There may even be a few among you who think that cigarette sales should be banned." But, Bleakley emphasized, that was not the issue of this case. "You may conclude at the close of this case that there are occasions or instances in which the tobacco companies have behaved foolishly, or badly, or even wrongly. You may conclude that the cigarette companies should have conceded years ago that smoking causes disease. You may have all those views . . .or even stronger ones."

But the issue the jurors needed to decide was whether wrongful conduct by the defendants increased health care costs on the three specific programs, Bleakley said. And the defense was united in the belief that they did not.

"Is the plaintiffs' side going to bring any smokers to testify that they were deceived? They are not," Bleakley said. "Not one.

"How do we know whether [the industry] in fact, deceived anyone?. . . . Keep that question in mind as you listen to the evidence in this case because the plaintiffs are not going to bring in anybody who can testify how many were deceived, how much, when, or to what degree. None of that. It's all going to be experts testifying that they think it happened. . . . You're certainly not going to hear about it from the statistical model that Mr. Ciresi talked about..."

Bleakley quoted from a deposition taken from one of the experts who designed the model, who was asked if he knew whether the plaintiffs would have paid more or less money for health care services if defendants had not committed the wrongs alleged in the complaint.

The answer, Bleakley quoted, "'No, I don't know that.'"

Instead, the attorney said, "We're going to offer evidence that these people were not in fact deceived."

While Ciresi reached back in time to 1953 for his assertions, Bleakley would go back centuries to support his contention that people had long been aware of tobacco's dangers, much as he had done in his opening remarks in the Cipollone trial. He quoted from Christopher Columbus' diary in 1490 in which tobacco-using inhabitants of the island of Espanola told the explorer they "were unable to cease from using it."

Moving ahead a hundred years, Bleakley quoted from England's King James, who wrote a famous treatise called a "Counter Blaste to Tobacco." The monarch stated, "Tobacco is a custom loathsome to the eye, hateful to the nose, harmful to the brain, and dangerous to the lungs."

Bleakley quoted from numerous national articles about the harmful effects of tobacco in the 1940s and 1950s before bringing it home to Minnesotans' own knowledge of the subject.

Bleakley told the jury that citizens of Minnesota had known for years that cigarette smoking was harmful. He said use of the slang words "coffin nails" and "cancer sticks" in reference to cigarettes was common in everyday conversation and had been for some time. He cited a 1935 textbook used in Minnesota schools entitled *Tobacco is a Poison.*

"In 1964, when the Surgeon General's report was issued, 80 percent of Minnesotans believed smoking is hazardous to health. By 1969, that number had gone up to 93 percent. By 1970. . . .that figure was up to 95 percent," Bleakley said, describing that figure as "universal awareness" since "you almost never have more than 95 percent of the people believe anything."

Even Andy Czajkowski, the Blue Cross CEO, said in 1984 that "the debate on smoking is closed," Bleakley informed jurors.

"As a result of this universal awareness in Minnesota and elsewhere, what you're going to learn and many of you probably already know is that millions and millions of Americans have quit smoking, addicted or not," said Bleakley, noting that upwards of 50 million have quit and that there were more ex-smokers than smokers in the country today.

Finally, Bleakley asserted that there was no documented evidence that it cost more to treat the illnesses of a smoker than those of a nonsmoker. And if that's the case, he said, neither the state nor Blue Cross is entitled to any of the $1.77 billion in damages being sought.

"And it doesn't make any difference, ladies and gentlemen, whether you don't like smoking, you don't like tobacco companies, whether you think the tobacco companies behaved badly or foolishly, it doesn't make any difference what you think about any of these issues, because when you go into the jury room to deliberate, the question you're going to be asked is what's the answer to the question? More or no more? And if the answer is no more, no increased health care costs, as I'm suggesting to you the evidence will establish, then you'll come back from the jury room with a verdict against the state and for the defendants."

Bleakley was followed by John Monica, an attorney with the Kansas City firm of Shook, Hardy & Bacon, well known for its long, aggressive defense of the tobacco industry. Monica represented Lorillard Tobacco Company, a relatively small player in the industry, with about 8 percent of the U.S. market. Its best-selling cigarette was Newport. It also manufactured Kent, True, and Old Gold.

In folksy, country-lawyer style, the grey-haired attorney denied that the industry targeted young people and attributed underage smoking to youthful exuberance and the thrill of risk taking. "The issue of advertising to kids is an attempt to inflame passions," he said in his brief opening statement.

Monica disputed the plaintiffs' claim that manufacturers used comic characters such as "Joe Camel" to market cigarettes to children. Monica said cartoon characters had long been used in adult-directed marketing efforts, citing "Speedy Alka Seltzer" and "Mr. Clean" among his examples.

Moving closer to the point, Monica mentioned an old Hamm's beer commercial. "Remember the little bear that was beating on the tom-toms all the time? There is obviously an adult product that used a cartoon-type character to appeal to adults."

The attorney attempted to deflect the particularly damaging Lorillard document Ciresi had used about high school students being the base business for the company's Newport cigarettes.

"This document was written by a man out in the field. His job was to call on stores, to make sure they were properly stocked. He gave the president of the company his views." Monica said that formal company marketing documents targeted smokers 21 through 44.

"We sold a legal product, we advertised a legal product, we put the warnings on our brands, on our packs, and on our advertising. We complied with the rules," Monica concluded. "Even though that was the understanding, we're now being asked to pay two billion dollars."

The first day of opening arguments concluded. As television reporters did their standup reports outside of the courtroom, Dorothy Hallen drove home and thought about her first day at the trial for which she had wished.

"It really was a blur," she recalled. "I think both sides got me very excited about the case. It was so lawyerly—getting up and expounding on what was going to happen. But by the afternoon, I kind of panicked. The stress and excitement had worn off and I was really tired."

Hallen stopped at her local drug store. "I asked the pharmacist, 'What can I do to stay awake? I don't want anything prescription.'

He suggested No Doz." Hallen quickly laid in a supply.

As the opening arguments resumed Tuesday, the march of defense attorneys to the podium continued. However, at a meeting in chambers, Judge Fitzpatrick gave Peter Bleakley some bad news. Ciresi's team had filed a motion asking that the judge make a corrective statement to the jury informing them of the inaccuracy of Bleakley's opening remark: "The case before you is about money."

Bleakley was incensed. "I said, 'Judge, I want you to understand that I made a very careful statement. I said the case *before* you is about money; and the case before this jury *is* about money. It is not about disgorgement or equitable relief and that kind of stuff.'"

Fitzpatrick disagreed. "You can come up with a corrective statement, or I'm going to," he told Bleakley.

During the morning recess, Bleakley had formulated his corrective statement and sought out Michelle Jones, saying he wanted to show his statement to the judge. She said, "You tell me what it is, and I'll find out whether it is acceptable to him."

Bleakley reiterated, "I would like to raise this directly with the judge."

Instead, he recalled, "She turned around and walked away and five minutes later the judge came in and made his own curative statement."

The judge told the jury, "Plaintiffs seek to recover health care expenses to treat diseases caused by smoking as well as other relief. At the conclusion of the evidence you will be called upon to evaluate the evidence and apply the law as I instruct you at the end of the case."

"It was bland; I doubt the jury even remembers it," Bleakley conceded. "However, it was a chilling moment. It certainly left me with the feeling that we were in trouble."

Next up was David Bernick, lead attorney for B&W, the nation's third largest cigarette manufacturer and part of B.A.T. Industries' consortium of companies. Bernick advised the jury that mounds of scientific research into the smoking question had been conducted since the 1950s. At one point, he deliberately dropped four thick volumes of publicly accessible studies and treatises on the floor with a thud to illustrate his contention that the tobacco industry's research on nicotine mimicked existing literature in scientific and medical arenas and wouldn't have changed smoker's minds about smoking.

Bernick characterized the documents presented by Ciresi as telling only part of the story, conceding, "We're not going to walk away from them. They are what they are."

Bernick, a handsome 43-year-old attorney from the Chicago office of Kirkland & Ellis (whose Washington, D.C., office was home to special prosecutor Kenneth Starr), was lithe and small in stature, though certainly not in intellect. Characterized as "brilliant" by attorneys who had faced him in court, Bernick would present the science and research portion of the defense's case. Although he'd never moved beyond basic science courses at the University of Chicago, Bernick had proven ability to portray scientific matters in a way that was effective with jurors.

That aptitude had been demonstrated most recently with some notable wins on behalf of Dow Corning, which was almost as besieged with breast implant suits as cigarette manufacturers were with tobacco litigation. Bernick would attempt to do the same for B&W, largely through restating the industry's controversial views about smoking and disease.

"The position on causation was not that cigarettes don't cause disease," Bernick maintained, "but that gaps remain in our knowledge that you can't use that word 'causation' in an absolute technical and scientific sense." He also shunned the word "addiction" for smoking, preferring to use the industry term, "habituation."

Bernick explained that some of the scientific research he referred to was funded by the industry through an independent arm called the Council for Tobacco Research (CTR). Ciresi characterized the CTR as a shell organization through which industry lawyers controlled the study of smoking and health issues.

However, Bernick countered by stating that the CTR awarded more than $284 million in grant and contracts—$600-plus million in today's dollars—and funded more than 1,365 projects for more than 1,100 researchers, including scientists at the Mayo Clinic in Rochester, the University of Minnesota, and three Nobel Prize winners. Grantees published more than 6,000 publications.

By 1989, there were 57,000 smoking-related articles in the scientific literature, Bernick said, adding that only a "sliver" were funded by CTR.

"We were not driving this car," Bernick maintained. "We were not steering the ship. It was out of our hands. It was in the hands of people who were responsible for public health, who wanted to deal with this issue because it was so big and so important.

"The industry sought to preserve itself. That can't be a shocker," Bernick said. "It sought to preserve the rights of smokers who choose to continue to smoke."

Bernick's opening remarks ran long, and, during a break, defense attorneys gathered in Fitzpatrick's chambers to ask for additional time to complete their statements. Michael Corrigan, the national attorney for B.A.T. Industries—the parent company to B&W, British-American Tobacco Company, and B.A.T., UK & Export, Ltd.—had filed a motion for summary judgment, asking to be dismissed from the case. Corrigan asked about the status of that motion. If he was going to remain a party to the case, he would need to make an opening statement. Corrigan's local counsel, Gerald Svoboda, recalled Fitzpatrick telling Corrigan that he hadn't yet ruled. "Mike said, 'Well then, I'll need to make an opening statement.'" The judge declined Corrigan's request.

"I've never heard of a case in which a party couldn't make an opening statement," said Svoboda, "It's just unbelievable."

The opening statement for RJR—the number-two cigarette manufacturer in the United States—whose Joe Camel advertising campaign became a flashpoint for antismoking advocates because of its youthful appeal, was delivered by Robert Weber.

Weber, 47, had the look of a Duke University linebacker, where he'd attended law school. The veteran of 20 product-liability trials, and the head of the product-liability group at Jones, Day, Reavis & Pogue's Cleveland office, Weber was a favorite RJR litigator. His claim to fame was successfully beating back "King of Torts" Melvin Belli's $100 million lawsuit filed against RJR in 1985, on behalf of deceased smoker Mark Galbraith in Santa Barbara, California. Weber, along with Bleakley and Bernick, had been poised to try the Florida Medicaid suit before it was settled in the summer of 1997. The attorney wore half glasses on a cord around his neck and constantly crunched Certs when he wasn't at the podium.

Weber opened with sarcastic reference to Ciresi's opening statement, saying, "*His* words, not mine."

He told the jury that the industry had spent millions of dollars on innovations to make the cigarette a better product, had tried thousands of filters, and was still seeking new ways to deliver smoking pleasure and meet public concerns over health issues. Weber disputed the plaintiffs' contention that the tobacco industry conspired to keep safer cigarettes off the market, saying the industry had considered as many as 100 tobacco substitutes, including "plant leaves, puffed grains, vegetables, vegetable hulls, shucks, skins—practically everything except bamboo."

Weber pointed to failed attempts to market two new cigarette brands: "NEXT," a "de-nicotined" cigarette which cost almost

$300 million to develop; and the smokeless cigarette, "Premier," an extraordinarily expensive flop which smokers said tasted terrible.

A cooperative venture between the CTR and the National Cancer Institute went on for 12 years, Weber said, until the effort was shut down by the federal government in 1978.

"But the companies continued working, studying, searching, researching, looking for new technology, taking actions that would count, actions approved by their highest executives, actions backed by hundred of millions of dollars of investment to bring about the types of results you see before you," he told jurors.

Weber turned next to the state's statistical model, used to calculate the $1.77 billion in damages plaintiffs' felt they were owed. The burly attorney insisted it was way out of whack. He called it "untrustworthy, unreliable." He said the state and Blue Cross were seeking $87 million of reimbursement based on the backgrounds of two 94-year-old nursing home residents, one of whom quit smoking 56 years ago and the other who started smoking one cigarette a day starting when she was 80 and quit when she was 87.

"The evidence will show you that an economics professor from the University of Minnesota will take that stand and say if a student gave him this work, he'd flunk. This is why, I'm sure, we heard nothing about these calculations from Mr. Ciresi, and this is why it's important throughout the course of this to listen to all of the evidence," Weber concluded.

The most unusual opening statement came from James Striker, an attorney from the New York firm of Kasowitz, Benson, Torres & Friedman, who represented the Liggett Group. Liggett was the maverick among the defendants—and a pariah to them. It had already settled with the state and had provided plaintiffs' attorneys with reams of confidential industry documents. It remained in the case as a defendant because charges brought by Blue Cross were still pending.

"Liggett is trying to do the right thing," Striker told jurors. "Liggett is the only company that admits that smoking causes disease. Liggett's pack says, 'Warning, smoking is addictive.' Liggett is different."

Striker repeated his "Liggett is different" assertion throughout his remarks, explaining that Liggett didn't advertise its cigarettes to anyone, and that the average age of its consumers was 50.

The attorney also said that Liggett never worked to manipulate nicotine levels, because it never conducted any laboratory research, and that, as the smallest of the cigarette companies, with only a 2 percent market share, it wasn't part of industrywide efforts to counter negative publicity about smoking and cigarettes.

"Liggett is different. Liggett has taken different positions from the 1950s to 1998. Liggett has not conspired, and is not conspiring with anyone," Striker concluded.

By midmorning Thursday, the jury had heard two completely differing versions on the relationship between smoking and health. They had been attentive and patient. They were starting to get to know one another and fall into a daily routine of court at 9:30 A.M., a midmorning break, 90 minutes for lunch, a midafternoon break and adjournment at 5:00 P.M. Only three-plus months to go. The smokers in the group had already made their needs felt.

Juror Terry Zaspel didn't know whether jurors would be allowed to go out for cigarettes, so she took the matter into her own hands. She put on her coat and stood by the jury room door. "I'd like a cigarette," she told the supervising deputy. Zaspel and the other smokers were taken outside to a loading dock behind the courthouse, where they puffed contentedly.

It was going to be a long three months for James Livingston, given the schedule he'd adopted. In order to compensate for his lost income, Livingston embarked on a grueling routine. He got up at 2:30 A.M., drove to his employer's Eagan welding shop, worked until 8 A.M., then drove back to St. Paul to be at the federal courthouse for the 9:30 A.M. start of the trial. It was exhausting, but, because he wouldn't get paid otherwise, Livingston felt he didn't have a choice.

Although he and David Olson had reiterated their concerns about their loss of income to law clerk Michelle Jones, there had been no response from the judge. Olson had attempted to go to work after the trial during the first few days, but in his job as an estimator for a Burnsville mechanical contracting firm, it just didn't work. He could send all the faxes he wanted at night, but he wouldn't be there during the day to answer questions. His February mortgage payment was due in just a few days. Olson decided not to pay it.

"At that time my house payments were $1,320 a month," Olson explained later. "I figured I might as well miss that one so I'd have some extra cash on hand to get through the first month for groceries for my kids, and everything else."

Mediawise, the trial's moment in the sun had been as fleeting as the sun itself during a Minnesota winter. With the exception of the ubiquitous CNN, most national media disappeared by Thursday night. The Monica Lewinsky scandal was raging at full throttle, the Pope was in Cuba, and the Olympics were gearing up in Japan. Set against that backdrop, Minnesota's Big Stogie registered as a tiny Tiparillo on the national media's radar screen.

But in St. Paul, the show was just getting started as the plaintiffs' first witness stepped up to the stand.

Chapter Five

Kicking Butts

The state and Blue Cross launched their medical case against smoking with a magic word in the world of medicine—Mayo. Michael Ciresi's first choice to introduce jurors to the world of nicotine and addiction was Dr. Richard Hurt, an internist at the famed facility in Rochester, Minnesota, who currently served as director of the Mayo Clinic's Nicotine Dependence Center.

Hurt was a commanding witness at six feet, five inches tall, an imposing man, even when seated in the jury box. He was an ex-chain smoker who still remembered the day he quit smoking—November 2, 1975, he would tell jurors several times. He was eloquent, authoritative and unbending in his opinions—none of them favorable to tobacco and its manufacturers.

The plaintiffs learned of Hurt's strong opinions on nicotine and addiction through testimony he had given to an FDA advisory committee. But clinic policy seldom allowed Mayo doctors to testify as expert witnesses in trials and Hurt had to obtain approval by the clinic's board of trustees. Hurt's participation in the case also was sensitive because Mayo's principal outside counsel was Dorsey & Whitney, a Minneapolis firm which also represented Philip Morris in the tobacco case. To avoid any conflict of interest, Minneapolis attorney Michael Berens was appointed to monitor Hurt's testimony.

A native of Kentucky, Hurt arrived at the Mayo Clinic in 1973 after a two-year stint in the Army. He became director of the clinic's Nicotine Dependence Center in 1988 and modeled it after standard addiction programs for other substances. The center had treated more than 15,000 people, Hurt said, more than 85 percent of them on referral from other Mayo physicians.

In 1975, Hurt testified, he and his wife both decided it was time to quit smoking. They attended the program offered by the dependence center's predecessor, the Mayo Smoking Clinic. "It was the hardest thing I ever did," Hurt said about kicking the habit, noting that he continued to crave cigarettes long afterward.

Hurt said quitting smoking wasn't easy for anyone and acknowledged that the success rate at the center was low. He said only about one in five people who quit smoking stayed smoke free a year after completion of the program. But, he said, that was better than the 5 percent success rate for those who attempt to stop on their own.

Ciresi's questions then guided him through the history of smoking in the United States and the corresponding rise in certain diseases, particularly lung cancer. Between 1869 and 1925, cigarette consumption rose from 2 million a year to 82.3 billion, he testified. Deaths from lung cancer rose correspondingly, he said, from being a rare cause of death in the early 1900s to being the leading cause of cancer deaths since the 1950s.

Jurors had now been issued notebooks, and scribbled busily as Hurt hammered home his belief that nicotine was an addictive drug.

"It has the same hallmarks as other addictions—rationalization, denial, loss of control," Hurt testified. "The cigarette is a better deliverer of nicotine to the brain than intravenous . . . The tendency is to blame the smoker. The smoker isn't the problem, the drug is the problem."

Hurt likened the death rate for cigarette smokers to three Boeing 747s "crashing every day, 356 days a year, with no survivors."

Through Hurt, the jury began to see the dozens of corporate documents accumulated by Ciresi and his team during three years of pretrial discovery. Ciresi used Hurt to introduce industry documents that demonstrated internal knowledge about nicotine's habit-forming characteristics.

In one of those documents, Philip Morris's William Dunn wrote to research director Dr. Helmut Wakeham in 1969 and asked, "Do we really want to tout cigarette smoke as a drug? It is, of course, but there are dangerous FDA implications to having such a conceptualization go beyond these walls."

A 1972 R. J. Reynolds Tobacco Company (RJR) memo from

researcher Claude Teague said the tobacco industry could be regarded as "a specialized, highly ritualized, and stylized segment" of the pharmaceutical industry.

That same year, Dunn wrote that a cigarette "should be conceived not as a product but as a package. The product is nicotine."

For each of the memos, Ciresi asked Hurt whether the tobacco companies repeated their conclusions publicly. "Not to my knowledge," Hurt replied.

Ciresi brought out the Frank Statement, the industry's 1954 pledge to research smoking and health issues. Appearing as an advertisement in newspapers across the United States, it read, "We accept an interest in people's health as a basic responsibility, paramount to every other consideration in business."

Ciresi asked Hurt what that meant to him. "To me that means that the consumer of that product should be assured that the product is safe to use, and that if they were to find out something that was bad about the product they would tell the public, the consumer, the medical community, and everyone else that had to do with these kinds of diseases that this product happens to cause," Hurt said, adding, "They did not live up to their promise."

Brown & Williamson's David Bernick promptly rose and asked Fitzpatrick to strike the last portion of Hurt's answer. Fitzpatrick agreed, but Hurt's conclusion still hung in the air.

His review of corporate documents in preparation for his testimony had been jaw-dropping, Hurt told the jury. He said it was revealing "in ways hard to describe."

"I had not even dreamed there was this much work that had been done over the years," he said.

Using charts and graphs, Hurt showed jurors how the bloodstream absorbed nicotine and sent it to the brain. He also told jurors how "free base" nicotine, with a higher pH concentration, was absorbed by the body faster, allowing the smoker to get a quicker "kick."

Hurt's testimony continued for a second day on Thursday when he startled the courtroom with the flat statement that Wednesday's death of long-time Twin Cities television anchor Dave Moore was caused by smoking. "Dave Moore died of coronary artery disease. But he really died of nicotine dependency, because he was a smoker."

Hurt didn't know Moore and his assertion surprised everyone in the courtroom. The defense team, though, did not object to the sudden claim. Many of their attorneys were from other parts of the country and weren't aware of the newscaster's prominence in the community. Furthermore, Moore died from pneumonia.

Bernick said later that he knew about Moore's death and popularity, but decided not to challenge Hurt. "It was a side show that was unlikely to yield a clear result," he explained. "It wasn't worth pursuing."

As Hurt testified for the second day on nicotine addiction, a group of tobacco company CEOs was holding forth with some rather surprising views of their own at a congressional hearing in

Washington, D.C.

After their disastrous congressional appearance in 1994, where tobacco company executives swore that nicotine wasn't addictive and that smoking didn't cause cancer, a group of new executives took their place, reflecting the forward-looking face tobacco had donned as it pursued passage of the proposed $368.5 billion tobacco settlement. This time, during a hearing held by the House Commerce Committee on January 29, the top officers admitted that nicotine could be addictive under some circumstances, and promised to step up efforts to see that cigarettes weren't marketed to children.

That issue arose as a result of the documents unearthed by Ciresi's team, which some committee members used to batter the executives. RJR Nabisco Holdings Corporation CEO Steven F. Goldstone told members of the House Commerce Committee, "I have real problems with these documents. I don't like them. I don't like them as chief executive of this company, and I don't like them as a father."

Goldstone reiterated his belief that marketing to children "is immoral and unethical, as well as illegal. I can't put it to you any more simply."

The tobacco company executives offered to make public the cache of almost 30 million pages of documents that had been supplied to the Minnesota trial team. Many observers felt it was not noble intention, but more an effort to reduce the negative impact the documents were generating daily in the media [and in

Congress], as they were introduced in the Minnesota trial.

Back in St. Paul, cross-examination of Dr. Hurt began at week's end by Bernick, who revealed himself to be a precise and thorough questioner. Bernick contended that Hurt's testimony in a number of areas—such as his lecture on the history of smoking—was beyond his scope of expertise on addiction. But as he sought to discredit that testimony and cast doubt on Hurt's addiction assertions, he found his progress blocked on two sides. Hurt wasn't going to just benignly answer Bernick's questions, and the judge wasn't going to make him. The Mayo Clinic doctor had no intentions of being a compliant witness.

Hurt was unyielding in his conclusion that nicotine was a drug, and that cigarette companies had tampered with the pH of smoke to boost nicotine absorption. He vehemently disputed Bernick's contention that people could quit smoking if they chose to.

"Choice is your word. That's the industry's word. It's a bad word," Hurt said. "I don't think they ever counted the number that died. They stopped smoking too."

Hurt, in Bernick's mind, had violated the court's order that no individual give testimony about smoking. "He was able to offer evidence about smoking. He made himself the plaintiffs' smoker. And that was highly improper," Bernick later contended.

Bernick continued his efforts. The cross-examination became frenzied, with frequent objections by Ciresi to Bernick's line of questioning. At one point, a frustrated Bernick had to ask for a break in order to reorganize his materials. At another, Bernick complained that Hurt's answers were not responsive to his questions, to which Fitzpatrick replied, dryly, "I think you got an answer, but it was probably more than you expected."

The competition between Ciresi and Bernick was keen. During Hurt's testimony, Bernick wrote several key points on a large notepad for the jury to read. When he offered sheets from the pad as evidence, he realized he didn't have any exhibit stickers. Ciresi quickly offered him stickers from the plaintiffs' table and Bernick dutifully attached them and numbered the exhibits. But when he offered the material, Ciresi objected on the grounds of relevance and the exhibits were denied.

As the trial entered its second week, and Hurt, his fourth day on the stand, Bernick initiated an activity that soon inspired attorneys and media observers to teasing comparisons between the attorney and the unctuous *Leave it to Beaver* television character, Eddie Haskell. As the courtroom filled up, Bernick would wander over to Mary Ann Fitzpatrick and her sister-in-law and chat them up until the day's proceedings began. In light of the pummeling he had endured from Ciresi and the judge the week prior, it seemed a prudent idea.

However, as his cross-examination of Hurt resumed, it became apparent that all the schmoozing in the world wasn't going to help him with this witness. Hurt's dislike of tobacco was all but palpable, and he stubbornly resisted Bernick's efforts to impeach his testimony. When he could, he threw in zingers of his own.

When Bernick questioned Hurt about similarities between the addictive qualities of caffeine and nicotine, Hurt interjected that caffeine, "certainly doesn't kill 400,000 people a year."

Bernick was frustrated but remained calm on the exterior. He was concerned that the jury was getting an uneven picture of the evidence because of the repeated objections and unfavorable rulings for the defendants from Fitzpatrick. He felt his right of cross-examination was being trampled.

If Bernick asked Hurt if he was familiar with the studies conducted by well-known researchers, Hurt would demand to see the exact article in question. When the article was produced, Ciresi would object, usually on grounds of relevance. The judge frequently sided with Ciresi. In this manner, the cross-examination sputtered along slowly and jerkily, like a truck in need of a tune-up. Jurors began to fidget. Finally, the judge lost patience, "I think we've pretty well covered that area. Let's move on."

Instead, Bernick suggested that a lunch break be taken. It had been an extremely unfruitful morning for the defense.

The afternoon wasn't much better. Bernick wanted Hurt to answer questions relating to tobacco companies' attempts to develop so-called "safer cigarettes." Hurt wouldn't bite. Instead, he had his own agenda. At one point he told Bernick, "The recurring theme, though, was that your companies knew these things decades before the rest of us. That's what came through loud and clear. And these people would be shocked to learn the things that I've learned."

Bernick's efforts to rein in his wildcat witness fell on deaf ears with Fitzpatrick.

The attorney's attempts to question Hurt about anything invariably backfired. In one exchange, Bernick asked Hurt, "Do you know that you've seen all of the documents that relate to what the companies thought internally about addiction? Do you know that you've seen them all?"

Hurt's retort, "No, but I've seen enough. They knew it and they didn't tell us."

Frustrated, Bernick turned to the judge, "I'm sorry, Your Honor, that's not responsive. My question is whether he knows whether he's seen them all."

Fitzpatrick responded mildly, telling Hurt, "Okay. Try to respond to the question."

One of Bernick's goals was to minimize any harm caused by Hurt's testimony about a 1995 issue of the *Journal of the American Medical Association*, which had been entered into evidence by Ciresi. In it was a series of articles written by Dr. Stanton Glantz and a team of scientists who interpreted several thousand internal documents from the files of Brown & Williamson (B & W). The documents, which came to Glantz anonymously, were highly damaging to the company and the industry.

An editorial accompanied the articles, which concluded, "We think that these documents and analyses merit the careful attention of our readership because they provide massive, detailed, and damning evidence of the tactics of the tobacco industry. They show us how this industry has managed to spread confusion by expressing, manipulating, and distorting the scientific record. They also make clear how the tobacco industry has been able to avoid paying a penny in damages, and how it has managed to remain hugely profitable from the sale of a substance long known by scientists and physicians to be lethal. We hope that publication of the articles will encourage all our readers to become even more active in the campaign against tobacco."

Bernick attempted to question Hurt about the motivation of the journal's editorial board and the veracity of the articles analyzing the B & W documents.

"Isn't the stated purpose as set forth by the American Medical Association itself, 'We hope that publication of the articles will encourage all our readers to become even more active in the campaign against tobacco?' Isn't that the purpose of these publications?" Bernick asked.

"No," responded Hurt. "I think the purpose of the publication is what they stated, which is to get out information to their readership that has heretofore been secret, that's been buried in your companies' files for decades. You all have known about the addictive nature of nicotine, you've known about the health risk to smoking, and you just forgot to tell anybody else. And not only that, you went beyond that by creating a public relations campaign that created doubt which affects the patients that I deal with because they're dependent upon this substance."

Bernick persisted. "Isn't it true the lead author of these articles is named Stanton Glantz?"

"He's the lead author of one of the articles. There's two of them. He's not the lead author on all of them," Hurt answered.

"And isn't it true that he has gone on record publicly stating that representatives of tobacco companies are cockroaches?" Bernick continued.

Hurt replied that he was familiar with Glantz's background, but denied that Glantz's opinion of the tobacco industry lessened the efficacy of his critique.

"The display of these articles was in my opinion as fair as it could have been for your companies. It could have been a lot worse had they known all the stuff that I know. This is only the tip of the iceberg. The documents that I have seen go beyond anything that these people have seen, period," Hurt declared.

Again Bernick attempted to undermine the validity of the documents, which resulted in a vigorous exchange between both attorneys and the judge.

"Is it true, Dr. Hurt, that these documents were stolen by a person who later used them to make threats against Brown & Williamson," Bernick asked.

Ciresi: "Your Honor, I'm going to object to the characterizations and the irrelevancy of the comments of counsel as totally inappropriate."

Fitzpatrick: "Sustained."

Bernick: "Do you know where the documents came from, Dr. Hurt?"

Ciresi: "Objection, irrelevant."

Fitzpatrick: "The objection is sustained."

Bernick: "Can you represent to this jury that these documents came from an unbiased source?"

Ciresi: "Objection, irrelevant to the line of questioning. I would ask that the court admonish counsel. This has been three or four times."

Fitzpatrick: "Okay."

Bernick: "Your Honor, we're trying . . ."

Fitzpatrick: "Counsel, the objection is sustained. Now if you want to move into a new area, that's appropriate, otherwise I'll consider your recross complete."

As Bernick's examination wrapped to a merciful close, Hurt fired one more shot and Bernick crossed Fitzpatrick's line of courtroom decorum one more time.

"The people that make the quotes in here work for Brown & Williamson. You can't run away from them," said Hurt.

"No one is running away from anything," Bernick shot back.

"Counsel, it is not proper for you to testify. Please limit yourself to questions," the judge said.

But by then, Bernick was all but out of them.

It had been a long four days of testimony by Hurt, and a clear indication of what the defendants could expect from a Ciresi witness. Smart, informed, and extremely uncooperative.

One juror noted Hurt's hostility on cross-examination, and didn't like it.

"He was good, but he showed too much of his feelings," David Olson commented. "I think it kind of took their credibility away in that sense."

Terry Zaspel agreed that Hurt was an antismoking advocate, but she felt his testimony was critical for the plaintiffs. "I thought he was a very credible witness," she said.

Dorothy Hallen felt Hurt was a strong witness to open the plaintiffs' case. "I thought Dr. Hurt was really good," she said. "I liked him because he's been through it. He was a smoker, he quit smoking, he works with people now, he knows about addictions, and he had a lot of credibility because he does have that clinic. He wasn't really exaggerating anything. He was a pretty powerful witness to me."

Slowly, the trial began to develop a personality. The jurors were growing accustomed to their role in the proceedings and became more comfortable with the courtroom's focus on them.

They started to give nicknames to the main players. Bernick became "Mouse," not only because of his small stature, but for the curled wire that protruded from the back of his suitcoat where his cordless microphone was hooked to his belt.

In the spectator section, Associated Press reporters Karren Mills and Steve Karnowski began to come up with nicknames for the jurors as well, since no one knew their real names. One they called "Hoss," after the character on *Bonanza*. James Livingston was nicknamed "Woody" (after actor Harrelson). Olson, with his long, wavy hair, was called Ashley after the Ashley Wilkes character in *Gone With The Wind*. Mills named other jurors after friends she felt they resembled. So, in place of jury numbers, there emerged a cast of characters known as "Eunice," "Ardell," "Christie," and "Allie." The juror who was born in Hungry was called "Otto."

After four days of Richard Hurt, Channing Robertson was, initially, a relaxing change. The Stanford University scientist immediately drew smiles from the jury when asked by Ciresi if he was married. "I think so. I mean—yes," came Robertson's flustered reply. "We won't tell your wife," Fitzpatrick said, chuckling.

Robertson and Ciresi weren't strangers. Robertson had been a Ciresi witness before, during the attorney's successful litigation against A. H. Robins and G. D. Searle on behalf of women injured by interuterine devices.

Robertson had a Ph.D. in chemical engineering and had been on the faculty of Stanford since 1970. His academic emphasis was in biochemical engineering. He'd been asked by Ciresi to investigate the chemical and physical aspects of cigarette design in late 1996.

Robertson was familiar with Ciresi's style and technique and answered questions easily as Ciresi led him through his expert testimony, which focused on the cigarette as a "drug delivery device."

That the two were previously acquainted could be seen in their easy give and take. At one point, Robertson explained that a capillary is about one-tenth the diameter of a human hair.

"For mine it would be nonexistent," retorted the balding attorney.

"That occurred to me," Robertson responded, dryly.

However, for all his playfulness with Robertson, Ciresi never lost sight of who he was playing to—the jury.

Later, as he and Robertson reviewed a document together, Ciresi pointed to a topic heading, saying, "Doctor, my French isn't very good, but under the subject it says 'Raison d'etre,'" pronouncing it "Raisin Dot."

The deliberate mispronunciation before the jury sent more than several eyebrows arcing skyward among lawyers and court observers alike, and even several jurors looked skeptical that such a learned attorney had never heard the phrase before.

Robertson testified that part of his study of cigarette design included weeks reviewing sensitive tobacco industry documents in Ciresi's top-secret, "electronically armed" section of his law firm. Robertson saw reports discussing nicotine delivery dating back to the 1960s, he testified, which convinced him that tobacco companies had long known that cigarettes were little more than vehicles for delivering doses of nicotine in levels high enough to keep smokers addicted.

The Stanford professor spent the first portion of his testimony much as Dr. Hurt had, introducing jurors to the anatomy of the lung via a flashy computer graphics presentation.

His conclusions were similarly unequivocal, "The defendants know that nicotine is a drug. They knew the lowest threshold for

it to be pharmacologically active, above which they had to operate to be successful. They knew if they removed nicotine, they'd
have no business."

Further, Robertson testified, the industry was concerned that
government regulation of nicotine would result in such low levels of nicotine in cigarettes that smokers would simply quit using
the product.

But Ciresi didn't stop at Robertson's expert opinion. He also
used Robertson to introduce almost 50 documents during the
scientist's two-and-a-half days of testimony. Ciresi introduced
memo after memo showing the deep extent to which the tobacco industry knew why people smoked, and their fear that nicotine would fall under government regulation.

A 1963 B & W document stated, "Nicotine is by far the most
characteristic single constituent in tobacco."

An RJR executive stated in another memorandum, "We are
basically in the nicotine business." A memo from an executive of
the British American Tobacco Company (BAT Co.) said similarly, "We are in a nicotine rather than a tobacco industry."

A 1974 memo from BAT Co. said, "classification of tobacco as a
drug should be avoided at all costs."

Robertson's testimony also included discussion of "compensation"—the altered patterns smokers adopt to maintain desired
nicotine levels even as lower nicotine cigarettes appeared on the
market. Robertson said "compensating" smokers maintained
nicotine levels by inhaling deeper and more often.

Robertson said tobacco companies developed methods to enhance the nicotine kick in cigarette smoke by increasing the smoke's pH, which could be done with increased ventilation in the cigarette filter and with more porous paper. "The defendants spent considerable effort searching for ways to continue nicotine delivery in cigarettes, no question about that," Robertson testified.

Outside the courtroom, Bernick called Robertson's testimony repetitive, saying it focused on a topic that has been known for 200 years — that nicotine is pharmacologically active. "The idea that there is some magical dose [of nicotine] has never been true," Bernick said. "People have a wide range of choices."

The next day, Bernick again stepped up to the podium as the attorney designated to cross-examine Robertson. It seemed an odd choice, given that the ashes were barely cool from the scorching he received from Hurt. But the witness assignments had been given to defense attorneys long before Ciresi announced his lineup, and Bernick was the attorney in charge of science and research.

Robertson was not as hostile as Hurt, but he proved just as intractable. About the only thing Bernick was able to get Robertson to admit was that he didn't have expertise in cigarette design prior to being retained as an expert witness for Ciresi. Ciresi was, again, a legal jack-in-the-box, objecting some 58 times within the first two hours of Robertson's cross-examination. Most were sustained.

When Bernick focused on Robertson's knowledge gap regarding independent scientific research on smoking, Robertson replied that he concentrated on the knowledge and research of the tobacco companies.

"I was focused on the internal documents. They told me about the activities going on behind the walls of the tobacco industry, activities of which no one on the outside had any direct information of," Robertson said.

Hamline trial law professor Joseph Daly, who'd come to court to watch some of the nation's best attorneys at work, professed amazement at Bernick's technique during one of the court recesses.

"Bernick keeps asking questions, rather than making statements for which the witness can only offer a yes or no answer," he commented. "That's a basic cross-examination technique that I teach to all my students—and he's not using it."

By the end of Robertson's appearance, jurors had a received a good introduction to Ciresi's methodology with his friendly witnesses. When the next witness took the stand, they'd find out how Ciresi dealt with hostile ones.

The jurors now had two weeks of trial under their belts. Their courtroom lives had fallen into a pattern. But burdens outside the courthouse, caused by the trial, were taking a toll on some. David Olson's outside employer was only paying him during the first two weeks of the trial. After that, his company would just cover health insurance. "Hey, I can't be here," Olson told law clerk Michelle

Jones when he asked for a letter from the judge to explain the situation to employers and creditors.

As the week ended, Fitzpatrick took note of concerns raised by jurors about financial problems the lengthy trial would impose. His staff faxed a letter to their employers asking for any assistance possible to ease the burden of jury duty, noting the court could offer nothing beyond the $30 per diem and lunch.

The letter also said, "Failure of a juror to appear constitutes a misdemeanor crime subject to penalties of this court as well as the immediate apprehension of the juror by deputies from the Ramsey County Sheriff's Office."

But the letter didn't help Olson's looming crisis. Having already skipped his February mortgage payment, he now faced other bills that were coming due. Olson relayed his concern to Fitzpatrick's law clerk.

"I said this isn't going to help my creditors out. They're going to think my boss is paying me," Olson recalled. But Jones told Olson that was all the judge could do.

It wasn't just the jurors who were suffering. Philip Morris attorney Peter Bleakley later said that he felt his lowest after Ciresi's first two witnesses.

"It was their high point," he said. " If they could have rested after Hurt and Robertson, who knows what would have happened."

By the end of those first six days, Bleakley recalled, "I don't remember anybody on the defense team who was in a good mood."

Hurt, Bleakley said, "was allowed to say anything he wanted to. Anything. Normally a witness wouldn't be allowed to do that on direct examination. Bernick tried to ask him about those things on cross, and he was blocked."

Bleakley had gotten a glimpse of what lay ahead in Fitzpatrick's courtroom for the next three or four months. He didn't like what he saw.

Chapter Six

Hostile Witnesses

Walker Merryman was no stranger to the tobacco industry. He'd served as Big Tobacco's official spokesperson since 1981, as vice president and director of communications for the Tobacco Institute, the public relations and lobbying arm funded by the industry's major players. Over the years, Merryman had become a fixture on the media circuit, trotted out whenever an opposing viewpoint was needed to balance antitobacco stories.

Because Merryman's organization was a defendant in the case, the spokesman was being called as an "adverse" or "hostile" witness, someone whose opinions were not favorable to the plaintiffs. It would be the jury's first look at Ciresi's legendary style of cross-examination, his relentless interrogation that didn't miss a beat, and his forceful, often cynical questioning that produced answers witnesses sometimes would later regret.

Ciresi's strategy was to use Merryman to discredit the industry for its use of what he called "propaganda" to deflect medical challenges to smoking and to deny any direct link between smoking and disease. The defense hoped that Merryman's measured, polite responses would portray him as a man of integrity and deflect Ciresi's aggressive questioning.

Merryman had abandoned a career in 1976 as a small-market television newsperson in the Midwest to work for the Tobacco Institute. Courtly in demeanor and stately in speech, he eventually became the industry's frontline mouthpiece, surviving years of hardball questions from such news Goliaths as Ted Koppel and the McNeil-Lehrer news team. As the industry's point man, he traveled across the country to give hundreds of other media interviews denying the link between smoking and disease.

Now he was on the witness stand in St. Paul, hoping he could deflect Ciresi's questions. A large man, Merryman politely appended most of his statements with "sir," although his responses quickly raised eyebrows throughout the courtroom. Merryman was soon in trouble.

Nonthreatening in appearance, Merryman was no Darth Vadar of the tobacco industry. But he was no Ronald Reagan either, when it came to deflecting questions he was either unprepared or unsuited to answer.

Ciresi expected Merryman to espouse the industry line, so it was no surprise when the spokesman testified that the industry didn't consider smoking to be addictive. "We don't believe it's ever been established that smoking is the cause of disease," Merryman said. He acknowledged a "statistical association" between smoking and disease, but claimed the link between the two remained unproven. The public was aware of the risks associated with the product, he declared, adding "if the risks aren't well known, then a company should tell people what it knows about the risks."

Ciresi then asked if tobacco companies had a greater obligation to inform the public about the risks of smoking in light of mounting evidence linking cigarettes to disease.

"That really isn't my job," Merryman answered. Ciresi was pleased with the admission. He wanted the jury to believe, as he did, that the mission of the industry's principal trade organization was to create confusion on the smoking-and-health front.

"That's not what I'm supposed to do at the Tobacco Institute," Merryman explained politely. "If you're asking me, personally, do I think that companies ought to reveal information that people don't already know or aren't already aware of, as a general proposition I'd say, yes, that's a good idea."

"If it's not your job, Mr. Merryman, whose job is it with regard to disseminating that information to the tobacco industry? Whose job is it?" Ciresi continued.

"Well in the case of health risks associated with smoking, I think that many different public health authorities for many, many years have done an extraordinary job of giving people information about the health charges against smoking," Merryman said.

"Whose responsibility is it on the part of the company, sir?" Ciresi countered.

"I don't know that, sir," Merryman replied.

At Ciresi's hands, Merryman became an "I-don't-know," whose credibility as vice president for communications for a tobacco industry–funded organization was strained.

Throughout his testimony, Merryman responded with a look of sincereness that he couldn't answer the questions because he didn't know, wasn't informed, or didn't have that information. His testimony was not a confidence builder for the industry.

Ciresi asked him why the Liggett Group pulled out of the Tobacco Institute in the early 1990s. Liggett was an industry maverick and had broken ranks with other manufacturers by admitting that smoking was addictive and did cause disease. Merryman replied that he didn't know.

"Well you know that it was when they admitted publicly that smoking was addictive; isn't that correct?" Ciresi asked.

"I don't know that. No, sir."

"Weren't they asked to leave at that time?"

"That's really an administrative detail. That's not something I'd be aware of, sir."

Ciresi continued to press as he further sought to undercut Merryman's veracity. "You mean you're the vice president of communications, Liggett quit or was forced out, and you didn't even ask?"

Merryman didn't waver. "That's not something that I'd be aware of. No, sir."

"Just had no curiosity about why Liggett left?"

"No, sir. That doesn't seem to be something that I would need to know in the general course of my business."

Shaking his head in disbelief, Ciresi refused to give up. "Just not a matter of concern at all, is that right?"

"If a company makes a decision or a decision is made with respect to that company, there's not really anything that I can have an impact on with respect to that decision," Merryman answered.

"Would you agree, Mr. Merryman, that the time that Liggett left was the time that they publicly admitted that cigarette smoking was addictive?"

"I can't tell you when Liggett left. I simply don't recall. It didn't make an impression on me."

Ciresi pushed further, letting the jury hear more about Liggett's defection and admission. "Didn't Liggett enter into a settlement with various states around the country and it was the first settlement ever by a tobacco company? Isn't that true?"

Merryman replied, "That's not an issue that we at the Tobacco Institute would have talked about to the news media. That's not something that we were—that we were authorized to speak to the news media about. So it's not something, sir, that I would have had information on."

Ciresi's voice strained with incredulity, "But you watch TV, don't you?"

"Oh, I'm generally aware of it, sir, but beyond that I don't have any specific knowledge of it."

"You watch TV; don't you?" Ciresi again asked the man designated by the tobacco industry to track media developments.

"I occasionally do."

"Read the papers?"

"Yes, sir."

"Listen to the radio?"

"Sometimes."

"Try to keep abreast of what's going on in your industry?"

"Yes, sir."

"And there was tremendous publicity, wasn't there, about the fact that Liggett admitted that cigarette smoking was addictive?"

Merryman, ever earnest, replied, "I don't know if I could characterize the nature of the publicity. Certainly there was some."

"Ah," declared Ciresi, triumphantly, "So you were aware of it, then?"

"I was aware of some publicity. As I said, I was generally aware of the subject."

"And that was when Liggett left the Tobacco Institute; isn't that right?"

And Merryman returned immediately to square one. "I do not know, sir."

Ciresi, by now openly cynical, just kept going, "Just don't recall?"

"I do not."

"Don't know one way or the other?"

"I do not."

From the jury box, Dorothy Hallen watched in rapt fascination. "This was like Perry Mason, where he'd do a hard cross-examination. I thought, 'Whoa—this is fun; it's just like the movies.'" But she didn't know how much weight to place on Merryman's testimony. "I just felt like he was their answer man."

Juror Jim Otis was similarly impressed with Ciresi's work on Merryman.

"That's when it started to get entertaining," he recalled. "At first I thought the guy knew more than he was letting on. Then I wondered if the higher ups were keeping him blind to a lot of things. I thought he was full of beans. Everybody was on the edge of their seats through that one. We all came out of there going, 'wow.'"

Indeed, it was a well-choreographed examination. Ciresi thrusted and parried; he cajoled and castigated. This was his strength, and his performance was Oscar-worthy. Ciresi continued to exploit Merryman's knowledge gap. Ciresi and Merryman also sparred over the term "addiction," with Merryman asserting that smoking cigarettes was not the same as using heroin or crack cocaine.

During his testimony, the tobacco spokesman acknowledged that he was a former smoker who gave up smoking a year and a half earlier after suffering a heart attack and undergoing bypass surgery. Ciresi jumped on the connection.

"I decided that I wanted to avoid as many risk factors in my life as I could; I gave up smoking," Merryman told Ciresi. "I started an exercise and diet program, tried to take as much stress out of my life as possible. I eat a low-fat diet and follow the advice of my physician."

Ciresi asked if Merryman's physician told him to quit smoking. No, said Merryman, his physician told him to reduce risk factors in his lifestyle, noting that his health problems could be hereditary.

"And he told you ought to consider quitting smoking, didn't he?" Ciresi continued.

"Yes," Merryman replied. "He didn't tell me to quit smoking. I made that decision on my own."

By the second day of his adverse examination, Ciresi grew increasingly aggressive. He hacked away at Merryman's denial that tobacco companies marketed to teens with a slew of incriminating documents, some never before seen by a jury in any court.

The documents revealed an industry that had tracked the smoking habits of children as young as 14, who, as one 1974 R. J. Reynolds marketing plan explained, "represent tomorrow's cigarette business."

The marketing plan stated "as the 14 to 24 age group matures, they will account for a key share of the total cigarette volume—for at least the next 25 years."

Ciresi used the document to berate Merryman for his repeated assertion that the industry did not market to underage smokers. "Did anyone say, 'We can't do this, we can't sell to a child of 14 years of age?'"

Merryman retorted, "I've seen documents where the company says we don't want 14-year-old customers."

Document after document was shown to Merryman to demonstrate the various cigarette companies' obsessions with the young adult market. A 1973 Brown & Williamson memo talked about the popularity of Kool cigarettes with young smokers.

"Kool has shown little or no growth in share of users in the 26-plus age group," the memo stated. "Growth is from 16 to 25-year-olds. At the present rate, a smoker in the 16 to 25-year age group will soon be three times as important to Kool as a prospect in any other broad age category."

Philip Morris documents outlined the strengths and weaknesses of its brands with young smokers. A 1979 document revealed that Marlboro dominated the "17-and-younger" category with more than 50 percent of the market. It also had the largest share—one third—of the 18 to 24 market.

Merryman's protestations about youth marketing continued, but Ciresi was unrelenting.

"You would have been deceived?" Ciresi barked, at the end of a question about youth marketing.

"Well, since we don't receive information on marketing from our member companies, I don't think the use of the word 'deceived' is proper," replied Merryman.

Ciresi hammered on. "Then you were deceived by them with regard to what they were doing, correct, sir?"

"If they were doing what you suggest, then we wouldn't have

been given accurate information by the companies," Merryman answered.

"You would have been deceived, correct?" Ciresi said.

"But I don't believe that there is a strong showing that that in fact happened," the weary Merryman answered.

"Sir, if you weren't given accurate information, you would have been deceived, correct?" Ciresi asked one more time.

"Correct," Merryman finally conceded.

After a day and a half of Ciresi's barrage of questions, Merryman looked exhausted. During a midafternoon break, Merryman quietly informed the court that he wasn't feeling well. Merryman asked to be excused for the remainder of the day to rest.

Next in line came one of the plaintiffs' star witnesses, Bennett LeBow, whose Brooke Investment Group was the sole owner of the Liggett Group, which manufactured the Chesterfield, Eve, L&M, and Lark cigarette brands.

LeBow had purchased Liggett in 1986. The executive's appearance at trial sent a ripple of reaction through lawyers in the courtroom. With the exception of his company's own attorneys, Liggett was universally despised by the tobacco companies as a traitor to the cause—little better than a mob informant. The Miami investor forever earned their enmity through his sudden settlement with class-action attorneys and state attorneys general, a settlement that included the acknowledgment that cigarettes addicted, killed, and were marketed to children—the very notions Big Tobacco had furiously contested for years.

Liggett had settled Medicaid lawsuits with 22 states, including Minnesota, in March 1997, pledging to turn over 25 percent of its pretax income, as paltry as that might be for the struggling company. LeBow's testimony in Medicaid trials, including Minnesota's, was also a condition of the settlement.

But he was appearing in St. Paul under unusual circumstances. Because Blue Cross was a private company, it was not a party to the states' settlement. Liggett thus remained a defendant in the Minnesota case with the insurer. Technically, LeBow was on the witness stand as a favorable witness for the state of Minnesota and an adverse witness for Blue Cross.

Ciresi took a breather after eight days on his feet and assigned the examination of LeBow to his colleague Richard Gill, whose light gray hair and fair complexion inspired the jury to nickname him "Pale Rider." It presented one of the most interesting challenges of the trial: on the one hand, Gill had to present LeBow as a credible witness to support the state's claims about Big Tobacco's conspiracy to defraud consumers; on the other, he had to convince the jury that Liggett's actions were still actionable and subject to damages for Blue Cross.

"It was schizo," Gill later acknowledged.

As a witness for the state, LeBow would be easy to examine and very cooperative. But Gill knew that the defense would attempt to portray LeBow as an opportunistic businessperson willing to say anything now that lawsuits against his company had been dropped. It was up to Gill to deflect as much of that as possible so there'd be no surprises for the jury when the defense had its shot at LeBow. At the same time, Gill realized, LeBow could have taken the same actions back in the 1980s as he did when he settled in 1997.

"He was hardly a hero," Gill said.

Gill had never met LeBow prior to his arrival in court on Monday, February 9, but he'd read a deposition the CEO gave in a Florida lawsuit. Gill recognized the pitfalls inherent in the examination, both for him, and LeBow. He knew LeBow gave the appearance of an industry turncoat who'd say anything to get a deal that was good for his company. Gill was not sure, however, whether LeBow understood clearly that he was still a defendant in this case and that his testimony could be used against him by Blue Cross.

And Gill had a plan for reaching that goal. "On the one hand, he was very cooperative. On the other hand, we wanted to wash our hands of him," Gill said. He approached the podium and faced LeBow.

LeBow seemed immediately comfortable on the stand. Dressed in a dark suit and flashy tie, the silver-haired businessman sported a close-cropped beard and looked more like the self-made entrepreneur that he was than a cigarette CEO.

Bennett LeBow graduated from Philadelphia's Drexel University in 1960 with a degree in electrical engineering. He continued his engineering education at Princeton, before entering the work force. From 1962 to 1964, LeBow served in the U.S. Army. After receiving his honorable discharge, LeBow stayed on with the Army in a civilian capacity, running all of the Army's computer systems at the Pentagon.

In 1967, LeBow left the Army for good and started his own company, moving from the world of computers and engineering into high finance. He bought and sold his way up the corporate food chain until he had enough money in 1986 to look at a larger acquisition. He saw a financial opportunity in Liggett and decided to acquire it.

When LeBow recruited the investment group to purchase Liggett, he gave little thought to the nature of his purchase. At the time, Liggett was selling four main brands, L&M, Lark, Eve, and Chesterfield. LeBow didn't give much thought either to smoking and health issues as they related to his new acquisition. A smoker until the 1960s, LeBow willed himself to quit, although it took him several months to get over the cravings. He'd heard about some litigation from company lawyers, but was told that he shouldn't be concerned. After all, there were health warnings on the cigarette packs informing the public that the product could be hazardous to health.

As the smallest tobacco company in the industry, with only a 2 percent market share, LeBow took his lead from the majors when it came to industry issues, he said. The industry position was that smoking didn't cause lung cancer, wasn't addictive, and was a matter of personal choice.

During the late 1980s and early 1990s, Liggett was still a member of the Tobacco Institute. LeBow didn't know much about the Institute's activities. What he did know—and often railed against—was why, given Liggett's tiny size, it paid dues to be a member at all.

LeBow testified that his awareness of Liggett's position on smoking and health issues began to increase in the early 1990s. For one thing, in 1993, he was deposed for a class-action lawsuit in Florida brought by airline attendants who claimed secondhand smoke caused cancer within their ranks. During the predeposition briefing, LeBow was told by his attorney that he'd probably be asked if he thought cigarette smoking was addictive. LeBow did not. After all, he'd been able to quit and knew a lot of other people who'd stopped smoking too.

By the fall of 1995, smoking and health issues began to intrude into the company's finances. LeBow was paid a visit by the outside attorneys who had been representing his company for the last 20 years. They wanted to move to another firm, Lathan & Watkins. And if he approved the move, Philip Morris would pay Liggett's legal bills, which were running about $8 million to $10 million dollars a year by that time.

The idea of a competitor picking up his legal bills was a first for LeBow. Nothing like that had ever before happened in his professional experience. In the tobacco industry, however, the stronger companies helped their weaker colleagues in this fashion to keep a united front on the smoking and health issue. But it was news to LeBow and he began to question the loyalty of his attorneys, but decided to let them move to Lathan & Watkins and see what happened.

Several months later, LeBow became involved in a shareholder effort to get RJR Nabisco Holdings Corporation to split its food and tobacco business into separate companies. He figured a later merger of Liggett and the RJR tobacco division could be effected—at great profit to him.

But LeBow's financial advisors told him such a move would be impossible because of all the pending lawsuits against R. J. Reynolds Tobacco Company (RJR) and the industry. RJR as a stand-alone company was considerably weaker than it was as a division of an international conglomerate with the financial wherewithal to respond to a crisis, in this instance, a legal loss.

LeBow said he was flabbergasted by that assessment. He believed the tobacco industry was virtually guaranteed ongoing success in the courtroom.

"I said 'Wait a minute. I've been told for 40 years we've never paid a penny, we have no liability.' I really started to smell a rat." LeBow said.

Prior to that, LeBow testified, he had never regarded the lawsuits as an economic threat to his company.

LeBow thought the easiest way to find out the truth was to contact the lawyers bringing all the smoking and health cases against the industry. Secretly, he instructed his personal attorney, Marc Kasowitz, to contact plaintiffs' attorneys and state attorneys general who had filed lawsuits against the industry, find out the basis for their suits, and why the industry was worried. He didn't want to talk to the lawyers at Lathan & Watkins. "I wasn't sure whose lawyers they were," LeBow testified.

Based upon Kasowitz's report, LeBow testified, he learned the industry's legal woes were indeed serious. He realized that if nicotine was found to be addictive, the defense of personal choice would collapse like a house of cards, taking his company along with it in the sure-to-be-astronomical judgments. LeBow decided to settle.

In an agreement with five attorneys general and class-action lawyers, Liggett agreed to FDA regulation of cigarettes. The company would make certain monetary payments to plaintiffs. And, if RJR Nabisco Holdings Corporation ever spun off its tobacco division, and if Liggett completed a merger, RJR Nabisco Holdings Corporation would be protected under the settlement as well, a factor that LeBow thought RJR Nabisco Holdings Corporation shareholders might appreciate.

Big Tobacco's reaction when the deal became public in March 1996, was "a firestorm," LeBow testified.

Lathan & Watkins quit Liggett as a client although LeBow was about to fire them anyway. LeBow instructed Kasowitz to retrieve all Liggett's documents from Lathan & Watkins and begin reviewing them. When the review was completed in the fall of 1996, Liggett dropped another bombshell.

"We had seen all the documents," LeBow testified. "I was convinced that smoking was addictive, that smoking does cause all these problems. I didn't want to have to go to court and lie about it."

LeBow went public. Liggett admitted that smoking caused disease and that it was addictive. It agreed to make public all its documents and to change the warnings on its cigarette packages to reflect its new attitude. It agreed to cooperate in upcoming trials. Liggett attorneys then negotiated a new settlement agreement that encompassed all the parties, including Minnesota (though not with Blue Cross and Blue Shield).

Liggett's cigarette brands now carried a new warning separate from the surgeon general's label, reading "Smoking is addictive." Nor would Liggett advertise its products, at all.

"You've disclosed all the ingredients in your cigarettes?" Gill asked.

"Absolutely. It's on all of our cartons."

"And how many of your competitors have done likewise?"

"None."

But Gill was also asking questions on behalf of Blue Cross, for whom LeBow was a defendant. Gill intended to show that LeBow's moral compass spin wasn't particularly timely.

"In all candor, Mr. LeBow, there is absolutely no reason why you could not have learned in 1986 what you learned in 1996, correct?"

"If I pushed the current lawyers at that time to show me all the documents, that's correct," LeBow responded. "But I did not."

"Because, in all candor, when you bought Liggett in 1986, you had the power to set policy, correct?"

"Correct."

"You had the power to get at the truth."

"Correct."

"And at that time you didn't care about it."

"I was told by all the lawyers not to worry about it."

Gill pressed. "You were focused on the potential profitability of the company, and your focus was not on smoking and health."

"That's correct."

Gill later recalled. "At that point he was looking at me like, 'What are you doing?' But once I got him to admit to all the bad things, it was too late for him to backslide. I don't think he realized what was happening until it was too late."

Gill had been correct, Liggett's attorneys hadn't foreseen this negative line of questioning, and they weren't happy.

"We didn't expect that," said Liggett local counsel Steven Kelley. "We didn't see the sense in that. That's an example of the Robins firm being snotty and nasty to us, despite the fact that we had settled with the state, and that settlement required us to cooperate in certain ways."

Finally, after a few more questions, Gill sat down, satisfied that he had identified all of LeBow's "dirty linen."

However, RJR's Robert Weber had a whole hamper full, and he was looking forward with delight to the task of exposing it.

Weber—nicknamed "The Duke" by the jury for his linebacker

build and John Wayne swagger—regarded LeBow as "no different than any other informant witness. He's a guy who has taken position A for years, and has now taken Position Z, and has done so as part of a deal."

Weber thought the plaintiffs had made a mistake in calling LeBow. "It was just stupid to interrupt the flow of their case with this guy. They put this guy on, had him tell his whole story, had him make stupid statements like 'I want to come clean. I want to get all the cards on the table,' then left us the delicious opportunity to show all the cards he didn't put on the table."

Weber came out swinging. He attacked LeBow as an opportunistic businessman who was far from being the good corporate citizen he claimed and whose only goal was to protect his investment in a company that was up to its cigarette butts in red ink. Weber treated LeBow like a government informer who'd turned on his partners to avoid jail time.

Initially LeBow took the punches almost indifferently, answering Weber's questions with a fatalistically cheery nonchalance.

Under Weber's forceful examination, LeBow admitted that his company had been unprofitable for nearly a decade, operating at a loss of some $150 million a year. Therefore, Weber pointed out, the terms of Liggett's settlement calling for the company to pay 25 percent of pretax profits actually amounted to nothing. LeBow said Liggett hoped to break even in the current fiscal year.

The real value of the settlement for the states, Weber suggested, was that Liggett agreed to participate in litigation as a witness against the other tobacco companies.

Pointing to a paragraph within the settlement, Weber said, "That says that you've agreed to actively assist the attorneys representing the attorneys general in locating witnesses, et cetera, correct?"

"Correct," LeBow replied.

"And you shall actively assist counsel in interpreting documents relating to litigation. You see that?"

"Yes."

"And that's what you were doing here yesterday on the stand; weren't you, actively assisting counsel?"

Weber also drew concessions from LeBow that he didn't know the difference among the definitions of "addiction," "dependence," or "habit," and that he hadn't discussed those differences with scientists, but had taken his attorneys' word for it.

And as for Liggett's proud new labeling, Weber pointed out that Liggett manufactured hundreds of private label cigarettes that didn't contain those warnings.

"You didn't tell the jury yesterday that you were still making cigarettes without putting the label on it; did you, sir?"

"No."

Jurors weren't sure what to make of LeBow's testimony. He was getting wrapped on the knuckles wherever he turned. For his part, LeBow, who initially argued with Weber's interpretation of the Liggett settlement and other matters, eventually gave up answers with little fight. He was getting tired.

"It seemed like he was selling out and covering himself and Liggett," said juror Hallen.

Her colleague, Jim Otis, agreed that the testimony might be self-serving, but he was still impressed. "Being the CEO, that must have taken a lot of guts to get up there and admit to all those wrongs they were doing. I think he did the right thing."

Weber also got LeBow to acknowledge that the advertising restrictions contained in the settlement were virtually meaningless because Liggett did very little advertising of its brands.

"You hadn't instructed your advertising people of anything at the time you signed this agreement, had you?" Weber demanded.

"We have very few advertising people," LeBow acknowledged.

Weber's cross-examination of LeBow lasted a little over two hours and crimped the effectiveness the Liggett CEO had served for the plaintiffs, although not as severely as the defense may have hoped.

"But even if he did it just to protect himself, he was still a CEO willing to say all that stuff in public about addiction, and it just reinforced it all," recalled Hallen.

But any satisfaction the defendants had from the grilling of LeBow was tempered outside the courtroom. The long-awaited determination from Special Master Mark Gehan on the validity of attorney-client privilege claims made by the industry was ready.

In a report to Fitzpatrick, Gehan determined that 39,000 industry documents were improperly classified and should be turned over to the plaintiffs.

Gehan's report was the result of an intensive, three-month review of the documents. More than 50 boxes of documents filled a secure office in the suite of offices occupied by his St. Paul law firm, Collins, Buckley, Sauntry & Haugh. Gehan systematically examined document samples, knowing full well that both the defendants and the plantiffs were anxiously waiting for his findings.

"The documents were delivered in November. That was certainly the worst period for me, reviewing all of those documents and trying to generate some conclusions," Gehan recalled.

Gehan was assisted by Fitzpatrick's law clerk, Michelle Jones, and court observer Patricia Miller who flagged particular documents for Gehan's attention. Without the sampling system, Gehan said, it would have been physically impossible to read every document.

Only a brief summary of Gehan's finding was publicly released, however. The full report was given to Fitzpatrick, under seal, for the judge's consideration. In the public filing, Gehan said attorney-client privilege claims were wrongly applied in 4 of 10 broad categories of information.

Gehan said the industry violated the crime-fraud provision which supersedes claims of attorney-client privilege for documents that are in futherance of a crime or fraud. His finding was similar to a September report on 800 documents from the files of the Liggett Group, which included material from other tobacco companies regarding joint-defense strategies.

Gehan based his finding on a sampling of documents from each category. If he determined the sample from a category constituted crime-fraud, then the whole category should be released to the plaintiffs.

It was a blow for the defendants, even though Gehan ruled favorably on the majority of the 240,000 documents for which attorney-client privilege was claimed. Gehan said among the types of documents which the plaintiffs could see were scientific research on smoking and health, special research projects directed by lawyers, and documents relating to public industry positions on health issues.

Both sides immediately rushed to claim victory. Weber, while objecting to the sampling technique the special master used in making his determination, said the industry was pleased to see its privilege claims upheld in 10 of 14 categories.

Ciresi called Gehan's ruling "extremely significant." Attorney General Humphrey, however, spared no adjectives, describing the 39,000 documents as "the crown jewels of the conspiracy," even though no one in his office had seen them.

But no one would see the actual report until Judge Fitzpatrick issued his final order on the matter. Just when that might be was anybody's guess, but probably before the trial concluded.

Documents of all kinds were on everybody's minds—in and out of Minnesota. Congress, in particular, also was interested to see what was on file in Minnesota. On February 12, three House

Commerce Committee members—Democrats Henry Waxman, Sherrod Brown, and John Dingall—wrote Fitzpatrick, urging him to support the industry's decision to release the 30 million pages of documents gathered in the Minnesota depository. Ciresi and Humphrey weren't entirely opposed to the idea—as long, they said, as the industry agreed to release the new 39,000 document batch as well.

Back in court, the Tobacco Institute's Walker Merryman returned to the witness stand and faced friendly questioning from Philip Morris attorney Peter Bleakley. Merryman described the Institute's 14-year effort to discourage youth smoking, including handbooks for parents and youth, and a program for retailers to more effectively card teen cigarette purchasers.

But Ciresi had another shot at Merryman during his re-direct examination—and he didn't buy into the Tobacco Institute's much vaunted programs to discourage teens from smoking. Using a giant pie chart, Ciresi pointed out that, from 1983 through 1994, the industry had spent just $22 million on those programs—an infinitesimal amount of the $16 billion it spent on advertising, promotion, and marketing during the same period.

In addition, Ciresi claimed, at the same time the Institute was working so hard to promote its antismoking programs, the tobacco industry was actively lobbying to kill a Minnesota bill that would make it costlier for underage smokers to buy cigarettes.

Ciresi continued his efforts to paint Merryman and his employer as participants in a campaign spanning decades to manipulate and undermine the public perception of the health risks of smoking.

At one point, Ciresi pulled out an internal 1972 Tobacco Institute memo from Vice President Fred Panzer to then-President Horace Kornegay describing the industry's 20-year strategy to defend itself against health claims.

"While the strategy was brilliantly conceived and executed over the years helping us win important battles, it is only fair to say that it is not—nor was it intended to be—a vehicle for victory," Panzer wrote. "On the contrary, it has always been a holding strategy, consisting of 'number one' creating doubt about the health charge without actually denying it."

Merryman could only assert that the memo reflected Panzer's personal opinion, not policy of the Tobacco Institute. He acknowledged, however, that he never saw a reply from Kornegay denying Panzer's conclusion.

Throughout his brutal four days on the witness stand, Merryman sought to portray himself as a good soldier who was merely following orders.

"So long as you got paid, year after year, you did exactly what they told you to say, isn't that right," Ciresi asked during the examination.

"Well, certainly as an employee I'd be expected to do as instructed," Merryman replied.

"Do as instructed. And that's what you've done, correct, sir?" Ciresi asked.

"Yes, sir, and honorably," said Merryman.

"And what?" queried Ciresi.

"Honorably," Merryman repeated.

"Honorably," Ciresi mimicked.

Ciresi was confident that Merryman's performance had demonstrated to the jury that the industry's public denial of wrongdoing was an orchestrated public relations campaign to obfuscate the reality that smoking causes disease and teen-age markets were considered areas of opportunity.

At one point during his examination, Ciresi asked how the Tobacco Institute could continue to deny the causal link between smoking and disease in the face of that very conclusion by organizations such as the American Medical Association, the American Lung Association, the American Cancer Society, the World Health Association, and the Centers for Disease Control.

"I don't agree that it's been established that smoking is a cause of lung cancer. No, sir," Merryman persisted with his standard name-rank-and-serial-number reply.

"You don't agree with that, do you, sir?" Ciresi asked one more time.

"No sir," Merryman answered.

"Do you believe the world is flat?" Ciresi quickly shot back, perking up the ears of everyone in the courtroom.

"Objection, your honor," cried Bleakley.

"Is that a serious question?" asked Merryman.

"I'll withdraw it," said Ciresi, his point already made.

Chapter Seven

Trial Life/The Specialists

"**S**ir, sir," I'm going to have to ask you to stop chewing gum," the courtroom security guard whispered, frowning, to a young defense attorney sitting in the spectator section one morning. The attorney, puzzled, turned to the guard and whispered back, "I'm not chewing gum."

Five minutes later, the guard was back at the attorney's side. "Sir, you're going to have to stop chewing gum or I'm going to ask you to leave."

Irritated, the attorney turned and hissed back, "I'm *not* chewing anything."

Behind the exasperated lawyer, two members of the media exchanged sidelong glances, eyebrows raised. Looked like it was going to be another one of those days in court.

From day one, the courtroom's dark-paneled, moody atmosphere had been further permeated with an almost claustrophobic paranoia, courtesy of Judge Fitzpatrick's erstwhile Palace

Guard, the private security staff hired especially for this trial to enforce His Honor's long list of restrictions.

Obviously, order was needed in the court, given the sheer number of attorneys seated in front of the bar. However, the lengths to which the judge had gone to keep his courtroom under wraps were incomprehensible. Even Ramsey County Chief Judge Lawrence Cohen, Fitzpatrick's boss, would comment after the case ended, "I wouldn't have that kind of security for a civil case." But, Cohen added, "I picked up from him an attitude that he had to have security."

Whether it was because, as Fitzpatrick had earlier stated, the trial's relocation to the federal courthouse made participants "guests" in that venue, or because he actually believed the courthouse would be mobbed with unruly observers, word quickly leaked out that a very strange situation was under way on Robert Street.

Minneapolis *Star Tribune* reporter David Peterson wrote a story entitled "Order in the Court," illustrated by an ominous drawing of a menacing court guard in dark glasses, in front of an equally spooky courtroom. It was widely praised as a dead-on account of court life, Judge Fitzpatrick–style.

Color-coded passes were required for anyone who wanted access to the courtroom (including the attorneys), a procedure said to be borrowed from the hi-octane criminal trials of Timothy McVeigh and O. J. Simpson. However, as a court official at one of those venues told Peterson, that procedure was instituted because of the crush of people trying to get into court each day.

For all but about four days of the Minnesota trial, seating was plentiful.

During his week in court, Peterson witnessed an encounter between one of the courtroom guards and a member of the public, retired Honeywell engineer Bob Matthys.

Matthys told Peterson that he'd strolled to the front of the gallery seating section to get a better look at the courtroom, while waiting for the proceedings to begin. "But some officious guard," he told Peterson, ordered him to stay back in the two back rows reserved for the public.

"The guard overhears this [the exchange between Peterson and Matthys] and approaches," Peterson wrote. "'Do you have some problem with the arrangements here? Because if you're going to be disruptive, I'm going to have to ask you to leave.'"

Matthys protested, "I'm not being disruptive."

Peterson wrote: "The two of them repeated the same words a couple of times, then the guard says, 'Sir, could you gather up your belongings and come with me.' Matthys can't believe it. He won't do it. 'Do I have to speak to the judge about this?' the guard asks. Matthys goes with him."

The guard then returned to Peterson and told him, "If someone approaches you with comments like that, it'd be in your best interest not to entertain that."

Ironically, Peterson noted, "While neither Matthys nor

reporters are allowed even to approach the railing that separates the gallery from the well of the courtroom, the judge's wife, who gets to sit in the well itself, was wandering around the courtroom. . . . at lunchtime, laughing as she fingered a lung and a heart on a life-sized anatomical exhibit."

Mrs. Fitzpatrick would be the only one so relaxed in such a setting.

A guard threatened one reporter with expulsion for turning his reporter's notebook pages too loudly one morning, as he recorded the day's testimony. Another day, observers were told "to keep all facial gestures in check—even things you might just do nervously." On yet another occasion, a reporter was ejected from the courtroom for "smiling and laughing at the jury" during a sidebar, although colleagues observed no such behavior.

One guard spent so much time staring menacingly at reporters that one of them finally wrote the judge to complain that his behavior was beginning to border on harassment.

The trial attorneys weren't immune either. R. J. Reynolds' Robert Weber recalled being admonished "for all sorts of things. It was just goofy. You kept waiting for Alan Funt to come in and tell us we were on *Candid Camera.*"

"I got yelled at for ripping a piece of paper. I got yelled at for chewing mints—we got into an argument over that one, because we told the guard we had a 'mint exception' to the candy rule. We were yelled at for passing notes. We were yelled at for talking. I was yelled at when one of my witnesses looked at the jury."

Philip Morris Associate General Counsel Greg Little, so constant a presence in the defendant's section of the court gallery that he got his own jury nickname, "Red Tie," was admonished one day for "smirking."

Brown & Williamson attorney David Bernick was chastised when his magic marker squeaked while he highlighted some notes.

B.A.T. Industries local counsel Gerald Svoboda compared the courtroom atmosphere to "being in Nazi Germany." The attorney recalled an incident during a courtroom break one day where "someone told a joke and we all started laughing. The guard came over and threatened to eject us unless we maintained the 'decorum' of the court. This was during a recess! It was pretty silly."

Woe to the poor unfortunate who forgot to turn off his or her cell phone or pager. On the rare occasions when one went off, everyone in the courtroom would freeze, shrinking in their seats like dysfunctional children of an abusive parent, as guards angrily scanned the room for the transgressor.

Once the offending pager actually belonged to law clerk Michelle Jones, but nothing happened to her.

"It was entirely inappropriate," said Weber. "If it was meant to show the judiciary in its best light, it backfired. Because it showed the judiciary as kind of insecure and intemperate."

Some members of the media and the defense team began

choosing to spend their time in front of video monitors in their conference rooms, rather than be subjected to the unrelenting tension on the seventh floor.

Ciresi and his team were the souls of propriety, at least as far as the court was concerned. However, several jurors had been irritated during the first few weeks of the trial about Ciresi's head wagging, eye rolling, and other facial contortions when the defense questioned witnesses. Juror Terry Zaspel wrote a letter to the judge, asking that it be stopped.

After the first complaint, Jill Burton recalled, "Michelle told us that the matter had been taken care of."

But Ciresi's facial contortions continued. Zaspel again complained. "Ciresi keeps peeking around and making faces," she wrote in a second note to the court.

"It made me mad," she said. "It was very distracting to me."

Finally, Zaspel recalled. "The word came back: 'That's Ciresi's way. Just live with it.'"

Ciresi's antics didn't bother Dorothy Hallen. "I thought it was funny," she said. "If they weren't lawyers, they'd be actors. I'm sure that he was trying to influence us, but I just wouldn't let it."

Ciresi's face making wasn't high on the list of jury problems. The group was beginning to chafe under the restrictions imposed on their courthouse lifestyle.

The days could be tedious for jurors, particularly when witnesses stayed on the stand for extended periods. They were confined primarily to their tiny, windowless jury room. Lunch was catered in each day from one of only three restaurants. The three smokers were the only ones who got a breath of fresh air when they were escorted to the courthouse's loading dock for daily smokes. Soon some of the nonsmokers joined them just to get out of the building.

"We went out behind the courthouse and walked in a circle, like dogs in a yard," said juror Jim Otis.

Their conversations were monitored by a Ramsey County bailiff and a private security guard. They were admonished if their conversation turned to any aspect of the trial. Newspapers were banned. The bailiff clipped anything relating to cigarettes and smoking from magazines.

Dorothy Hallen had started to read *Soap Opera Digest* to check up on the progress of a couple of shows she followed. "There would always be a cigarette ad on the front cover. . . . so, there would go the cover. We thought it got pretty ridiculous. I would leave court and drive down the street and there was a huge cigarette billboard, so it wasn't like we weren't seeing tobacco stuff during this whole time."

Conversations in the jury room would be halted summarily when the guard or the bailiff thought the jurors were treading toward forbidden territory. David Olson and Jim Livingston had been sharing their mounting financial problems with their new group of friends, having all but given up on ever getting a response from Judge Fitzpatrick or his law clerk. They were silenced on that subject as well.

"We were actually told not to discuss our personal problems with the other jurors," Olson recalled. "So that was the end of that."

The constant monitoring finally got on their nerves. Hallen recalled one day "during court, Jim [Otis] put something in his notebook. Jill [Burton] looked over and snickered, and the guard just let them have it. He claimed the lawyers might think they were laughing at them. I don't think the lawyers cared what we were doing. We just couldn't believe that anybody would care as much as the guard thought they would."

The incident with Burton and Otis was the last straw. During a break, Zaspel told the other jurors, "'We're not second graders. We've got to have a meeting here. Let's get somebody in here.' We were being smothered. We couldn't say anything. One day one of the jurors got reprimanded for leaving a pack of cigarettes on the table. Who cares? It was things like that."

Jim Otis agreed. "We felt like we were being treated like criminals, and we were just doing our civic duty."

Michelle Jones was summoned. "'We're tired of being treated like babies,'" Zaspel recalls a juror telling the law clerk.

"'This is just too much,'" Hallen recalled jurors saying. "'We can't say anything. These people are on us, they're just watching us constantly and yelling at us. Give us a list of what words we can and cannot use.'"

"We felt like prisoners. We told her to get them off our backs."

After that, Hallen said, the pressure eased up. The guard and bailiff started to spend more time outside of the jury room. They became more friendly. The bailiff confessed that it was the first trial she'd seen handled in this manner. In addition, the decision was made to expand the jurors' lunch options and a variety of restaurants were subsequently used. However, the jurors were still restricted in the amount of food they were allowed to order each day—nothing over $10.

Jurors spent their downtime playing cards or Scrabble (although they were forbidden to bring in a dictionary), and snacked on goodies some in the group brought from home. Everyone started to gain weight.

"We were joking that our posttrial reunion would have to be held at Jenny Craig," said Jill Burton.

David Olson said he gained about 20 pounds during the trial, which created yet another economic problem for him: "I couldn't afford to buy any clothes."

Days were long and punctuated by breaks that could range from 20 to 40 minutes, allowing smokers—including those on the jury, several defense attorneys, and one of the court stenographers—time for one or two cigarettes.

Some attorneys found the lengthy breaks and lunches aggravating.

"The pace was glacial," Robert Weber commented.

With no defined time limits, the trial's participants and observers took their cue to return to the courtroom from Mrs.

Fitzpatrick and her sister-in-law, who'd visit with the judge in chambers and then return to their seats just before trial resumed. The women were better than watches. However, their special seating accommodations continued to irritate several defense attorneys.

"It was just bizarre," said Gerald Svoboda. "You're in a court of law where, according to American constitutional law, everyone is supposed to be treated equally, and here the judge was according them special privilege. Governor Arne Carlson could enter any court tomorrow, and I guarantee you no one associated with the judge or the lawyers would make any special arrangements for him whatsoever."

Only Brown & Williamson's David Bernick chose to make the best of the awkward situation, continuing his daily chats with the two women. "I feel more comfortable if I have some kind of relationship with the people I'm going to be around every day of the week," he explained. "I thought they were very, very sweet women and I genuinely enjoyed my conversations with them. I talked about my kids, where I was going to go have dinner that evening, what Chicago was like. . . the weather."

But Bernick was also pragmatic. "Other people in the court-room can have a big impact on atmospherics. If every time I stand up, people who are sitting where the judge's wife and sister were are scowling, or crossing their arms, or shaking their heads and reacting—well, that's going to affect the jurors. If they come to know me and believe that I am good at what I do and am sincere in expressing my beliefs, and they respect it, that will be reflected in the way they act around me."

Members of the media were split between sitting in the courtroom to record events or watching the testimony on closed-circuit television in the first-floor pressroom, where they had access to laptops and telephones. However, the television pictures came from two fixed cameras and didn't provide the atmosphere and dynamics of the real thing. The jury also couldn't be seen on television.

The media room also had another feature not found in the courtroom—spin doctors. Publicists for the attorney general's office, Blue Cross, Ciresi's firm, and the defense team were never far from reporters. The attorney general's press secretary, Leslie Sandberg, liked to keep her spin succinct. "Skip good; tobacco bad," she'd remind the media regularly.

Often at noon and always at the end of the day, reporters would gather outside the courthouse to catch attorneys for comments on the day's developments. Weber and Bernick became the principal sound bites for the industry while it was always Ciresi who spoke for the plaintiffs' trial team.

After the heady early days and weeks of the case, however, local media interest waned. Trial stories moved off the front pages of the local newspapers. Broadcast media crews all but disappeared. That trend would continue as the state moved into an important, but decidedly unphotogenic part of its case—the medical case against smoking and the unveiling of the state's statistical model calculating plaintiffs' damages.

It began with Dr. Jonathan Samet, the head of the Epidemiology Department at the Johns Hopkins School of Public Health in Baltimore. Samet, a highly respected, nationally known researcher, provided precise testimony that started to lay the foundation for the plaintiffs' damages case.

He testified that smoking caused a range of diseases, from cancer to heart failure to stroke. What's more, he said, smokers needed more frequent hospitalization and missed more days of work than their nonsmoking peers.

Jurors received a first-hand look at the consequences of smoking when lung segments from smokers and nonsmokers were placed into evidence. A court clerk, carrying two plastic bags, moved down the jury row as jurors leaned forward to see the two samples, each about the size of the palm of a hand. The nonsmoker's lung was grayish brown and smooth, while the tumor on the cancerous lung segment was a light, lumpy, black-flecked spot.

Juror Terry Zaspel grew pale as the specimens passed by her. Her father had died from lung cancer. "It could have been his lung," she said. "They didn't need to do that; it was overkill."

Samet helped the state prepare for the case, he said, by reviewing and compiling a computer database of more than 900 studies from scientific journals. As proof, six file boxes filled with Samet's materials stood near the jury box.

"The findings of studies have shown over and over that the

relative risk of lung cancer is increased by cigarette smoking," Samet told plaintiffs' attorney Thomas Hamlin, illustrating his points with detailed charts and graphs.

"No one has ever found any alternative explanation to these findings except that smoking causes lung cancer," Samet said.

In response, Philip Morris attorney Murray Garnick sought to establish that cigarette smokers tended to be overweight, exercise less, and drink more alcohol, and that these factors could explain their higher rates of disease.

Samet's cross-examination concluded at about 4:45 P.M. on a Friday afternoon, the beginning of a three-day weekend. But if jurors and defense attorneys thought they might be released early, those hopes quickly were dashed. Mike Ciresi had other plans. He wanted the jury to meet Dr. Thomas Osdene.

Osdene, who had worked at Philip Morris' Research and Development Center, in South Richmond, Virginia, held key positions within the company over his 28-year career, serving at various times as a researcher, research director, and, finally, vice president.

His signature was all over some of the most controversial tobacco documents, and his name had been high on Ciresi's witness list. Ciresi wasn't the only one interested in Osdene. In 1997, Osdene sought legal immunity from the U.S. Justice Department, apparently distancing himself from his employer. Because of his situation with the Justice Department, during his deposition for the Minnesota case, Osdene repeatedly invoked his Fifth Amendment right against self-incrimination—135 times in all.

It was that videotape that Ciresi planned to show to the jury, in its entirety. Defense attorneys had vigorously fought the playing of the videotape of Osdene on the grounds that it was highly prejudicial and left the impression that the industry was guilty of misconduct. However, Judge Fitzpatrick ruled that Osdene's testimony was "relevant and its value is not outweighed by [the] potential for prejudice." Ciresi wanted Osdene's image to remain fixed in jurors' minds over the long weekend. He'd play as much of the deposition as he could before court adjourned for the day.

Thomas Osdene, a former four-pack-a-day smoker, was the living embodiment of Jonathan Samet's testimony on the effects of smoking. As the former researcher's face came up on the large courtroom video projection screen, it was clear that he was very ill. Osdene acknowledged that he suffered from diabetes, hypertension, bladder cancer, cardiac problems (he had two angioplasties), and high cholesterol. Gray-faced, frail, and wheezing, Osdene had to pause frequently to catch his breath or to cough. Not that his testimony was particularly long-winded. In the first 15 minutes of his testimony, Osdene took the Fifth Amendment 11 times during questioning about his 28-year career at Philip Morris. It wasn't what Osdene said, but what he refused to say that made the testimony compelling.

When asked if he had served as research director, Osdene

replied, "On advice of counsel, I decline to answer based on my Fifth Amendment privilege against self-incrimination, because there is an ongoing, parallel criminal investigation."

Osdene also refused to answer if he had once supervised biological research projects outside the company.

He was shown a 1980 memorandum he wrote to top Philip Morris officials and board members about research and development programs, but took the Fifth on all questions.

Osdene did answer one question directly. He acknowledged that a federal grand jury had subpoenaed him to testify about his work for Philip Morris. He said he hadn't yet testified and didn't know the nature of the investigation.

For the defense, it was a devastating performance. Whether Osdene had anything to hide or not, he certainly gave the appearance of guilt. It was the lingering final image Ciresi had intended.

While jurors enjoyed the President's Day holiday at home Monday, attorneys for both sides appeared before Fitzpatrick to argue the merits of Special Master Mark Gehan's February 10 recommendation that 39,000 documents previously protected by attorney-client privilege be turned over to the plaintiffs for review.

Fitzpatrick had not yet ruled on the special master's report, but he had followed Gehan's previous recommendation by releasing a set of Liggett documents in the fall of 1997.

Arguing for the state and Blue Cross, Roberta Walburn suggested that the documents were "perhaps the most significant and important" material to be produced in the Minnesota lawsuit. "It's been a long journey to arrive at where we are today on the issue of privilege," Walburn said. "The issues raised by defendants are issues that have been addressed repeatedly by the special master, this court, the Supreme Court, and the appeals court. It's a massive abuse of the process."

RJR's Bob Weber countered, "It is plainly an impermissable intrusion into the workings of counsel. It is fundamentally and profoundly impermissable."

Defense attorneys weren't hopeful that their position would prevail.

Jurors returned to court on Tuesday, fresh from their holiday, and resumed viewing the Osdene deposition.

The 70-year-old Osdene's voice was a tired monotone as he peered over half glasses to read his prepared statement that, on the advice of counsel, he declined to answer potentially incriminating questions. As a result, the jury heard evidence in the form of questions by Corey Gordon, an attorney at Ciresi's firm. Gordon wasn't part of the courtroom trial team, but played a key role in document discovery and pretrial depositions of tobacco industry witnesses.

Gordon patiently led the frail scientist through a litany of documents he either wrote or received from other Philip Morris scientists at Philip Morris. The volume of material was considerable, and damning.

In a 1980 memo, Osdene wrote, "I believe the thing we sell most is nicotine."

Gordon then cited a 1969 draft of a presentation to the Philip Morris board in which Osdene wrote, "We have, then, as our first premise, that the primary motivation for smoking is to obtain the pharmacological effect of nicotine."

Each time Gordon asked Osdene if that was his view on a subject or if those were his words, the retired research director would read his self incrimination statement. Eventually, Gordon told Osdene it would be okay to say "same response" rather than the entire Fifth Amendment clause in order to speed things up.

One by one, Gordon placed damaging documents in front of Osdene about the industry's views on why people smoked and why they kept smoking.

In the same 1969 draft to the corporate board, Osdene continued, "In the past, we at R&D have said that we're not in the cigarette business, we're in the smoke business. It might be more pointed to observe that the cigarette is the vehicle of smoke, smoke is the vehicle of nicotine, and nicotine is the agent of a pleasurable body response."

The memo also offered Osdene's view of the psychology of a beginning smoker. "We are not suggesting that the effect of nicotine is responsible for the initiation of the habit. To the contrary. The first cigarette is a noxious experience to the novitiate. To account for the fact that the beginning smoker will tolerate the unpleasantness, we must invoke a psychological motive. Smoking a cigarette for the beginner is a symbolic act. The smoker is telling his world, 'This is the kind of person I am.' Surely there are many variants of the theme: 'I am no longer my mother's child.' 'I'm tough.' 'I am an adventurer.' 'I'm not a square.' Whatever the individual intent, the act of smoking remains a symbolic declaration of personal identity."

Osdene went on to write, "As the force from the psychological symbolism subsides, the pharmacological effect takes over to sustain the habit, augmented by the secondary gratifications."

In the course of 90 minutes, Gordon got nothing of substance from Osdene, but managed to enter dozens of sensitive internal company documents regarding smoking-and-health issues.

Some discussed biological research, including research areas to be avoided. Others discussed increasing pH in smoke to enhance nicotine delivery to the body and another reported that smoking by pregnant women resulted in low birth-weight babies. There was even a memo from Philip Morris' "Nicotine Kid," William Dunn, about a proposed study by researcher Carolyn Levy on the withdrawal effects of nicotine.

"I have given Carolyn approval to proceed with this study. If she is able to demonstrate, as she anticipates, no withdrawal effects of nicotine, we will want to pursue this avenue with some vigor," Dunn wrote in the 1977 memo. "If, however, the results with nicotine are similar to those gotten with morphine and caffeine, we will want to bury it." Gordon asked Osdene if the study was ever completed. Osdene took the Fifth.

In a 1978 Osdene memo cited by Gordon, the scientist opposed a proposed Roper public opinion survey on whether the industry should take the position that smoking should not be done in excess. "An admission by the industry that excessive cigarette smoking is bad for you is tantamount to an admission of guilt with regard to the lung cancer problem," Osdene wrote. "This could open the door to legal suits to which the industry would have no defense."

Osdene was asked at length about Philip Morris' overseas research operation which plaintiffs' attorneys asserted was an attempt to maintain sensitive studies, especially biological research, out of the jurisdiction of American courts. Philip Morris owned a German facility called INBIFO located in Cologne, Germany.

A handwritten Osdene memo seemed to strongly support the plaintiffs' view that the German subsidiary was a dumping ground for scientific research that Philip Morris did not want to fall into the hands of litigating lawyers.

"1. Ship all documents to Cologne," Osdene's memo said. "2. Keep in Cologne. 3. Okay to phone and telex (these will be destroyed). 4. Please make available file cabinet. Jim will put into shape end of August or beginning of September. 5. We will monitor in person every 2-3 months. 6. If important letters or documents have to be sent, please send to home—I will act on them and destroy."

As with the Tobacco Institute's Walker Merryman and Liggett's Bennett LeBow, Ciresi's team was using documents to make the most out of their hostile witnesses—even if those witnesses had absolutely nothing to say.

Outside the courthouse during the noon break, Philip Morris's Peter Bleakley expressed concern over the impact on the jury of Osdene's testimony and his repeated use of the Fifth Amendment. "It's certainly not what we wanted," Bleakley told reporters. "Philip Morris asked Dr. Osdene to testify fully and truthfully. We wanted him to come here. . . . The reference to document destruction goes unanswered. The fact is, there weren't any documents destroyed."

Following Osdene, the state presented Dr. Scott Davies, director of pulmonary and critical care at the Hennepin County Medical Center. Davies discussed at length the cause of chronic obstructive pulmonary disease, or COPD, the most common manifestation of which is emphysema.

The doctor also brought along visual aids. Davies showed two freeze-dried human lungs to the jurors—the clean lung of a nonsmoker and the stained, moth-eaten-looking lung of a smoker. Several jurors touched the lungs and squeezed them as law clerk Michelle Jones carried them on trays along the jury box. A person with COPD breathed faster, "because your lungs are hungry for air," Davies said. "Your diaphragm can't help you. You have to use your neck and chest muscles. It's very hard work."

He said lifetime smokers generally developed COPD by their late 50s and died in their early 60s. He said it was the fourth-leading cause of death in the United States, and that smoking was the overwhelming cause. "If smoking was stopped, in one generation COPD would be a rare condition," Davies testified.

Jurors were shown a videotape of one Davies' patient with COPD who needed a portable oxygen canister to help perform even simple tasks like taking out the garbage. The patient, a 52-year-old nurse, began smoking when she was 13 and had a pack-a-day habit by age 14. She took a disability retirement at age 50. The soundless video was painful to watch as she labored up and down her south Minneapolis driveway, stopping halfway back to her house just to catch her breath.

Driving home that night, juror Jill Burton was struck with a horrible thought. Davies' lungs had come from the Hennepin County Medical Center. Burton's grandmother had recently died of lung cancer and had willed her body to science. "All I could think was 'What if that was grandma?'" Burton said later. "It made me feel really strange."

The state's medical witnesses were on and off the stand fairly quickly.

Davies was followed by Dr. Kevin Graham, a specialist in cardiovascular disease with the Minneapolis Heart Institute. Graham said smoking causes blockage of the arteries by preventing red blood cells from adequately absorbing oxygen.

"Smoking is the most powerful, modifiable, risk factor for

coronary heart disease," Graham told the jury. "Cardiovascular disease is the biggest killer in Minnesota. Cigarettes are the biggest cause."

Under cross-examination by Lorillard's local counsel, David Martin, Graham acknowledged that a sedentary lifestyle and poor diet could lead to heart disease, but maintained that they were nowhere near the risk factors that smoking added.

Two more video depositions of retired Philip Morris scientists were played for the jury as the trial moved at an uncharacteristically—albeit relatively—brisk pace.

James Charles, who worked for Osdene and succeeded him as director of research in 1984, discussed the INBIFO work and said reports and studies were routinely sent there to be filed when Philip Morris scientists in the United States "had no further use for it." Charles said he visited the facility several times a year and that there was a floor-to-ceiling cabinet, apparently the one referred to by Osdene in his "Ship all documents to Cologne" memo, where reports were stored.

"That was a management decision made by Dr. Osdene to return those to INBIFO," Charles said.

"Didn't you think that was strange?" Charles was asked.

"I don't know what I thought," Charles responded.

"Wouldn't it make more sense to keep them in Richmond? Wouldn't it be easier?"

"Probably," Charles answered.

The parade of videotaped witnesses was like a time warp, giving the jury a picture of the industry mindset from the 1950s and 1960s, when DeSotos were still driven on Main Street, U.S.A., television was in black and white, and frozen pot pies were the newest convenience.

Perhaps the biggest throwback to that era was Robert Heimann, the one-time chief executive and president of the American Tobacco Company. Heimann's videotaped deposition was taken in 1986 during a lawsuit brought by the family of a dead smoker in Holmes County, Mississippi.

With no subtleties or nuances, Heimann flatly stated that there was no proof that smoking caused disease or that nicotine was addictive. In the face of far-reaching reports by the U.S. surgeon general to the contrary, Heimann was unwavering in his belief.

He called the 1979 Surgeon General's Report showing a causal link between smoking and lung cancer, "a rehash," "misguided," and "dead wrong." It certainly was no reason for a change in the corporate position denying the link, he believed.

"The real nub of this question is the proper use of statistics," Heimann lectured. "Most physicians have little or no knowledge of statistical nuances and could be easily taken in by the misguided use of statistics."

The plaintiffs finally returned to the present with Dr. James F. Glenn, chairman and chief executive of the Council for Tobacco Research (CTR), an industry trade group subsidized by Big Tobacco. Although Glenn didn't join CTR until 1987, he would be faced with questions about the organization dating back to its inception in the early 1950s, when it was known as the Tobacco Industry Research Committee (TIRC). It would not be a subtle cross-examination. Ciresi seemed to rub his hands in anticipation.

In the early 1950s, a number of reports emerged that linked smoking to disease, especially lung cancer. With the help of the public relations firm Hill & Knowlton, industry executives met at the Plaza Hotel in New York on a December day in 1953 and created the TIRC to help diffuse the health issue. It was basically a public relations ploy that resulted in the Frank Statement, which was published the following month.

Ciresi quoted from Hill & Knowlton documents indicating that tobacco companies felt "grave concern" that the value of their stock prices were being pushed down by the health concerns surrounding their products. Ciresi claimed the companies were well aware of the link between smoking and health.

"A company that puts out a product has a responsibility to put out all information it knows about that product. When dealing with the issue of life and death, you'd expect a company to do everything, wouldn't you?" Ciresi asked Glenn.

"I think the companies acted responsibly by setting up a research committee," Glenn replied.

"A company that mass markets a product should get out all the information it knows about the hazard of that product that causes death?" Ciresi continued.

"I can't answer that. I don't think anyone can," said Glenn.

Citing a Hill & Knowlton memo, Ciresi quoted a tobacco company research director as saying "Wouldn't it be wonderful to produce a cancer-free cigarette? What we could do to the competition!"

Glenn acknowledged that cigarettes were habit forming, but said that was significantly different from the term "addicting." He also said carcinogenic agents had been found in cigarette smoke, but it remained undetermined whether those agents caused cancer.

"Has the surgeon general said smoking causes cancer?" Ciresi wanted to know.

"Yes," said Glenn.

"Has the American Lung Association said smoking causes cancer?" Ciresi pressed.

"Yes," said Glenn.

"Has the American Medical Association said that smoking causes cancer?" Ciresi asked.

"Yes," said Glenn.

Ciresi was like a bulldog yanking on Glenn's sleeve. His questions left his witness room only for single-sentence answers.

"From 1954 until today, how many Americans have died of lung cancer?" Ciresi asked.

"I don't know," said Glenn.

"From 1954 until today, how many Americans have died of heart disease?" Ciresi persisted.

"I don't know," said Glenn.

"From 1954 until today, how many Americans have died of COPD?" Ciresi inquired.

"I don't know," said Glenn.

Ciresi then asked Glenn which companies had informed him that smoking causes cancer.

"We never discussed the issue," Glenn replied. "There is a tacit acknowledgment that they've got a product that carries a risk factor and we know what those risk factors are."

Midway through his testimony, Glenn acknowledged that he had asked his four children not to smoke.

"Have you ever told the nation's children not to take up smoking?" Ciresi queried sarcastically.

"That's not my responsibility," Glenn answered.

During his second day under examination by Ciresi, Glenn was confronted with industry criticism of CTR's work. A 1977 letter written by the prolific Thomas Osdene illustrated concern by manufacturers about the quality and type of research funded by the council.

"It is my strong feeling that with the progress that has been claimed, we are in the process of digging our own grave," Osdene wrote about CTR studies linking smoking and disease. "I am very much afraid that the direction of the work being taken by CTR is totally detrimental to our position and undermines the public posture we have taken to outsiders."

In a memo from the files of the British-American Tobacco

Company, Osdene also was quoted as saying that the CTR "did virtually no useful work and cost a vast amount of money."

Moreover, Ciresi, in his continuing effort to undercut the credibility of Glenn and the CTR, introduced a 1958 letter from Philip Morris Chief Financial Officer J. E. Lincoln that benzopyrene, a carcinogen found in cigarette smoke, "must be removed" or "sharply reduced."

Lincoln added, "We must do this not because we think it is harmful, but simply because those who are in a better position to know than ourselves suspect it may be harmful." His admission came less than a year after the CTR, then known as the TIRC, issued a press release that said cigarette smoke did not contain benzopyrene.

Other company documents introduced by Ciresi showed that RJR and B&W had also identified the presence of benzopyrene in smoke by the early 1950s.

"I don't think the companies had any obligation to make (the TIRC) aware of their internal research," Glenn replied.

Under questioning by badly needed ally RJR attorney Robert Weber, Glenn tried to put a positive spin on CTR's work. He noted that, as of 1992, the council had spent $204 million on research grants for 1,329 investigations by 932 scientists at 300 medical schools. He said grant recipients were encouraged to publish their findings.

A controversial grant program called "special projects" received just a fraction of the funds, Glenn testified. The special projects section was under the direction of a group of industry lawyers, known as the Committee of Counsel. The plaintiffs alleged that attorneys ran the program to keep projects under the protection of attorney-client privilege. Glenn said it was not unreasonable that attorneys would be consulted on sensitive projects.

But Ciresi took one last crack at Glenn. "When," he asked, "did CTR survey all those imminent scientists to determine whether or not smoking caused" any of a variety of diseases?

"Never," Glenn replied.

Glenn was a wounded witness when he left the stand on February 23. But now, the most difficult part of the state's case followed. Its damage experts would now have to prove to the jury, through the use of a complex statistical model, that the state and Blue Cross had suffered actual losses of $1.77 billion through the treatment of smoking-related illnesses.

The damage model represented a real departure from tobacco trials of old, replacing testimony by individual smokers with statistical calculations. This case would mark the first time one of these models would be actually tested at trial. The model's purpose was to provide a statistical estimation of the actual costs paid by Blue Cross and the state to treat smoking-related illnesses.

The defense had planned to attack the model by using the so-called death benefit argument—that smokers didn't cost more to treat than non smokers, because they died earlier—and by claiming that the state, through its cigarette excise taxes, had already more than compensated itself for treating sick smokers. The judge had thrown out both arguments shortly before the trial began. When the defense then asked to be allowed to put forth its own damages model, the plaintiffs' argued that it was too late in the case. Judge Fitzpatrick agreed.

Different damage models had been prepared for the Mississippi, Florida, and Texas cases. Ciresi had his team commission an entirely new model, and they considered it a winner. Still, the damage model testimony would have to be simple enough for a layperson to understand and thorough enough to justify the requested $1.77 billion award.

The Ciresi team first turned to Scott Zeger, chairman of the biostatistics department at Johns Hopkins University's School of Public Health. His testimony was offered under the direction of Robins attorney Thomas Hamlin, a meticulous, deliberate litigator whose specialty was complex litigation. His full head of longish, prematurely gray locks inspired the nickname, "Hairboy," from the jury.

Zeger was part of a damages team that included Dr. Samet and Dr. Timothy Wyant, another Johns Hopkins–trained biostatistician. Their review covered the years 1978 to 1996. The team developed their model from three sources. They evaluated 280 million medical claims to the state and Blue Cross during that period and found 90,000 claims for diseases associated with smoking, such as lung cancer, COPD, heart disease, and stroke.

They supplemented those findings with additional data from a U.S. Department of Health survey of 35,000 Minnesotans on their health behaviors, including smoking. Then they added additional data from 28,000 respondents to a National Medical Expenditure survey conducted every decade to evaluate factors that influence health care expenditures.

Zeger and his team used those sources to build two models, a "core model," and a "refined model."

Zeger explained that the core model, which addressed the costs of treating patients with lung cancer and COPD, showed that the state and Blue Cross paid $626 million from 1978 to 1994. The refined model, which included data from the core model, added additional costs, such as nursing home expenses, and other diseases influenced by smoking, such as heart disease, stroke, and a variety of other cancers (pancreatic, bladder, and oral, among others). The plaintiffs' total smoking-related expenditures on the refined model totaled $1.77 billion.

Philip Morris attorney Murray Garnick returned again to questions regarding smokers' lifestyles, which he claimed weren't addressed in the model. He zeroed in on factors such as family medical history, high blood pressure, exercise, weight, and diet.

"Isn't it true that smokers tend to exercise less than non-smokers?" Garnick asked.

"I don't have expert knowledge," Zeger replied.

"Isn't it true that smokers drink more alcohol than nonsmokers?" Garnick persisted.

"I have no knowledge," answered Zeger, who maintained those lifestyle issues were irrelevant to the factors of age, gender, and disease.

"Does it take into account any behavioral differences between smokers and nonsmokers," Garnick asked.

"That is not taken into account," Zeger responded as Garnick completed his cross-examination.

After listening to nearly a month of testimony, jurors got a break in the routine. On Wednesday, February 27, they were left largely on their own to review nearly 300 documents submitted as evidence by the state and Blue Cross, about half of which had not been introduced at trial. Ciresi called it "document day." The defense called the highly unusual procedure ridiculous.

B&W attorney David Bernick told Fitzpatrick that it was "incredibly far fetched" to think jurors would gain anything meaningful from the exercise. However, the judge promptly denied a defense motion for a mistrial based on the free juror access to documents.

During "document day," the jury would be free to roam the courtroom and sift through 15 boxes of material at their leisure. A bailiff, a security guard, and representatives from both trial teams would be the only people observing them.

In open court, Fitzpatrick explained the procedure to the jury, asking, finally, if they had any questions. One hand rose.

"Can we sit in your seat?" one juror asked, causing laughter.

"Would you like to take turns?" Fitzpatrick retorted.

Later, jurors admitted, they did just that.

The hundreds of pages of material covered a broad range of subjects, including addiction, low-tar cigarettes, nicotine, and smoker compensation.

The documents reinforced the points made by the plaintiffs earlier in the trial about industry knowledge of addiction and the vulnerability of smokers. Some demonstrated outright cynicism.

A 1983 B&W memo about a coupon redemption program for its Raleigh and Belair customers said, "Raleigh and Belair smokers are addicted to smoking. They smoke primarily to reduce negative feeling states rather than for pleasure. Given their low income, smoking represents a financial drain on family resources. Saving coupons for household items helps reduce the guilt associated with smoking."

A 1972 RJR marketing memo stated, "I believe that for the typical smoker nicotine satisfaction is the dominant desire, as opposed to flavor and other satisfactions."

A Philip Morris memo from the same year contained drug culture references. "Kool is considered to be good for 'after marijuana' to maintain the 'high' or for mixing with marijuana, or 'instead.'"

The state's case as presented in the documents grew stronger. But the damages model remained troublesome.

Testimony resumed after document day with Dr. Timothy

Wyant, an independent statistical consultant, who had worked previously with Ciresi estimating damages for women injured in the Dalkon Shield IUD case.

Wyant said about 7 percent of the money the state spent for Medicaid and general assistance programs went to treating smoking-related illnesses. About 15 percent of the money Blue Cross spent for its subscribers was smoking-related. He said his first estimate of total smoking-related damages was $1.42 billion, but after defense lawyers criticized the methodology, the statistical team recalculated the total using different methods. The total subsequently increased to $1.77 billion.

Wyant's testimony was cluttered with statistical jargon, but in the midst of it some rather startling figures emerged. In discussing "estimated relative error," that is, the estimate of the margin of difference that might occur if the study were repeated, Wyant explained to Hamlin that the relative error in the various segments of the damage model ranged from plus-or-minus 41 percent for major smoking-related diseases, to a whopping 176 percent for the cost of nursing home care for smokers. That made the range of error in the nursing home component encompass anywhere from zero to more than $700 million dollars, he acknowledged.

Wyant, however, dismissed the wild variations, saying that confidence levels normally weren't calculated in regard to statistical estimates of damage.

RJR's Peter Biersteker wasn't so sure. During his detailed cross-examination of Wyant, frequently punctuated with objections from Hamlin, he returned to the relative error figure. Wyant acknowledged that many studies did use a margin of error of plus-or-minus 5 percent.

"Is there a lower standard when you're asking defendants to get out their checkbooks and write a check for $1.77 billion than when you're writing for a peer-review journal?" Biersteker asked.

Wyant, however, said he stood by his findings. "I believe it is a reliable model."

Biersteker, veering away from numbers, probed weaknesses in the model with words the jury would understand.

Turning to the portion of the model that covered medical costs of 19 to 34 year-old male smokers, Biersteker asked, "Do you know why they were in the hospital?"

Wyant said he hadn't studied the records, but knew of at least one case of pneumonia. "Many of those people had other smoking-related conditions in their histories that would have led to complications of treatment."

But Biersteker pointed out that hospital records showed some 19 to 34 year-old male smokers were hospitalized for hemorrhoids, schizophrenia, and, in one case, to act as a kidney donor.

"I don't believe that makes any difference to the fundamental workings of the model," Wyant responded.

Wyant also acknowledged that the survey data used to compile the model had incomplete smoking information from participants.

"And when you were missing the information for those people, you just assumed the person was a smoker, right?" Biersteker asked.

"That was the working assumption," Wyant responded.

In response to Biersteker's questions, Wyant also acknowledged that the model classified smokers as anyone who smoked more than 100 cigarettes in their lifetime, regardless of whether or not they had quit or when they had quit. Nor did it matter whether they smoked low-tar or high-tar cigarettes.

Biersteker was particularly interested in how the model evaluated two 94-year-old women, classified as smokers, who were part of the nursing home portion of the model. If the model were recalculated using a sensitivity test, he asked Wyant, "and this time we just excluded 94-year-old women, wouldn't your estimate be $87 million lower?"

However, Wyant never had to directly respond to the question. Hamlin's subsequent objection was sustained. Biersteker moved on, but he wasn't done with the two 94-year-women. He would bring them back to haunt the plaintiffs during the defense's portion of the case.

However, the model itself and the accompanying testimony had been confusing, and at least one juror already was skeptical. "As the state was going through it, I had a lot of questions in my mind," David Olson said after the trial. "It didn't sound right."

Jill Burton agreed, "I hated the damage model from the beginning. Especially when he sat up there and talked about all the plus and minus numbers. I thought 'Excuse me while you pick a number.' Times like that I wondered if I could just raise my hand and say something."

Media reports on the testimony were equally lukewarm, most mentioning the large relative error figures. However, Ciresi, game face locked in place, brushed aside criticism of the damages model. He remained convinced the case for the state and Blue Cross was going well and felt the otherwise stoic jury was siding with the plaintiffs. "Our witnesses have done extraordinarily well," he said between court sessions late in the week.

And he was especially looking forward to his next guests on the witness stand.

Chapter Eight

The Marlboro Man
and the King of Camels

I
f any tobacco industry witness could be characterized as a
celebrity, Philip Morris Chairman and Chief Executive
Officer Geoffrey Bible was it. In the world of Big Tobacco,
Bible reigned as king, sitting atop Philip Morris Companies,
Inc., one of the world's largest packaged goods conglomerates,
thanks to subsidiaries such as Kraft Foods and Miller Brewing, in
addition to its namesake cigarette company.

Bible wasn't the first Philip Morris executive to testify on
March 2, nor would he be the last CEO to appear that week.
Bible would be followed by R. J. Reynolds President and CEO
Andrew Schindler. The testimony of these executives was considered critical, not only to the case in St. Paul, but the national
debate as well. Would they continue their pacifistic overtones
toward resolving tobacco's legal and political problems, or would
they parrot past assertions by other tobacco executives and deny
the link between their product and disease? Their appearances
would be closely watched, from Washington to Wall Street.

And Ciresi had planned it that way. Judge Fitzpatrick had ruled
that each of the 11 defendants had to produce at trial, one "live"
(rather than videotaped) witness of the plaintiffs' choice—and
Ciresi aimed high on the corporate food chain.

With Geoffrey Bible—who had been deposed once, but never
appeared live at a tobacco trial—Mike Ciresi had a triple-A witness, the man at whose desk Philip Morris' megabucks stopped.
The litigator prepared to take his witness on a roller-coaster ride
through document hell.

Bible, 60, arrived in court flanked by a cadre of corporate attorneys and accompanied by his wife, Sarah. A small, neatly dressed
man with silvery white hair and an engaging smile, Bible looked
more like a favorite uncle than the ruler of what antitobacco
activists considered to be the "evil empire."

On top of this kindly visage, he spoke with a highly cultured
Australian accent that sounded more like Alec Guinness than
Crocodile Dundee. His carefully modulated answers floated like
music across the courtroom and would bedevil Ciresi during the
first of Bible's three days on the stand.

The attorney at first ignored the possibility that the staccato
harshness of his feisty Jimmy Cagney courtroom technique might
backfire with jurors when it butted up against Bible's suave, unruffled demeanor.

After questioning Bible about his citizenship (Australian, he
became a U.S. citizen in 1994), his multimillion dollar compensation package (estimated at $8 million annually in 1995), and

Philip Morris' operating revenues ($68 billion in 1996), Ciresi shot straight to the point. He asked Bible how he'd respond if it were proven that his product killed 100,000 people a year.

"It's not an assumption I would make," Bible replied.

"How many would it have to kill?" Ciresi repeated.

"I don't find that a very fair question, sir," Bible answered gently. "I can't assume something of that nature when it's not something I believe occurs."

Ciresi persisted. "How many would have to die from smoking before you would reassess your duties? One? A hundred? Five thousand? How many, sir?"

"Well sir," Bible responded. "I don't know that anybody does [die]."

Ciresi devoted much of his early assault trying to push the CEO into acknowledging a link between smoking and disease. But Bible wouldn't take the bait. He responded, almost apologetically, that he believed that there were risks associated with smoking, but no proof that it caused disease.

Ciresi pressed the question so relentlessly that Judge Fitzpatrick delivered one of the few reprimands the attorney received during the trial, telling him, "Please don't interrupt the witness."

Ciresi turned his questioning toward the plaintiffs' Rosetta Stone, the Frank Statement. Earlier witnesses had stumbled badly when confronted with it. Now it was Bible's turn.

But the CEO was not about to falter. As Ciresi queried him about his knowledge of the 1954 document, Bible responded,

"When I took over as CEO, I concluded I could do one of two things. I could spend the rest of my life looking backwards to examine what had gone on for the last 40 years, or try to do something to resolve the issues that have been confronting us. I decided to spend my time looking forward, trying to resolve the issues that are confronting us."

Bible would return to his "looking forward" statement many times during his three days on the stand. When he did, Ciresi would return to his favorite question, about the link between smoking and health.

"Sir, in the four years that you've been CEO and you wanted to look forward, have you had a concern whether or not people are dying from your product?"

"Well, of course I've been concerned about it," Bible responded, adding—again—that he didn't know whether a link between smoking and disease existed, only that it "might."

The questioning ran in similar circles throughout the morning.

When court broke for lunch, Bible stepped outside to smoke a cigarette. The television camera crews were on him like flies. They wanted a shot of the CEO of the largest tobacco manufacturer in the world smoking. Asked what brand he smoked, Bible smiled. "I'm a Marlboro man," he said, puffing on Philip Morris' most popular brand.

Bible continued to deflect Ciresi's best efforts throughout the afternoon.

"I don't think smoking causes lung cancer," he repeated. "It's a very significant risk factor. If there was anything in cigarettes con-sidered risky that could be taken out, I'd be delighted."

"You don't know if it can be done?" Ciresi asked.

"I am not a scientist," Bible answered.

"How many of your average smokers *are* scientists?" Ciresi retorted.

Bible acknowledged attempts by Philip Morris to develop a smokeless cigarette that would reduce health concerns. But after $300 million in development costs, he said, the company con-cluded the product wouldn't sell.

Ciresi returned to the Frank Statement again and again that first day, but couldn't wrestle the answer he wanted from the CEO:

"Now, the Frank Statement arose out of an alarm in the indus-try back in the 1950s, didn't it, sir?"

"I have no idea, sir."

"You have no idea?"

"No idea, no. In 1954, I was battling away in Australia to sur-vive, so I don't know what happened."

Still, on that first day in court, Bible's "I don't knows" and oft-expressed confusion about the scientific content of some of the documents Ciresi showed him played in his favor. It wasn't that Ciresi wasn't scoring some direct hits during his questioning, it was just that Bible seemed particularly adept at absorbing them.

At one point, Ciresi returned again to the issue of dying smokers.

"Do you know what other industry where it has been reported

Smoked

that over 400,000 people per year in the United States died from the product?"

"No, I don't."

"Any other industry?"

Bible again responded. "No, I don't know. I don't know of any other, but I don't pretend to be a historian. I don't know what other events have occurred, but I don't know. I'm not going to argue or quibble over it."

Toward the end of the day, Ciresi again attempted to pressure Bible to acknowledge that smoking caused cancer.

"Do you accept that smoking causes disease?" Ciresi demanded.

"I've said that I think that cigarette smoking is a very significant risk factor in certain diseases, sir."

"That's not what I asked you," Ciresi snapped. "This is a simple word here."

Unruffled, Bible responded. "Okay. Well, let me have it again."

"It's 'cause.'"

"Uh huh." Bible waited.

"C-A-U-S-E," Ciresi spelled out sarcastically. "Cause. Do you understand that? That's what I'm asking you about."

"Object to the snide remarks of counsel," Bleakley protested.

Fitzpatrick agreed. "Counsel, just ask your question."

Courtroom observers buzzed with speculation at the end of Bible's first day of testimony. Could this charming CEO actually survive a Ciresi examination? Could Bible be a Teflon witness?

Nothing Ciresi threw at him seemed to stick. And, the rougher the attorney played, the worse it bounced back on him. Philip Morris attorneys were all smiles as they escorted the CEO and his wife from the courthouse.

"They were looking at appearances, an affable Aussie," Ciresi would later say. In fact, he felt good that night. He'd anticipated that Bible's theme would be forward-looking and he'd been right. Ciresi knew that Bible would attempt to appear gentlemanly on the witness stand. "This guy had gone to charm school," Ciresi acknowledged, but added, "We got some tremendous admissions that first day."

However, the magic the CEO had worked on the courtroom slowly ebbed away as the examination continued Tuesday. While Bible's overall demeanor remained the same, Ciresi had modified his pugnacious attitude to better match that of his witness. The strategy began to work.

A long string of "I don't knows" during his second day of testimony created the impression that Bible was unaware of his company's long internal debate about the dangers of smoking. He acknowledged to Ciresi that he'd never asked the company's scientific staff about smoking, nicotine, and other health issues until he was subpoenaed to testify in a lawsuit in Florida in 1997.

Bible was confronted with a memo revealing Philip Morris' knowledge—six years before the surgeon general ordered a warning put on cigarette packs—that pregnant women who smoked tended to have low-birth-weight babies. Philip Morris hadn't publicized that information.

"Why didn't the company do it?" Ciresi asked.

"You know, I wonder if anybody in America believes cigarette companies when we say something like that, sir," Bible replied, somewhat disingenuously.

Bible claimed ignorance of a 1992 Philip Morris memo that said "the primary reason [people smoke] is to deliver nicotine to their bodies."

Ciresi responded: "Would you agree that if people are addicted to cigarettes, then your company couldn't very well defend cases by saying people had a free choice?"

"I find that a bit difficult to answer. I'm not a lawyer, but I would say that your choice is limited if you are addicted to something. I'd understand that certainly," Bible answered.

Ciresi continued his polite, but unrelenting attack.

He confronted Bible with a 1969 internal presentation to the Philip Morris board of directors that analyzed the smoking psychology of 16 to 20-year-olds "Does the term 'adolescent' ring a bell with regard to the age we're talking about?" he asked.

"Yes, it does," Bible replied, "I'm ashamed of that. I don't like to see anything about the company talking about 16-year-olds. I can tell you categorically today we do not market cigarettes to under-age people."

"Well, we just have to take your word on that, don't we, sir?" Ciresi asked.

"I'd like you to." said Bible.

Ciresi didn't. For the rest of the day, he barraged Bible with documents that produced similar sorrowful responses.

Asked about a 1974 Roper study of underage smoking, Bible said, "If they were actually conducting a survey of children that age to do with smoking habits, yes, I'd be ashamed of that."

"That's another one you're ashamed of, correct?"

"Yes, I'm very sorry about that."

"Are you shocked by these?"

"I am shocked, yes," Bible acknowledged.

Another document, written on Philip Morris letterhead in 1979, discussed Marlboro's domination in the 17-and-younger age group, where it had captured over 50 percent of the market.

"Are you ashamed by this document?"

"I'm sorry about it, yes I am," Bible replied.

Another section in the document discussed marketing efforts undertaken during spring school breaks at beaches and other places where young adults congregated.

"But if young adults were under 17 and went all the way down to 14, you'd be ashamed, wouldn't you?

"I'd be very sorry and ashamed, that we should not be marketing cigarettes to young people, but I believe that we can market them to adults," Bible responded.

By the executive's third day on the witness stand, Ciresi had worn down Bible's patience. He occasionally became testy. The youth marketing memos continued to drown him, as did Ciresi's repeated, increasingly sarcastic queries regarding his shame, sorrow, and embarrassment.

Ciresi produced a 1981 memo about a study on "The Effect of Government Regulation on Teenage Smoking," discussing how best to pass along an excise tax increase in a manner that would not stop teens from starting to smoke because of the price of cigarettes.

"Now, are you ashamed of the document?" Ciresi asked.

"I'm embarrassed," said Bible.

A similar document written six years later, produced a similar exchange.

"Is this one you're ashamed of?"

"Yes, I'm embarrassed by that."

"Ashamed?" pressed Ciresi.

"Well, I'm embarrassed." Bible retorted. "I don't see the distinction between the two, frankly."

Bible also characterized each of the shame-producing documents as "an anomaly." By the third day, Ciresi had had enough of that term as well.

After reviewing a memorandum discussing the greater impact of cigarette price increases on teenagers, Ciresi asked, "Is this another anomaly?"

Bible showed a rare flash of annoyance. "Sir, I don't know. I think we've used that word on five or six occasions. It's something that I've not seen in my career at Philip Morris. We do not market cigarettes to teenagers, I can tell you that. I never have. And if this is one of five or six, I would say it's certainly an anomaly."

Ciresi's marathon examination had begun to exact a toll on the defense attorneys watching it. Although they sat ramrod straight at the onset of Bible's testimony, by now they rocked back in their chairs, or slumped forward, elbows on the table, just waiting for the pain to end.

"I thought it was a real mistake to have Geoffrey Bible apologize," said B.A.T. Industries local counsel Gerald Svoboda.

When it came time for Philip Morris attorney Peter Bleakley to question Bible, he wasted no time in burnishing Bible's larger-than-life status. He focused on Bible's rags-to-riches rise to the top, a story Bible was happy to relate.

Geoffrey Bible was born in Canberra, Australia. During World War II, the family moved to Sydney. When Bible's father died, his mother was hospitalized, and he left school at age 14 to run his father's retail shop. After his mother recovered and took over the store's operation, Bible joined an accounting firm as an office boy, attending accounting school at night until he graduated as the equivalent of a certified public accountant.

In 1959, Bible left Australia for Lebanon, where he joined the United Nations' Relief and Works Agency for Palestinian Refugees as an internal auditor. From there, he moved to the International Labor Office in Geneva, Switzerland, for a year, then to ESSO (the precursor to Exxon), where he worked as a financial analyst. Bible joined Philip Morris in 1968. With the exception of a six-year period in which he left the company, Bible had been a Philip Morris employee ever since.

He moved up the organization through various positions in Europe and Australia, until he relocated to the United States in 1984 and became executive vice president of Philip Morris International (PMI). He became president of PMI in 1987, then moved to subsidiary Kraft Foods in Chicago as its president and CEO in 1990. Returning to New York in 1991, Bible became executive vice president of parent organization Philip Morris Companies, International.

When he took over the company in 1994, Bible said, he sensed the tobacco industry was in turmoil, with threats of litigation increasing and congressional investigations under way. "I saw the growing concern about cigarette smoking and youth smoking. I concluded that there had to be a better way than what the past was and what the current future held, given the explosion."

Bible decided that it would make a lot of sense if Philip Morris could reach out to "the people who were suing us, and I worked with Philip Morris U.S.A. to see what they could do to address the concern of youth marketing and youth smoking."

Bible said he and the rest of the industry decided to turn to Congress for a national resolution to resolve the future of the tobacco industry, even though it would result in fewer cigarettes being sold because of higher taxes, more regulation, and advertising restrictions.

It was a highly unusual admission in the middle of a trial to discuss a settlement, but Ciresi had mentioned it briefly during his initial questioning. The defense wanted the jury to hear about the industry's desire to settle its legal uncertainties in a uniform way.

Bleakley found Ciresi's settlement reference "clearly misleading. The jury now knew nothing except that it's been suggested to them that the defense was trying to get immunity. What choice did we have, but to explain the context of the national settlement overall?"

Instead of continuing to deny a direct link between smoking and disease, Bible said, the company would "disengage from the debate" outside of the courtroom. They would no longer fight about whether or not cigarettes were addictive, outside of the courtroom. New warning labels would be put on cigarettes, Bible said. "They will read, 'cigarettes are addictive, tobacco can harm your children, cigarettes can cause fatal lung disease, cigarettes cause cancer, cigarettes cause strokes and heart disease, smoking during pregnancy can harm your baby, smoking can kill you, tobacco causes fatal lung disease in nonsmokers, and quitting smoking now greatly reduced serious risk to your health.'"

From the jury box, Dorothy Hallen listened to Bible's explanation with growing confusion. "I didn't understand why he said that, when the whole time he was saying it, it didn't happen."

Ciresi was overjoyed that the settlement issue had been raised in greater detail. It allowed him to show that the industry was willing to pay large sums of money to obtain immunity from lawsuits similar to Minnesota's. It also permitted him to attack the proposed settlement's shortcomings.

"The settlement has been roundly criticized by leading organizations in this country which deal with the public health, correct?"

Bible agreed. "Yes, I'm aware of that."

"And numerous senators and congressmen and even the White House have criticized this proposed settlement."

Bleakley objected, but the judge overruled him, saying, "You opened the door, counsel."

Ciresi took issue with Bible's stated concern that continued litigation could hurt the company and its investors, saying, "Not a word about the victims of your company's conduct, correct? What about the people who are dying from your product? What about those people? You didn't mention them, did you?"

"If they are ill and they are adult smokers, they've made their free choice," Bible replied.

Ciresi continued to batter Bible with a staccato barrage of questions.

"When you became CEO in June of 1994, did you say, 'Open up the vaults, get the documents out.' Did you say that?"

"No, I did not."

"Did you do it in 1996?"

"No."

"Did you do it in 1997?"

"No, I did it in 1998."

"Yes, when you went to Congress asking for certain things."

Ciresi scoffed at Bible, noting it took the Minnesota case for the industry to turn over millions of previously secret documents about its knowledge of smoking, addiction, and disease.

"You fought those documents in this case up to the Minnesota Supreme Court and to the U.S. Supreme Court," he stated. "Tell me what other attorney general other than Skip Humphrey took you to the Supreme Court?"

Ciresi abandoned any pretense of civility as he hammered away at the CEO, at one point banging the large poster-board "Frank Statement" exhibit down so hard, it drew another admonishment from the bench.

After three days on the witness stand, with his wife watching from the defense seats in the spectator section of the courtroom, Bible was excused. The CEO remained a gentleman until the end, finally asking the judge, almost wistfully, "May I step down?"

Although he'd faltered out of the gate, Ciresi had accomplished his goal with Geoffrey Bible. "A trial is a series of impressions, of evidence, of position," the attorney later reflected. "Bible enabled us to establish many, many impressions that were important to our case."

One trial analyst later said of the examination, "Geoffrey Bible's idea of hell may be eternal cross-examination by Mike Ciresi."

Still, the overall impression Bible left on several jurors was not unfavorable. James Livingston liked "his accent." Terry Zaspel described him as "sincere and believable." Dorothy Hallen found him "so nice, so pleasant. I believed him when he talked about looking to the future. But I think he had a rude awakening. I hope he took some of it back with him. Maybe I'm being naive, but I hope something good comes of this."

However, juror Jim Otis felt differently. "I don't think it was fair that he denied knowing anything happened. If you're taking over a corporation like that, you've got to know. If they were screwing up in the past, well, he's in charge; he should be taking measures to correct that."

Attorney Bleakley was highly critical of Ciresi's methods with the chief executive. "It was clearly improper for Ciresi to be allowed to use defense witnesses as vehicles to read to the jury what he perceived to be repeated passages from bad documents when it was clear [Bible] had no knowledge of the subject matter. That was improper. Plain and simple—improper. And I think, by itself, would have resulted in a reversal on appeal. That's what bothered me.

"Obviously those were uncomfortable moments because we had made our objections, they were clearly going to be overruled, so you just had to sit and live with all of it."

However, Ciresi countered, "Corporations talk through documents, and you can't bring everyone in to testify. Documents are admissions. They show a course of conduct and you can ask the head of the company, 'Is that appropriate conduct?'"

Ciresi's next industry target was Andrew Schindler, chief executive of R. J. Reynolds, the tobacco subsidiary of RJR Nabisco Holdings Corporation, another international food and cigarette conglomerate. Schindler had arrived in the Twin Cities several days earlier to review documents and prepare for his testimony. He visited the court one day and watched a few minutes of Ciresi's scorching examination of Bible on the industry's closed circuit transmission in their downstairs conference room. After 15 minutes, he'd seen enough.

R. J. Reynolds attorney Robert Weber told Schindler what to expect. "The plaintiffs wouldn't ask questions about anything he knew about or had done. They would ask questions about what he *didn't* know about, and ancient events and documents he'd never seen. The CEOs were just sounding boards for the plaintiffs to read and reread documents. We knew what was coming. We told Andy to be ready for this, and that he shouldn't worry that it wouldn't appear fair to him, because it wasn't going to be fair."

About the only thing Schindler shared in common with Bible was an executive status. The two witnesses were as different as night and day. Schindler was tall and handsome, with graying brown hair worn in a stylish cut, and thinly framed glasses perched on his angular face. The RJR CEO, at 53, was roughly a peer of Ciresi's—the attorney wasn't going to worry about having to be deferential. Neither was Schindler. Sparks flew between the two men as they faced off. A Vietnam veteran, Schindler was a combative witness who drummed his fingers on the witness stand and audibly sighed in frustration with Ciresi's unrelenting questions.

Schindler rose to chief executive in 1995 after spending 21 years with the company in a variety of positions at both RJR and RJR Nabisco, Inc. During his career he had overseen sales, manufacturing, and personnel. He was a no-nonsense executive who believed firmly in the chain of command.

With 25 percent of the domestic market, RJR ranked as the number-two cigarette manufacturer in the United States. Its brands included Winston, Salem, Camel, and Doral. As RJR lost market share to Philip Morris' Marlboro in the 1970s and 1980s, it countered with the now infamous Joe Camel campaign. While a success in terms of sales, Joe Camel was roundly criticized for its youth-oriented, party-hearty message, and was discontinued in 1997.

"We don't market to youth," Schindler told Ciresi, repeating the line established by Bible earlier in the week. "I've been with the company 24 years and I've never seen a marketing plan directed at underage smokers."

But Ciresi had some internal RJR documents to share with Schindler. One was a 1975 outline of a presentation for the RJR board of directors about targeting the "young adult franchise."

"They represent tomorrow's cigarette business," the memo said. "As this 14 to 24 age group matures, they will account for a key share of the total cigarette volume—for at least the next 25 years."

An exasperated Schindler said that sort of thinking did not represent the corporate mindset on his watch. "If someone said, 'Andy, here's a way to get 14-year-olds,' they'd be in serious trouble."

Said Ciresi, "Mr. Bible—when faced with documents like these—said he was ashamed. Are you ashamed?"

But Schindler wasn't about to wander down the path of "shame" that Bible had taken. He shot back:

"They were wrong to be doing analyses of brand selection of people 14, 15, 16 years old. We don't do that today. It shouldn't have been done then. I'm not ashamed. It shouldn't have been done. It's stupid and it shouldn't have been done and it's unnecessary. I'm not ashamed of something someone did 25 years ago," Schindler replied.

Ciresi countered with a 1975 memo sent to C. A. Tucker, then marketing and sales vice president. Schindler at the time worked under Tucker. "To ensure increased and longer-term growth for Camel filters, the brand must increase penetration among the 14 to 24 age group which have a new set of more liberal values and which represent tomorrow's cigarette business," the document stated.

"Look, Mr. Ciresi, I can only answer from my own experience," Schindler replied. "I don't have any memory of people talking about developing marketing plans for 14-year-olds."

Like Bible, Schindler couldn't escape from the words of company executives regarding starting smokers, even if they were written two decades earlier. In a surprising admission, Schindler said RJR stopped tracking the smoking habits of minors in the 1980s, tacitly acknowledging that it had once been company policy, despite his earlier protestations that the authors of the memos cited by Ciresi were rogue employees.

In the mid-1980s, RJR began the research that would eventually lead to its Joe Camel advertising campaign in 1988. The company started its study with focus groups of smokers 18 to 24 years old and saw favorable results with the cartoon character, although one researcher reported the animal's appeal to smokers younger than 18 years old was a "main drawback."

But Schindler denied that a marketing campaign such as Joe Camel would prompt someone to take up smoking on the spur of the moment.

"I don't think that has anything to do with people starting to smoke," Schindler said. "I don't think someone drives down the street, looks at a billboard, and says, 'I think I'm going to start smoking.' Once they've made the choice to smoke, a marketing campaign can influence brand choice and brand switching."

The jury watched the witness with interest. Jim Otis later described Schindler as "a nice guy," adding with a chuckle, "The girls liked him."

When he returned to court for more of Ciresi's questioning on Friday, Schindler tried to go on the offensive, vigorously challenging the notion that nicotine is addictive. He said addicts were socially dysfunctional and needed to be institutionalized to kick their habits.

"I bet there's been more coffee users who went through hospitalization than smokers," Schindler said.

"How many people a year does coffee kill?" Ciresi shot back.

Ciresi was brash, swaggering, and often sarcastic with RJR's CEO, and drew numerous objections from Weber, who, at one point, objected to Ciresi's "sarcasm, snide comments, and smiling when the witness is answering." The judge declined to get involved, but later told Ciresi "not to get carried away" after he'd banged one exhibit around so much that Weber objected to the "pounding and yelling."

The noisemaking stopped when Weber stepped up to the podium to question his client. Schindler said RJR was proactive in discouraging underage smoking and had backed campaigns in schools and stores to keep cigarettes out of the hands of minors.

Schindler also testified that RJR had spent approximately $1 billion to develop a lower-tar cigarette with a different delivery system. But the product, called Premier, flopped in the marketplace because its smell and taste were unacceptable.

"I believe we have managed the company in a way that lowered the risk of products, and I am proud of that," Schindler said.

Weber also elicited some information from Schindler on a subject supposedly forbidden to be discussed before the jury—Minnesota's cigarette excise taxes. Surprisingly, Judge Fitzpatrick allowed Schindler to tell the jury that the state of Minnesota earned far more profit on each pack of cigarettes sold—48 cents—than did the federal government, which levied a 24-cent tax, or RJR itself.

But Ciresi wasn't about to let Weber proceed smoothly with his examination. Ciresi popped up and down like a jack-in-the-box with objections to Weber's questions. At one point, while Schindler was in the middle of an answer, Ciresi slowly began rising from his seat. Schindler stopped, midsentence, waiting for the objection. Instead, Ciresi, by now smirking, merely sat back down.

Fitzpatrick turned to Schindler. "That's called paranoia."

"Just been here too long," Schindler replied wearily.

It had been a good week for Ciresi, and a draining one. He'd been on his feet for most of it, displaying reams of documents to hostile witnesses as nerves on both sides frayed.

"Yeah, you're good," Schindler said sarcastically late in his testimony.

Weber was pleased with his witness, but remained frustrated by what he perceived as the continuing bias of the court. "We had two different sets of rules." He felt Schindler's exasperation with Ciresi was justified and understood by the jury. "It was entirely human and entirely proper. Juries don't expect people to be automatons, and Andy isn't. He's a guy who's been through a lot in his life, and who has fairness and integrity about him. I think it bothered him that this process was working the way it did."

Ciresi had little pleasant to say about either witness.

He described Schindler as "a smart-ass."

His characterization of Bible was far worse. "I thought he was a liar. I think the jury liked him because he had an accent. He was there as a showman."

Wall Street apparently didn't share Ciresi's disdain for the two executives. In fact, by the end of their week-long appearances in St. Paul, both Philip Morris and RJR stock rose by a few dollars per share.

Court adjourned Friday, but the trial wasn't over for the weekend. Not by a long shot.

Chapter Nine

Explosion

On Saturday morning, March 7, coffee cup in hand, Roberta Walburn walked the 50 feet separating her 11th floor room in the St. Paul Hotel from the trial team's makeshift office in a nearby suite. Not sleeping well during the trial, Walburn was an early riser, even on Saturdays, when she and her colleagues prepared for the week's coming witnesses.

After breakfast in the hotel dining room, Walburn made her second computer visit of the morning to check for electronically filed orders from Judge Fitzpatrick. Fitzpatrick had already issued several late-night and weekend orders, so it became routine to watch for new case developments around the clock.

Walburn was not disappointed with what she found. Filed at 8:04 A.M. was an explosive order that would alter the course of the trial. In yet another scathing indictment of tobacco industry conduct, Fitzpatrick ordered the release of the controversial 39,000 internal company documents, invalidating their protection under the claim of attorney-client privilege.

Fitzpatrick ruled that the industry "blatantly abused" the privilege assertion to hide incriminating documents from the state and Blue Cross.

"We were excited and glad that the documents would finally be coming out," recalled Walburn, who'd been tagged "the Diva of Documents" in a story in *Minnesota Law & Politics*. "We didn't think it would be the end, though. We knew there'd be appeals."

At his Inver Grove Heights home, R. J. Reynolds (RJR) local attorney Jonathan Redgrave was making the same discovery on his laptop computer, though not as happily as Walburn. He quickly alerted other defense attorneys, many of whom were out of town for the weekend.

To the defendants' alarm, Fitzpatrick ordered that the documents be turned over to the plaintiffs' attorneys within 48 hours. That meant the deadline for production of some 209,000 pages of material would arrive 26 minutes before the Minnesota Court of Appeals opened its doors on Monday, the earliest an appeal could be filed in the normal course of business.

Industry attorneys huddled via conference calls all day Saturday pondering their next step.

"We didn't know when he would rule," Redgrave said of the Saturday order. "But we didn't anticipate it would come on a Saturday morning and we certainly didn't anticipate it would come with a 48-hour deadline."

Peter Sipkins, lead counsel among the local defense attorneys, was in Palm Springs, California, for his mother's 75th birthday. "I got a call around 9:00 A.M. about the order," recalled Sipkins, a Dorsey & Whitney attorney who represented Philip Morris. "Everybody was going crazy."

Lorillard attorney David Martin, with the Twin Cities firm of Doherty, Rumble & Butler, thought Fitzpatrick had gone too far. "It was a stunt. He, in effect, said 'I'm tired of you appealing things so I'm going to deny you the right to appeal.' It was intentional."

Defense attorneys studied the Appeals Court's rules for extra-ordinary relief and by early Sunday afternoon were on the phone with Cynthia Lehr, chief staff attorney for the court. Lehr, who was in the middle of baking a cake, got on a conference call with Redgrave and James Simonson for RJR, Sipkins for Philip Morris, Brown & Williamson's local attorney, Jack Fribley, and lead plain-tiffs' attorney Mike Ciresi.

Lehr listened to both sides and contacted Chief Judge Edward Toussaint Jr. to report on her discussions with the attorneys. Late Sunday afternoon, Toussaint agreed to enter a temporary stay on Fitzpatrick's order and gave the defendants 24 hours to file an appeal.

The contents of Fitzpatrick's order did not come as a complete surprise to either side. Nonetheless, his order carried landmark significance because of the volume of material covered under his ruling and the potential contents of that material. Although the plaintiffs were more than halfway through their portion of the case, they figured they could call additional witnesses later and enter the new documents as exhibits then.

In his adoption of Special Master Mark Gehan's recommenda-tion to release the documents, Fitzpatrick was blunt with his con-clusions. "The intentional and repeated misuse of claims of privilege is intolerable in a court of law, and an appropriate sanc-tion for such abuse is release of all documents for which privilege is improperly claimed," he wrote.

Although Gehan had found no evidence of crime or fraud for the category covering youth marketing, Fitzpatrick asked him to review that category a second time, noting in his order the exis-tence of a memo from the files of Brown & Williamson (B&W) that was a marketing research report on the smoking conduct of 16- and 17-year-olds.

Fitzpatrick also unsealed Gehan's 147-page report from February 10. The special master had sampled categories of documents and determined the industry's claim of privilege was invalid in four categories, including smoking-and-health research. Gehan said he concluded there was a "high probability" that the industry knew about the addictive qualities of nicotine and failed to tell the public.

Ciresi was confident the material would be damning. "A 40-year wall of fraud and deceit has been breached," he said from his hotel war-room Saturday afternoon. "We will take that wall down brick by brick."

"It's another example of the court ruling on the basis of so-called tobacco law—where an industry is so unpopular that it has a law unto itself," said Philip Morris spokesman Michael York that weekend.

As Ciresi's team mobilized for a breakneck review of the newly declassified material, defense attorneys plotted another strategy. Convinced that Fitzpatrick had been running a biased courtroom for the last seven weeks, the defense was ready to attempt something dramatic—and risky.

The industry was reeling and in shock. The plaintiffs had presented a strong case to date on the issues of fraud and conspiracy, culminating with Ciresi's hostile examination of two of the highest-ranking executives in the cigarette business, Philip Morris's Geoffrey Bible and RJR's Andrew Schindler. It was time for an offensive move.

The uproar over Fitzpatrick's Saturday order hadn't diminished by Monday. Editors not familiar with the slow pace of the Minnesota trial or with the nuances of appellate law wanted their reporters ready to comb the 39,000 secret documents as soon as possible. News producers from ABC and CBS quickly arrived at the trial—too late for the weekend's big story and too early for any news of the appeal, which defense attorneys filed later that day. The documents would remain in limbo for an uncertain period.

In asking the Minnesota Court of Appeals to overturn Fitzpatrick's order for the release of the 39,000 documents, the defendants wrote, "The trial court has given the state of Minnesota a road map to defense counsel's strategies and opinions in the middle of an ongoing trial."

A three-judge panel was expected to consider the issue within a week or possibly two, but certainly soon. As would happen often in the days and weeks to come, the actual trial played second fiddle to the judicial orders, motions, and appeals swirling outside the jury's presence. The media section of the courtroom stood practically empty during each session. Nobody wanted to be confined for hours at a time listening to testimony, with news threatening to break on the other side of the courtroom's double doors.

That Monday evening, the principal defense attorneys met for dinner at Goodfellow's restaurant in downtown Minneapolis. They decided to seek Fitzpatrick's removal from the case, even though the risk of further alienating the judge left nobody comfortable.

"Judge Fitzpatrick is a very good, decent person," Sipkins said in retrospect, several months after the trial ended. "But the size of the case overwhelmed him. He'd lost control of it and he didn't recognize it."

There was a tinge of reluctance to seek Fitzpatrick's removal, but the weekend order on the privilege issue pushed doves into the camp of the hawks who felt the judge was openly biased against the defense. Sipkins planned to poll local defense attorneys to determine their appetite for such a direct challenge to Fitzpatrick's ability to run the case.

Only one of the Twin Cities–based defense attorneys, Faegre & Benson's Jack Fribley, had previously been involved in a recusal attempt, so the team was moving into uncharted waters. Unlike most of the national defense attorneys, who hadn't appeared before Fitzpatrick until shortly before the trial began, the Twin Cities lawyers had been with Fitzpatrick for the duration of the case and had developed professional relationships with the judge.

The Monday, March 9, episode of ABC TV's prime-time legal drama, *The Practice*, was the talk of the media room early Tuesday morning. It was as if the show had been lifted directly from the trial events of the past two weeks. The subject matter that night dealt with Big Tobacco: document discovery, attorney-client privilege, a court-appointed special master, and advertising to children. The parallels were incredible—and incredibly anti-tobacco.

As defense attorneys walked down the long hall leading past the media room to their courthouse conference room, they were asked if they'd seen the show. More importantly—were they worried that jury members might have been watching? They listened in horrified fascination to the plot line, but weren't about to talk about it with Fitzpatrick. Philip Morris associate general counsel Greg Little joked, darkly, "With that judge? No way! He'd probably show it to the jury—then tell them to disregard it." The joking would prove to be an eerie foreshadowing of what would unfold over the next few days.

That day, Sipkins found that his colleagues were more than willing to step forward and sign the recusal motion.

"A decision was made that we had to go public with the conduct of the court," Sipkins recalled. "We felt we were getting beat up in the media. We felt the public wasn't getting a complete view of what was going on."

Before dawn on Wednesday, March 11, 335,000 copies of the Minneapolis *Star Tribune* were delivered across the Twin Cities with a top-of-the-page story headlined, "For the Defense: Tobacco Firms' Lead Attorney Finds Trial 'Absurd,' 'Grossly Unfair.'" A picture of Philip Morris attorney Peter Bleakley, his cheek resting on his fist, ran next to it. Bleakley, whose responses to media questions up until now had been fairly circumspect, took an entirely different posture with reporter David Peterson.

The defense wasn't getting a fair trial, he said, not even close. "Whatever you may think of tobacco companies," Bleakley told Peterson, "they are entitled to all the same protections in this courtroom as anyone else—and they are not getting them. All rules have been suspended because these are the reviled tobacco companies."

He came armed with a long list of grievances, most of them centered around judicial decisions and orders, which he described variously as, "very unusual," "absurd," "grossly unfair," and, in one example, "the most ridiculous thing I've ever seen in my life."

These were harsh words seldom uttered in public by an attorney about a judge, certainly not during a trial. But Bleakley, and the team of defense attorneys he ostensibly led, felt the judge was controlling the case in a manner unfair to them.

Bleakley acknowledged that he'd been unhappy at trial before, most notably at the Cipollone tobacco trial in 1988, where Judge H. Lee Sarokin ultimately concluded that "the tobacco industry may be the king of concealment and disinformation." Sarokin eventually was removed from the case. However, Bleakley claimed, the atmosphere of that case was "nothing like this."

"We had problems with Judge Sarokin, but they were very different and vastly less troublesome," Bleakley said after the Minnesota trial ended. "Sarokin was no fan of the tobacco industry and his reputation was well known. . . . But he was a very smart, fair, and honest judge."

That wasn't Bleakley's assessment with Fitzpatrick. "The state is presenting a fraudulent case to the jury. They are deceiving this jury. And unfortunately, they are getting away with it," Bleakley told the *Star Tribune*.

At the core of Bleakley's anger was Fitzpatrick's ruling on the so-called "death benefit," the defense's position that smokers don't cost more to treat than nonsmokers because they die earlier. Although Bleakley conceded that this legal position was "not normally a defense," he maintained, "There has been an enormous effort to keep this evidence from the jury. The fact is that because smokers tend to die sooner, there are no increased costs. If [plaintiffs] want $1.7 billion, they ought to damn well be required to prove it—and so far that ain't happening."

Fitzpatrick had been adamant in two pretrial hearings that any reference to a death benefit would be hostilely met. The very notion of arguing that society saves money from a product that kills seemed to touch a raw moral nerve with Fitzpatrick, a former seminarian.

Bleakley was equally contemptuous of the state's damages model, used to calculate the extra costs of treating smoking-related illness. "It's baloney. . . but the judge bought it."

He also spoke out on the jury's composition, wondering, "Why call 180 jurors and have them fill out 26-page questionnaires if we're only ever going to see 35 of them? It's absurd." [Actually, 38 prospective jurors were interviewed.]

Bleakley further claimed that, "The court did not sustain a single motion of ours [that Ciresi contested] to strike a juror for cause."

Bleakley's outburst for readers of the *Star Tribune* was followed by a dramatic motion by the defendants asking Fitzpatrick to remove himself from the case, declare a mistrial, and allow it to start over with a new judge. The recusal motion was signed only by the local attorneys to demonstrate that it was Minnesota lawyers complaining about a Minnesota judge, not out-of-towners who were new to the scene.

"The undersigned senior counsel do not take this matter lightly," attorneys said in the pleading. "Regrettably, however, the rulings, conduct, and commentary by the court have created an atmosphere that has been unfairly prejudicial and effectively destroyed the right of these defendants to a fair trial."

The trial had become, in their words, "a show trial."

The 35-page memorandum attached to the recusal motion

outlined what the defense felt was a pattern of biased comments and rulings by Fitzpatrick, all the way back to pretrial issues.

"The Court has sent a clear message to the jury that the Court thinks the defendants should lose," the defense attorneys stated in their memorandum. "A fair trial is an impossibility in such a setting."

Among other examples, the memorandum cited Fitzpatrick's behavior during jury selection, where he refused to strike jurors who voiced opinions against the tobacco industry, forcing the defendants to use their six preemptory strikes instead.

"Time after time, prospective jurors were seated who acknowledged being biased against defendants, but promised to try to be fair when questioned by the court or plaintiffs," the motion said.

The defense team also questioned Fitzpatrick's decision to have only one attorney speak for the 11 defendants at any time, forcing "defendants to act out—for the jury—the 'conspiracy' that plaintiffs alleged. The court's order requires defendants to act in a 'conspiratorial' fashion in front of the jury, every single day of this trial."

The memorandum also found fault with the language contained in an early Fitzpatrick order. In it, the judge referred to previously unseen industry documents as coming from "some of the darkest bowels of the tobacco industry," and accused the defendants of engaging in a "conspiracy of silence."

The sound bites that day at the by-now obligatory posttrial attorney interviews were equally inflammatory.

Ciresi called the move "an act of desperation by desperate people who have seen their 40-year wall of deceit come crumbling down."

Peter Sipkins, who was surrounded by his local defense colleagues as he addressed the media, was adamant that the decision had been "heartfelt and deep-felt by all counsel."

Lorillard's David Martin had briefed his firm's board of directors before signing the motion. "It's your call," he was told. Initially opposed to any attempt to remove Fitzpatrick, Martin changed his mind following the weekend order.

"My feeling before the recusal was that we weren't going to win it," Martin said. But after Fitzpatrick's Saturday order, "I felt we had to. We had to make a statement to him at that point and tell him that what he was doing was wrong."

For Fitzpatrick, the attempt to remove him delivered a professional and personal blow. In 35 years of public service, he had never experienced such an uproar over his conduct. The development rocked his previously steady stewardship of this historic case. On the outside, his demeanor remained calm, but it masked a growing wound. The headliner trial of his career was on the verge of falling into chaos and ignominy.

Ramsey District Court Chief Judge Lawrence Cohen watched the developments from the Ramsey County Courthouse, aware that the removal issue could one day be at his doorstep. He also felt concern for a colleague "whose ethics were beyond reproach."

"They weren't sweet and gentle with Fitzpatrick. I think that hurt him," Cohen said after the trial was over. "It weighed heavily on him. It bothered him a lot."

Born and raised in St. Paul, Fitzpatrick had studied for the priesthood before turning to law. Since his graduation from William Mitchell College of Law in 1962, Fitzpatrick had been a public servant. He had never practiced as a private attorney nor billed his hours at handsome rates.

Fitzpatrick came from a dirt-poor background, where religion was a centerpiece of family life. He told the *St. Paul Pioneer Press* in a pretrial interview that his parents, who both died before he was 18, sometimes didn't know if there'd be enough money at the end of the week to buy food.

"I'm not ashamed of being poor even though a lot of people today seem to be," Fitzpatrick said in the interview. "I found that living in poverty made me a stronger person."

His legal career began as an assistant attorney general on the staff of Attorney General Walter Mondale. He moved to the St. Paul City Attorney's Office as an assistant in 1966, rising to city attorney in 1972. Fitzpatrick was appointed a municipal judge in 1973 by Governor Wendell Anderson. He became a district court judge in 1986 and eventually served as chief judge until late 1996.

Quiet in demeanor, Fitzpatrick generally was hard to read in court, and had a reputation for running a disciplined courtroom and letting lawyers try their case without interference.

For three-and-one-half years, Fitzpatrick marshaled the tobacco case through pretrial proceedings, including perhaps the most exhaustive discovery effort ever overseen in a Minnesota court, if anywhere. His monthly status conferences with the case's attorneys were marathons. Fitzpatrick would patiently give all parties the opportunity to make their points, and would sit for hours on the bench without taking a break.

Even attorneys for the plaintiffs were frustrated by his forbearance with the defendants. "For three-and-one-half years, I listened to our lawyers say, 'Is this judge ever going to rule in our favor?'" remembered Ciresi. "They were bemoaning the fact that these people would get seven, eight, nine shots, or bites of the apple, that every single order would be reargued, that the judge would give them more time."

From August 1994, when the case was filed, Fitzpatrick attempted to run an orderly court. At one pretrial hearing, he admonished attorneys after a testy exchange between the two sides, "This court is not impressed with any chippy comments. I would hope. . . that all counsel will perform with dignity and respect for each other."

In a 1997 interview with the Minneapolis *Star Tribune*, Fitzpatrick complimented the quality of the lawyers on both sides of the tobacco case. "There's nothing more enjoyable for a judge than to try a case that's being tried by good lawyers," he said.

"There's nothing I saw that indicated he started this case with an attitude," said Cohen. "He was pretty evenhanded with both sides."

The tobacco industry's delay tactics were well known over 40 years of litigation. Ciresi frequently quoted an industry attorney, who wrote 10 years earlier, "To paraphrase General Patton, the way we won these cases was not by spending all of [the company's] money, but by making that other son of a bitch spend all of his."

Fitzpatrick's patience began to wear thin in the latter half of 1997, when he felt the tobacco industry was not complying with some of his orders, particularly those relating to document production.

"He was becoming frustrated over the discovery process," said Cohen. "He saw the defendants circumventing the process."

Cohen, who was St. Paul mayor when Fitzpatrick was city attorney, called his colleague a "very righteous" individual. "He was a very patient judge who listened well and made decisions based on the evidence."

Fitzpatrick's now fractured relationship with the defendants had been strained a month earlier when defense attorneys asked the judge to remove law clerk Michelle Jones from the case because of a possible conflict of interest. Jones was deeply loyal to Fitzpatrick and he relied on her to help keep the case in order, especially as motions challenging his rulings were filed almost daily. During the trial, she often worked late into the evening and frequently slept overnight on a couch in the judge's chambers.

In the months prior to the trial, Jones had assisted Gehan in his special master role by helping him sort through samples of documents for which privilege was claimed. Jones and Patricia

Miller, an attorney retained by Fitzpatrick to help monitor the case, reviewed documents and wrote reports to Gehan. But the defendants believed Jones should not be doing work for Gehan while she also had a role in Fitzpatrick's courtroom, where Gehan's work would eventually be ruled upon. They also noted she had been paid an astounding $53,900 for six months of work, more than twice what she earned in a year as a law clerk.

Jones was hurt by the assertions from the defendants, and Fitzpatrick was very supportive of her. "He came back to the clerk's office and said, 'You've got to expect this kind of thing in this kind of a trial,'" Miller recalled. "He said, 'You can't take this personally.'"

In a letter to Judge Cohen, who investigated the Jones matter, Ciresi labeled the attempt to remove the law clerk as a further example of "scorched earth litigation tactics" by the industry to sidetrack the case and divert Fitzpatrick's attention from the trial. He urged Cohen to reject the industry motion to remove Jones and not to "condone in any way the efforts of this industry to cast a shadow on the integrity of this court."

Cohen investigated the Jones matter and determined that she may have violated some court personnel rules, but did not break any laws. Cohen went to the federal courthouse to meet with Fitzpatrick and said later that the challenge to Jones upset Fitzpatrick greatly.

"These people said, 'Don't worry, you'll get our support [to run the case],'" recalled Cohen. "When they challenged him, he felt that they stabbed him in the back."

Cohen advised Fitzpatrick that Jones should no longer work for the special master since court personnel rules limited the outside income that employees could earn. That was the end of the matter, although Cohen said Fitzpatrick seemed concerned that Cohen's role in the matter had undermined Fitzpatrick's control over the case.

In reflection, Cohen questioned his colleague's decision to move the trial out of the Ramsey County Courthouse to the federal building simply to use a larger courtroom. "I think he got too far away from the support system," Cohen said. "He got too far away from bumping into us in the hallway or the elevator. He should have kept it here. The case got too big for its britches."

Cohen said Fitzpatrick told him, "One would not understand the large number of motions being filed on a daily basis."

When the trial was over, Fitzpatrick told his 12 jurors that the efforts challenging his authority were distressing.

"He was hurt," said juror Dorothy Hallen. "He said in his 25 years that had never happened to him. By the end I think he was pretty mad at them. He was pretty hurt by what they were doing." Ciresi remained openly contemptuous of the recusal issue long after the final gavel banged.

"You didn't see anybody but the Minnesota lawyers on that. For chrissakes, if you were trying the case it would be a different story. They weren't even trying the lawsuit and all of a sudden you have that motion and they all sign it. Most of them weren't even in the courtroom. I thought it was a disgrace.

"To say a judge is biased is like kid's stuff if it weren't so serious—attacking a 40-year public servant who's been an outstanding jurist," said Ciresi.

Sipkins still defends the decision. "This wasn't a typical case," he maintains. "This was a case where things happened on a daily basis. What happened here had precedential impact on 35 other cases around the country. We had to make it clear to other judges that what was going on in Minnesota was aberrational.

"As much as we tried to style it so it wasn't personal, he viewed it as an unfair act by local counsel who he thought were his friends," Sipkins added.

As defendants and plaintiffs alike awaited word from the Minnesota Court of Appeals regarding release of the 39,000 documents, interested parties in Washington and on Wall Street watched closely as well. Wall Street was trying to figure out where the stock prices of the major tobacco companies would go based on the outcome of the Minnesota case; Washington wanted the documents for its debate on a national tobacco settlement.

Martin Feldman, a tobacco industry stock analyst for Salomon Smith Barney, was closely following the Minnesota trial. He had been predicting an eventual out-of-court settlement, but as a hedge had calculated that a loss in the case would mean a 10 percent reduction in valuation for industry leader Philip Morris. Feldman also had concluded that Fitzpatrick's role in the trial made predictions difficult.

Meanwhile, the list of tobacco lawsuits grew by one. On the same day defendants sought the ouster of Fitzpatrick, Blue Cross learned it finally was no longer the only health insurer daring to challenge the tobacco industry. On March 11, Twin Cities–based competitors Medica and Allina announced plans to file a joint lawsuit to recover health care costs related to tobacco use, citing the release of new documentation, much of it from the Minnesota case, as the reason behind their decision.

"The revelation of the additional documents which apparently show that the tobacco industry targeted children and teenagers as tomorrow's smokers strengthens our resolve to hold the industry accountable for their fraud and deceit," the companies said in a press statement.

Blue Cross CEO Andy Czajkowski praised the development. "We've been flying alone for four years. We're glad to have other health plans follow our lead."

By Friday, March 13, jurors were given a break from live testimony and placed in a vacant courtroom for another day of reviewing documents. Fitzpatrick and trial attorneys stayed in the usual courtroom and tried to figure out what to do about Congress' interest in Minnesota's document depository and the 39,000 documents currently sealed by virtue of appeal.

Fitzpatrick appeared unperturbed by the events that had transpired that week and treated attorneys for both sides in a pleasant, evenhanded manner. If he seemed concerned about anything, it was the continuing demands for documents from

Washington, D.C. At one point, almost out of the blue, he asked RJR's young local attorney, Jonathan Redgrave, "What's your position with regard to the letter from Congress, counsel?"

"You're talking about the letter from the three members of the commerce committee?" Redgrave asked.

"Yes. I don't know what your executives, what their agreement may or may not have been with Congress, so I don't know—I don't have any background on that," Fitzpatrick said, referring to a late January pledge to Congress from industry executives to turn over vast quantities of documents and open portions of the Minnesota depository to the public.

Redgrave was frank with Fitzpatrick. "Your Honor, my contact with that is limited. But I understand that to the extent that Congress and the companies need to work out something further or want to work out something further, that should be between Congress and the companies. . ."

Fitzpatrick interrupted. "Well, the letter was addressed to the court, and I guess—I guess what I'm asking is what should I tell them? To—to go jump?"

Redgrave, startled, began, "Well, Your Honor, I mean...."

"I mean, you want to negotiate with them or..." Fitzpatrick trailed off.

Redgrave was caught off guard by Fitzpatrick's questioning and wasn't sure how to respond. "It seemed to me he didn't want to be a mediator between Congress and the defendants," Redgrave recalled later. "He didn't want to deal with it."

Redgrave reviewed the bidding for the judge, pointing out that some of the documents requested had already been offered to Congress by the tobacco companies, and other things they'd requested were under court seal. He concluded, "So, I think that you're not telling them to go jump by entering the order that we provided. I think the court would be telling them that most of the provisions that they sought have been met."

Fitzpatrick, deadpan, retorted. "I was hoping that you would be the one that would tell them to go jump."

Redgrave, flustered, replied, "Well, Your Honor, I don't believe I want to go tell anyone to go jump in any circumstance. I believe."

Fitzpatrick cut him off. "I don't mean to be sarcastic. Can you — I mean, could the parties agree? I'm not really in this business, you know, and if the parties can agree on an appropriate response to the letter, I would certainly prefer that. I don't want to get into the middle of what your people told Congress or what Congress told your people. I don't have any knowledge, background, or expertise in that area, nor do I wish to."

Fitzpatrick was clearly uncomfortable under the Washington spotlight, and wanted both sides to work it out for him. But "jumping" remained on his mind. In a later exchange with B&W attorney David Bernick regarding documents at the Guildford depository in England, Fitzpatrick said:

"So, as I understand your position, you would like to tell Congress to go jump as to the Guildford depository. Would that be a fair summary?"

Bernick replied smoothly, "I might like to do that, Your Honor, but I don't really have to do that at the end, because I don't think this dialogue has really involved the Guildford depository."

Bernick was uncomfortable with the subject as well, telling Fitzpatrick, "Now what happens in our relationship with Congress, Your Honor, I frankly have to tell you I can't address either. I'm here to deal with this litigation and to follow the rules of this court. I understand Your Honor's not real anxious to get involved in Washington, D.C."

"Not one bit," Fitzpatrick agreed.

"Neither am I," replied Bernick. "Neither am I."

Fitzpatrick looked around. "Okay. Anybody here anxious to get involved?"

As the attorneys laughed, one of them rose.

"I am, Your Honor," said Ciresi.

"All right. Let's hear from someone who is anxious," Fitzpatrick said.

Bernick was right on his heels. "Then maybe Mr. Ciresi should take his request a little further east" to the nation's Capitol.

But Ciresi wasn't going anywhere. In an impassioned statement, he asked that all the defense documents, including those in England, be released to the public, using the words of Philip Morris CEO Geoffrey Bible to bolster his argument: "As Mr. Bible said, 'I want to look forward.' Well, then, look forward and get all of the documents out—Guildford and Minnesota."

Ciresi went on to assure Fitzpatrick. "I don't think the court should be involved in this and in the middle between Congress and these defendants. If they want to get the information out, they should go to Congress and say we're going to get all the information out."

Fitzpatrick had heard enough. "Should we move on?"

When told later of the judge's confusion and concern about the Washington requests, U.S. Representative Waxman, one of the three letter writers, said their request was not meant to interfere with the trial. Their interest in the material was for use in the debate over a national settlement then under way in Washington.

"We didn't in any way try to influence the trial," Waxman said. "But Congress was starting up and we felt it was important to have those documents."

The week had been a tough one on Fitzpatrick. Although he showed no signs of anger throughout it all, his memory of the events would run long and deep, surfacing in an astounding way later that spring.

Chapter Ten

Kids, Marketing, Antitrust, and the Witness Who Imploded

As the trial exploded outside the courtroom, a memorable witness was about to implode on the stand.

Cheryl Perry, a professor in the division of Epidemiology at the University of Minnesota's School of Public Health, stepped up to the witness box Friday afternoon, March 6. Unlike the string of out-of-towners who'd appeared in court during the past six weeks, she represented one of the few hometown experts called to testify. Perry's testimony marked another first, the trial's speaking debut of Ciresi's key associate, Roberta Walburn.

Perry's background was impressive. She received her undergraduate degree in mathematics from UCLA, followed by a master's degree in education from the University of California at Davis. After teaching in secondary education for four years, she attended Stanford University, receiving a Ph.D. in education with a specialty in adolescent behavior.

Leaving California for the Midwest, Perry explained that she had lived in Minnesota "about 18 winters."

Fitzpatrick, in one of his rare extemporaneous interjections, asked, "Do you ever stay for summer?"

As chuckles rippled through the courtroom, Perry, smiling, added, "I *love* summer."

"So do we all," said the judge.

Perry told the court that her duties at the university included teaching two courses for doctoral students on the principles of human behavior, as well as a master's level course called "Preventing High Risk Behavior among Young People."

Her main research area for the past 18 years, she added, had been large-scale, community-wide programs to improve the health of children and adolescents. She'd published more than 150 articles in peer-reviewed journals. More than half of them addressed adolescent smoking.

In addition to her responsibilities at the School of Public Health, Perry served as scientific editor for the 1994 *Surgeon General's Report*, which focused on preventing tobacco use among young people.

To prepare for this case, Ciresi's team asked Perry to review tobacco industry documents relating to youth smoking, many of them never made public.

Perry found those documents "quite shocking. I was shocked at how explicit they were in terms of targeting youth, particularly underage youth."

Those new, young smokers, Perry said, were targeted by

tobacco companies as "replacement smokers for those who quit or die."

Under questioning from Walburn, Perry unleashed a torrent of statistics about youth and smoking. Using figures from the government-funded National Household Survey on Drug Abuse, Perry said three million people lit up their first cigarette in 1994, two-and-a-half million of them under the age of 18. The surgeon general's report estimated that, of those first-time smokers, two out of three would became daily smokers at some time during their lives. The overwhelming majority of those kids who *didn't* start smoking by age 18, she said, never would smoke at all.

At the beginning of the century, Perry testified, only 1.3 percent of 17-year-old females smoked. Starting in the mid-1950s, that number began to sharply increase until, by the end of the 1980s, females were smoking at a higher rate than males, a trend that continued into the 1990s. About 23.7 percent of 17-year-old males smoked at the beginning of the century. That rate continued to increase until the 1940s, when it began a slow decline. In the 1990s, however, the rate again began to increase. Sharply.

According to Perry, that increase could be attributed, in large part, to Big Tobacco's advertising and marketing campaigns, which, she testified, clearly were geared toward attracting young smokers. Young smokers played key roles in the tobacco industry's marketing efforts, Perry said, and Walburn quickly furnished the documents to back her up.

A 1971 R. J. Reynolds (RJR) marketing department memo

broke down smoking preferences among 14- to 20-year-olds.

A 1973 internal marketing and research report at Philip Morris detailed questions asked of 452 teenagers nationally, "aged 12–17."

Walburn asked Perry to review a letter written in May 1979 by then–Brown & Williamson Chairman C.I. McCarty to Joseph Califano, then–Secretary of Health, Education and Welfare, in which McCarty stated, "because of our policy against advertising or in any way promoting the sale of cigarettes to persons under 21, Brown & Williamson does not have at hand the research data and other information necessary for a responsible analysis of the suggestion made in your letter. . ."

Walburn asked Perry, "Based on your review. . . did Brown & Williamson have information on smoking by teenagers prior to the time this letter was written?"

"Yes," the researcher replied, "They regularly reported information on 16- to-25-year-olds."

When marketing studies were translated into actual advertising, Perry felt, the ultimate impact on adolescents was "potent and influential," even though she acknowledged that they might not even be aware that cigarette advertising contributed to their decision to smoke.

Perry also brought to court a selection of print and broadcast cigarette advertisements, some not seen in almost 30 years. Jurors watched on courtroom monitors as Marlboro Country sprang back to life in all its glory. As the theme from the *Magnificent Seven* played, horses raced across the untamed West with rugged-

ly handsome cowboys in pursuit. Advertising aficionados considered these commercials some of the best of that period, or maybe
ever. For Cheryl Perry, they were invidious.

"The Marlboro Man is clearly independent, out there doing his
thing. This is a young, attractive man who's established his identity as a cowboy," she testified. "An adolescent watching an ad like
that would associate smoking with being independent and on
your own. And, you know, there are no parents in Marlboro
Country."

The jury watched Fred Flintstone and Barney Rubble light up
Winstons behind their Bedrock homes, as Wilma mowed the
front lawn. In another, Fred Flintstone chided a shopkeeper for
asking what brand of cigarettes he wanted. "It's what's up front
that counts," Flintstone said, adding, "You know, I never smoke
anything else," before proclaiming that "Winston tastes good, like
a cigarette should."

So long had it been since cigarette commercials appeared on
television that the whole presentation had a surreal air about it.
In another ad that ran during the opening of *The Beverly
Hillbillies*, the Clampett family pulled up alongside a Winston
truck, while the sitcom's bluegrass theme song incorporated the
sponsor: "The folks who make Winston cigarettes."

"These advertisements," Perry said, "which kind of blended in
with the credits to the show, would, for a young person, make
smoking seem a normal part of everyday life."

Down in the media room, baby-boom members of the press,

watching the ads on the courtroom's closed-circuit television set, sang along with the old television theme songs. Broadcast media members rushed to obtain copies for their nightly newscasts.

But Perry's point hardly was to entertain. She concluded that Marlboro's advertising campaign had everything to do with the product's wild success—and its widespread use among teens. Turning to a 1981 Philip Morris marketing report, entitled "Young Smokers, Prevalence, Trends, Implications, and Related Demographic Trends," she read:

> *It is important to know as much as possible about teen-age smoking patterns and attitudes. Today's teen-ager is tomorrow's potential regular customer, and the overwhelming majority of smokers first begin to smoke while still in their teens. The smoking patterns of teen-agers are particularly important to Philip Morris. Furthermore, it is during the teen-age years that the initial brand choice is made: At least a part of the success of Marlboro Red during its most rapid growth period was because it became the brand of choice among teen-agers, who then stuck with it as they grew older—this combined with the rapid growth in the absolute number of teen-agers.*

By the time Joe Camel came along in 1988, cigarette commercials were long gone from the nation's airwaves, but RJR had a similar strategy with its smooth cartoon camel, Perry said. A 1987 Reynolds white paper on young adult smokers advised, "The advertising will position Camel as an authentic brand for smokers who are admired and respected by their peers because their attitudes and lifestyles distinguish them as individuals who challenge convention and stand tall."

The research must have worked, according to Perry. Quoting from a 1994 report from the Centers for Disease Control, Perry testified that, between 1989 and 1993, sales of Camels among 12- to 18-year-olds rose 5.2 percent.

In attacking the infamous Joe Camel campaign, Perry didn't see a cartoon camel—she saw a subliminal, manipulative creature designed to appeal to a teenager's need for peer approval.

Pointing to an ad featuring Joe Camel in a card game, Perry claimed, "You can see Joe Camel with his peer group. He's part of the 'in' group. And you can see that there's some card playing going on; it's slightly risky. But, primarily, this is an advertisement that would appeal to wanting to be part of a peer group. An adolescent would see smoking as associated with the peer group."

In Perry's expert opinion, the tobacco industry knew that the majority of starting smokers were under 18 and marketed to them. That conduct was a major contributor in causing young people to start smoking. Walburn concluded her examination late Monday afternoon on March 9.

RJR's Robert Weber would cross-examine Perry. He knew that

her testimony had been powerful. Backed by statistics, secret documents, visual aids, and old television commercials, Perry had strongly established Big Tobacco's need for and solicitation of young, underage smokers to replace older smokers who had quit and/or died. Yet, by the end of Weber's cross-examination, all jurors would remember is that they couldn't stand Cheryl Perry.

Richard Hurt's hostility toward his cross-examination by David Bernick was no match for the petite professor from the University of Minnesota. Weber took his position at the podium, politely introduced himself, and began some cursory questioning on Perry's background. His witness refused even to look at him, directing her answers instead toward the jurors.

Less than five minutes into Weber's cross-examination, Perry began to display clear signs of what had become known among some court observers as being a "Ciresi witness." Where Perry had been attentive and succinct in responding to Walburn's questions, her attitude toward Weber was quite the opposite. His simplest queries produced convoluted, wordy, nonresponsive replies. It took Weber five tries to elicit a response to the simple question: Had she ever developed programs for private businesses that sold consumer products?

A minute later, the whole process repeated itself, when Weber asked if her articles had ever been published in peer-review journals devoted exclusively to advertising and marketing.

Turning to the jury, Perry replied, "The journals that I publish in are the journals that relate to behavioral health, so I would publish in *Behavioral Medicine*, the *Journal of the American Medical Association*, the *American Journal of Public Health*, and other journals that relate to smoking behavior among adolescents. And that's where the bulk of the research is on smoking behavior among adolescents. It's not in the advertising journals, it's in the journals that are the ones in my area."

Weber repeated himself. "Is it true, professor, that you have never published in a peer-reviewed journal in the fields of advertising or marketing?"

And Perry repeated herself, "The journals that I publish in often publish articles on advertising and its effects on youth—on smoking behavior, it may be adult or youth, so that it clearly is [sic] the kind of journals that are interested in this relationship between cigarette smoking and advertising or other aspects of public health and advertising."

"Is the answer to my question, 'no', you have never published in a peer-reviewed journal in the field of marketing or advertising?"

Walburn objected—the question had already been asked and answered. The judge demurred, saying that Perry could answer the question, seeming to ignore the fact that Perry wasn't going to comply.

"I would consider the kinds of journals that I published in, having an interest in and publishing research that would be considered advertising research," she said.

Calmly, Weber reminded his witness, "But the question is: Have you published in peer–reviewed journals that are devoted to the fields of advertising or marketing?"

Again Walburn objected, asked and answered.

Fitzpatrick repeated himself. "You may answer that."

And Perry, not answering the question for the fourth time, told jurors, "The journals that I publish in, such as the *American Journal of Public Health*, and certainly you've heard quite bit about the *Journal of the American Medical Association*, spend a great deal of their time on the issue of advertising and promotion and its effects on people's behavior. So in that sense, those are highly regarded peer-reviewed journals that deal with this subject of advertising and promotion. So I would say in that sense, yes, I have published in those journals."

Asked Weber, "Is the *American Journal of Public Health* and the *Journal of the American Medical Association*—are either of those peer-reviewed journals that are devoted exclusively to the analysis of scholarly study in the fields of advertising or marketing?"

"Both of those journals are devoted to the improvement of the health of people, not just in the U.S., but globally."

The unanswered questions and nonresponsive answers on this subject continued for several more minutes, before Weber moved on and through other subjects at a molasses-like pace.

This, then, would be the game with this witness. Weber had watched David Bernick become increasingly frustrated during his questioning of Richard Hurt and Channing Robertson. Cheryl Perry was cut from the same cloth.

The defense attorney knew he had a problem on his hands. "By the third question, it was obvious what was going on because she wouldn't look at me, and she wouldn't answer the question. She wouldn't shut up. It was every lawyer's worst nightmare."

Weber couldn't control her, and he knew the judge wouldn't help. "She was a woman and she was from Minnesota. He was going to side with her against me," he said later.

Weber chuckled at the recollection. "Well, I was a tobacco lawyer—he was going to side with *anybody* against me."

Weber quickly charted his course. He would maintain an unwaveringly pleasant and respectful manner, "like a patient adult with a disobedient child." He hoped his witness' stubborn refusal to provide simple answers to his simple questions would be noticed by jurors.

It was.

By the end of the morning's session, Weber's strategy was beginning to pay off. Perry's elusiveness was not playing well with the jury. Several jurors were openly frowning.

"Cheryl Perry was very good with the state," Dorothy Hallen recalled. "I thought it was really good that she was working with youth and trying to get them not to smoke or quit. But on cross-examination, she was arrogant. She was like one of those people who just quit smoking and now hates it. They're the biggest pills on earth. She wouldn't answer the questions and she would go on and on and on."

James Otis agreed. "Perry started out okay, then she got on her soapbox and even the judge couldn't control her."

When Perry returned to the stand after lunch, it appeared as if someone on the plaintiffs' team had talked with her during the break. When court resumed, Perry started off noticeably more cooperative. But not for long.

By midafternoon, Perry had gotten to the point where, when asked to read aloud from a document by Weber, she responded. "Well, first I'd like to remind the jury. . ."

"Professor," Weber politely cautioned. "The question was, 'Please read that.'"

"Do I have to do that exactly?" Perry asked no one in particular.

Weber chose to answer, "Well, I can't tell you what to do, only His Honor can."

Perry persisted. "Can I have a preface to my reading?"

Finally Fitzpatrick got involved. "Professor, maybe you can just read it for him."

"Okay."

Fitzpatrick explained, "You'll have a chance, through your attorneys, to preface and sequelize and do whatever you choose practically. At this time, why don't you just read it?"

Perry didn't get it. "Okay. Can I say something after I read it?"

Fitzpatrick was unmoved. "Well, we're trying to do a question and answer here."

Perry cooperated, but she didn't follow the judge's instructions for long.

During a later exchange, where Weber asked Perry to read

aloud a paragraph from a press release, she retorted, "I'll read the second paragraph if I can read another paragraph in this press release."

"I'm sure your lawyer will give you a chance to do that," Weber responded. "Right now I want to ask you to read the second paragraph, professor."

Perry read only a portion of the text Weber requested, deliberately skipping over several sentences.

"You didn't read that quite right, did you, professor?" Weber commented.

"I did read what I wanted to," Perry snipped.

Adopting the good-parent, disobedient-child tone, Weber pressed. "You skipped over a sentence, didn't you?

"It wasn't part of my point. . . . I didn't need to read your point."

Juror Jill Burton was astounded. "I couldn't even believe this!" she said later. "I thought, 'This is the Shrine Circus. Somebody make her shut up!' '

During a courtroom break, Dorothy Hallen recalled, the jurors quietly discussed the discrepancy in the judge's attitude between witnesses favorable to the defense and those favorable to the plaintiffs, like Perry.

"Someone asked, 'Why does the judge make the defense's witnesses stop talking, but not her?' We all saw that."

The self-professed expert on adolescents also made some amazing gaffes during her cross-examination.

When asked whether 18 was considered a legal age for many

activities. Perry ticked off activities that were not allowed at that age, one being "We don't vote until we're 21."

Weber, seizing the opportunity, sought a repetition of that assertion. "And you can vote when you're 18, can't you?"

"I'm not sure. I thought you had to be 21 to vote."

"Well, you've studied adolescents these numbers of years. Do you know whether adolescents who are 18 are given the right to vote?"

Perry looked nervous. "It's escaping me right now."

"Do you know whether they have the right to vote for president, representatives, and senators?"

"No, I believe that's age 21."

More than anything else Perry testified to during her four days on the stand, some jurors remembered that pronouncement as most crippling to her testimony.

For juror David Olson, that was it: "She was supposed to be an expert and she didn't know you only had to be 18 to vote. I'm sorry, but her credibility went right down the tubes."

Coming in a close second was Perry's stubborn belief that cigarette advertising was at the root of all teen smoking behavior, and other behavior as well.

"Are you saying that cigarette advertising causes youth to carry guns to school?" Weber asked at one point.

"I'm not going to rule it out," Perry replied.

Weber couldn't believe his luck. "You couldn't pay a witness enough to do that," he said later. "It was extraordinary."

For Jill Burton, the breaking point came with Perry's assertion that it didn't matter if a child was raised in a home where the parents smoked; it was advertising that ultimately motivated the habit.

"I thought to myself at one point, 'I'm going to stand up and bring this to an end.' Her testimony was never cut off, she continued to drone and drone, and that's what go to us."

The jury was subjected to more of the same labored cross-examination for another full day. By the end of Wednesday, Cheryl Perry's nonresponsiveness had shredded the nerves of almost everyone, except for Bob Weber, who pleasantly concluded his masterful examination as if nothing out of the ordinary had happened. Without it, Perry's extremely damaging initial testimony about the subtle ways in which the industry marketed to youth would still be resonating with jurors. As it was, although Perry still turned toward the jury with her answers, none of the 12 would even look at her anymore.

"By the end, we wanted to strangle her," Hallen recalled. "We hated her."

It was time for Perry to leave the stand. By midmorning Thursday, after some brief redirect examination by Roberta Walburn, she had.

Perry was later named unanimously by jurors interviewed as the most universally disliked witness of the entire trial.

Roberta Walburn still considered Perry an effective witness about youth and marketing. However, Walburn reflected later,

"Litigation is a very, very strange process, particularly for people who have never been involved in it before. For some people it's easier than others."

Ciresi claimed Perry was "nervous and uncomfortable in a courtroom setting," which made her defensive.

Defense counsel was less generous. "She was one of the worst witnesses I've ever seen," Peter Bleakley declared.

For the rest of the week, testimony returned to the video screen with taped depositions from top scientists at RJR and American Tobacco Company.

Murray Senkus, RJR's former director of scientific affairs, testified about the 1970 decision by RJR to close its biological testing lab in favor of research performed by outside scientists. He called the move "a business decision."

American Tobacco Company scientist Byron Price acknowledged that, although scientists at his company had discovered animal carcinogens in its research into cigarette smoke, the results were never published.

If the jury didn't understand the significance of those pronouncements at the time, they soon would.

Friday, the jurors settled in for another "document day." As they worked, they discussed plans they had for a stunt they planned to pull in court in the very near future. The stringent supervision they'd endured was beginning to ease up. Some days they even sang in the jury room during breaks, laughing because they wondered if anyone could hear them. The jury had definitely bonded, as the rest of the court would quickly find out.

The trial's eighth week started relatively uneventfully. Mike Ciresi called to the stand Harvard Graduate School of Business professor Robert Dolan. Dolan had been teaching at Harvard for almost 18 years, but he was no ivory tower theorist. He'd coauthored several books on marketing management, spent his time at Harvard reviewing actual business case histories with his students, and worked as a private consultant to a variety of major corporations, including Coca-Cola, Citibank, and IBM.

Ciresi wanted Dolan to explain the tobacco industry's marketing and advertising strategies, and—more important to the plaintiffs—whom the industry was targeting for its products.

Dolan's testimony provided a welcome respite for a jury that had grown weary of pH levels, statistics, and graphs. He amplified his remarks with lots of accessible examples—describing advertising strategies a tobacco company might use in buying an ad in *Sports Illustrated*'s annual swimsuit issue; explaining promotion by using a fictional example with the Minnesota Twins; and using the Nike "swoosh" for his example of sponsorship.

Dolan outlined four main marketing objectives pursued by tobacco companies: to attract new smokers, to stop smokers from quitting, to reacquire lapsed smokers, and to persuade smokers to switch brands and subsequently maintain that brand loyalty.

He echoed Cheryl Perry's contention that young adults were the industry's main source of replacement smokers for those who quit or died.

"If you can get a person to adopt your brand, it'll be easier to keep them," he testified. "You attract them at the very earliest opportunity and reap the benefits as consumption increases over time."

Dolan reviewed a 1989 Reynolds marketing document illustrating the tobacco companies' preoccupation with young smokers, and how the industry sought to push young adults' "hot buttons" with its advertising campaigns. The themes pursued by Reynolds were "excitement, humor, irreverence, romanticism, and sex," he testified.

Dolan's testimony was cut short when court recessed after Juror Number Six, James Otis, became ill and had to leave the courtroom. "I was sick and throwing up," he explained later.

But, as had become the norm in this trial, news was breaking outside the courtroom. In a one-sentence order issued that day, Fitzpatrick denied the motion for his recusal. The ball was back in defense's court. There was no word that day on whether they'd take their request to the next level, asking Ramsey County Chief Justice Lawrence Cohen to remove the judge for them.

Defense counsel was split over the matter. Some felt that Fitzpatrick had been behaving more fairly, so there was no need to force the issue. Others thought they had no choice but to finish what they had started.

"The debate raged on the defense side for another week to 10 days," Philip Morris local counsel Peter Sipkins recalled.

Court resumed the next day on March 17, a very special occasion each year in St. Paul. St. Patrick's Day assumes the importance of a high holy day among the heavily Irish-Catholic population, so it was no surprise to see most of the attorneys for both sides arrive that morning bedecked in green ties of varying shades. Sipkins wore a stylish green-and-white striped shirt, the judge's wife and sister wore green suits. It was no surprise to see the jury arrive in a similarly vermilion condition. What was surprising was their unified and exuberant greeting to Fitzpatrick.

"Top of the morning to you!" they cried in unison. It was the first outward sign that the jury had coalesced as a group. The courtroom broke up.

"And a happy St. Patrick's Day," Fitzpatrick responded. Doing his part, he announced, "In observance of this grand occasion, we'll be taking a two-hour lunch period," ostensibly to accommodate the St. Patrick's Day parade, which would pass alongside the courthouse at noon.

The luck of the Irish wasn't with the defense that day. A three-judge panel from the Minnesota Court of Appeals refused to overturn Fitzpatrick's March 7 order calling for the release of the 39,000 documents.

In making its ruling, the appellate panel rejected defense attorneys' arguments that, since only samples of the 240,000 pages of documents were reviewed to evaluate tobacco companies' claims of privilege, the claim was unfairly discarded. The appellate ruling noted that it had denied relief on a similar petition defendants filed on another batch of documents the year before.

The court ruled that the defendants "have not established that specific documents are *clearly* not discoverable, that the remedies afforded them are or were inadequate, or that the trial court exceeded its legitimate powers."

The Appeals Court ordered the documents turned over to plaintiffs by noon Thursday, March 19. Defense attorneys immediately appealed the decision to the Minnesota Supreme Court.

Back in court, Dolan continued his review of Big Tobacco's marketing strategies, focusing on the introduction of lower-tar-and-nicotine brands, which were advertised in the 1970s as safe alternatives to regular cigarettes.

As an example, Dolan used Lorillard's True cigarette brand, which he said was advertised as "a substitute for quitting."

A 1980 RJR document reflected that company's interest in low-tar-and-nicotine smokers, stating, "These smokers are well aware of the smoking-and-health controversy and have switched to ULT [ultra low-tar] products in an effort to decrease 'tar' intake.

"Many of these smokers are victims of pressure from peers and loved ones to quit or reduce smoking. Therefore, they smoke ULT brands to 'get people off their backs.' They are referred to as the 'get-off-my-backers,'" the memo continued.

Dolan said he saw no data that ever indicated that low-tar-and-nicotine cigarettes were any safer than regular cigarettes.

Dolan concluded his testimony by saying that tobacco companies marketed their products to underage smokers, sought to provide false assurance that their low-tar-and-nicotine products were safer to smoke, and that the industry had failed to warn consumers about the addictiveness of nicotine. In short: new witness, same points.

Bleakley began his cross-examination that St. Patrick's Day afternoon by apologizing to jurors for not wearing anything green. It was yet another demonstration of the out-of-town attorney's unfamiliarity with the customs and make-up of the local jury.

Dolan was no Cheryl Perry when it came to his cross-examination. He willingly answered any question Bleakley tossed at him. Bleakley was in good form that day and the exchange was lively, and rather damaging to the witness.

Dolan acknowledged that he'd read approximately 4,000 documents before he issued his expert report. He wasn't aware, until Bleakley told him, that the defense had furnished some 250,000 documents to the plaintiffs, "but it wouldn't surprise me." He also admitted that, although he traditionally liked to interview marketing executives at companies he was studying, he hadn't read any of the depositions taken of the cigarette company executives for this trial.

Bleakley pointedly challenged Dolan's assertions that the marketing strategies outlined in some of the documents admitted into evidence proved that companies were targeting underage smokers for their product.

One RJR marketing document referred to four life changes observed in the target market: "became unemployed, got a promotion, returned to work, and became responsible for own support."

"Do those sound like characteristics of people under 18?" Bleakley asked Dolan.

Dolan hedged, before finally answering, "I don't have a basis for answering that question."

Bleakley referred to another, highly inflammatory Lorillard document which stated "the base of our business is high school students."

"Does it say that they targeted high school students?" Bleakley asked.

Dolan responded, "It says we got them, but it doesn't explicitly say they targeted them."

Bleakley also got Dolan to admit, over repeated objections from Ciresi, that advertising played no significant role in attracting new smokers.

Dolan's assertions that cigarette companies had falsely mislead consumers about the health benefits of low tar-and-nicotine cigarettes also came under attack.

After being presented with a surgeon general's report statement that, "Today's filter-tipped, lower-tar-and-nicotine cigarettes produce lower rates of lung cancer than do their higher-tar-and-nicotine predecessors," Dolan acknowledged that many governmental and public health agencies had been saying the same thing.

By the time Bleakley finished, Dolan's testimony hadn't been discredited, but the expert had been neutralized.

On Thursday, March 19, the Minnesota Supreme Court granted the defendants a stay of Fitzpatrick's document release order until it could review the question.

The state's case was winding down and beginning to sound somewhat redundant. However, that would change when Adam Jaffe took the stand.

Jaffe was a professor of economics at Boston's Brandeis University, and also worked privately as an economic consultant. He was pedigreed from two of the country's finest universities, receiving his undergraduate and master's degrees from MIT, and his Ph.D. in economics from Harvard. He taught economics at Harvard until 1993, then moved to Brandeis. Jaffe also had served as a senior staff economist on the President's Council of Economic Advisors in Washington, D.C. His specialty was antitrust economics.

Richard Gill would have the job of putting Jaffe through his paces—a delightful task, according to the attorney.

"He was a quick study and had a great personality with the jury," said Gill. "You could picture him as the next door neighbor that you could talk to about sports or weather or kids."

Or conspiracies. The professor planned to detail the story of the conception and execution of what he considered to be one of the longest-running antitrust conspiracies in the United States.

Jaffe asserted that tobacco companies began conspiring in the early 1950s at the now-legendary meeting at New York's Plaza

Hotel, when Big Tobacco's CEOs met to discuss their options in the face of mounting public concern about smoking and health. That meeting led to the creation of the Tobacco Industry Research Committee (which later split into the Council for Tobacco Research—the science and research arm—and the Tobacco Institute, the public relations arm).

"How long has this conspiracy been in progress, professor?" Gill asked.

"Well, I haven't been able to find any evidence that the conspiracy has ended," Jaffe responded, "except that Liggett appears to have left the conspiracy in connection with its settlement of some of the litigation in the last few years."

He described the world of tobacco companies as one of collusion and closely kept secrets. After reading through hundreds of formerly secret industry documents, Jaffe had no qualms stating that there had been rampant antitrust activity by all the firms, spanning decades.

Although the cigarette brands always had competed against each other in the marketplace, Jaffe pointed out four areas in which competition appeared nonexistent.

They included:

• a "Gentleman's Agreement" that no in-house animal research be conducted related to smoking and health, as the possibility that such research might show a positive correlation would prove too damaging;

• an agreement that the companies would collectively reassure smokers (through the Tobacco Institute) and work to suppress unfavorable research about the health consequences of smoking (through the Center for Tobacco Research);

• an agreement by the companies not to engage in specific product warnings unless ordered to do so by a government agency;

• a joint agreement not to "engage in competitive exploitation of safer products in a manner relying on consumers' health fears."

Using dozens of once-hidden documents, Jaffe took three days to weave a tapestry that incorporated the names and faces of many of the people jurors had already met during the trial into one dark panorama of four decades worth of business, Big Tobacco–style.

Jaffe began with the Gentleman's Agreement, telling a story of competitors who, rather than maintaining distance, engaged in more intercompany gossip and chitchat than a ladies sewing circle.

To illustrate his point, Jaffe discussed the draft of a 1968 memo in which Philip Morris Research Director Dr. Helmut Wakeham warned company officials that, "in spite of a gentleman's agreement from the tobacco industry in previous years, at least some of the major companies have been increasing biological studies within their own facilities." Wakeham excised the term "gentleman's agreement" from his final memo, but suggested that Philip Morris undertake its own in-house animal studies in response.

In 1969, Wakeham and a researcher from another cigarette company were given a tour of RJR's in-house testing facilities, which included smoking inhalation equipment for rats designed by RJR scientist Dr. Murray Senkus. Wakeham reported that fact to Philip Morris CEO Joseph Cullman III. Wakeham discussed his conversation with Cullman with Dr. D. G. Felton, a researcher at yet *another* tobacco company, British-American Tobacco Company (BATCo).

Felton then reported Wakeham's version of the events to his superiors. Felton's memo stated, "Cullman had been incredulous and had phoned Galloway, the President of R. J. Reynolds, who had denied Reynolds were doing any bioassay [research]." The memo added that, when Cullman told Wakeham about Galloway's denial, "Wakeham's response had been to quote the Reynolds work on the Senkus smoking machine, and to claim that he had floor plans showing outline area allocations."

Cullman subsequently got back on the phone with Galloway, according to the memo, and within a month of the CEOs' conversation, RJR's "mouse house," as it was known, was suddenly shut down, and its staff laid off.

"The notion that the CEO of one company would call up the CEO of a competitor and tell them, 'I know you're doing research of a certain kind which I think you shouldn't be doing,' is incredible," Jaffe said. "The notion that Galloway took those calls or paid any attention to them would not be the kind of behavior you would expect from competitive firms."

Ironically, ten years later, a 1978 RJR memo fretted that Philip Morris had evidently made good on Wakeham's original suggestion, stating, "A wholly owned [Philip Morris] subsidiary in Cologne, Germany, engages in carcinogenic biological research in violation of the verbal agreement among domestic companies not to perform animal testing in-house."

Jaffe next turned to his claim that the industry suppressed smoking-and-health research. To assist in this portion of Jaffe's story, Gill provided a couple of exhibits with which the jury was more than familiar: the Frank Statement (now just known as "Frank" in the jury box) and a report from the three BATCo scientists about their 1958 visit to the United States.

According to Jaffe, instead of "scientific research into all phases of tobacco use and health," as the Frank Statement had promised, the industry had done almost the opposite. Two Liggett scientists told the BATCo scientists that the tobacco industry's research arm had done "little if anything constructive . . . in the face of mounting contrary evidence." Furthermore, they stated that the industry had supported "almost without exception, projects which are not related directly to smoking and lung cancer."

Jaffe pointed out the Center for Tobacco Research's (CTR) James Glenn told a congressional committee in 1994 that only 10 of 296 CTR studies listed in the index of the organization's 1993 report pertained to tobacco.

The professor also discussed an example of how CTR behaved in regard to tobacco-related studies it *didn't* fund. In the late 1960s, New Jersey pathologist Oscar Auerbach conducted a series of experiments on dogs, seeking a direct link between smoking and lung cancer. The "Auerbach beagle experiments" involved giving tracheotomies to 100 beagles, and forcing them to smoke through their windpipes. Several of the dogs in the experiment, according to Auerbach, developed lung cancer.

After reading Auerbach's study, B&W scientist I. W. Hughes reported to his superiors in a February 1970 memo, "Although open to criticism on several counts, the general standard of the paper is good. I am of the view that this shows it is now possible to produce tumors in the respiratory system of an animal by direct inhalation." Hughes reflected, "I would imagine that the industry could be asked what it's going to do following the Auerbach publication."

The question came up during a meeting at CTR held on November 3, 1970, attended by CTR staff, scientists from the major tobacco companies, three attorneys, and two representatives of the Tobacco Working Group (TWG). The TWG had been established by the government through the National Cancer Institute to study the possibility of manufacturing a safer cigarette. Auerbach would present his paper to that group on November 9, just six days after the CTR meeting.

Jaffe said minutes of that CTR meeting told of criticisms about Auerbach's study, his techniques, and his conclusions, which one participant called "meaningless."

A year later, when Auerbach sought additional funding from the National Cancer Institute for further smoking-related beagle studies, the CTR had another meeting. Jaffe reviewed the minutes of the December 21, 1971, gathering of CTR officials, industry scientists, and attorneys from Philip Morris and RJR, who agreed that the Auerbach experiments should be abandoned and that the cancer institute be notified of their concerns.

Jaffe concluded that, "It seems to me it's anticompetitive for the CTR and the research directors of the companies . . . to expend their efforts at trying to convince some other agency of the national government not to fund this research."

CTR's behavior even proved offensive to industry scientists. In a December 8, 1970, memo Philip Morris scientist Wakeham commented to CEO Joseph Cullman, "It has been stated that CTR is a program to find out 'the truth about smoking and health.' What is truth to one is false to another. CTR and the Industry have publicly and frequently denied what others find as 'truth.' Let's face it. We are interested in evidence which we believe denies the allegation that cigarette smoking causes disease."

Jaffe concluded that the CTR was used essentially as a cover. "They funded scientific research, they funded good scientific research, but the scientific research that they funded was aimed generally at understanding the mechanisms of disease," Jaffe said. "It was not primarily focused on determining whether or not smoking was harmful, and in those occurrences where they *did* fund research that found evidence that smoking was harmful, that information was not treated as significant information, was not highlighted by the scientific director, or presented to the public as being the significant findings that in 1954 they said they were going to pursue."

For its part, the Tobacco Institute spent much of the same time period casting controversy on the studies that had found their way into the public literature, Jaffe said. Tobacco Institute press releases emphasized "that causation had not been proven, that there was still a controversy, and that more research needed to be done before it could be concluded that smoking caused disease."

At the top of this conspiracy, Jaffe maintained, was the Committee of Counsel, a group of attorneys representing all the tobacco companies. Their control of U.S. cigarette manufacturers was mentioned in 1964 in a BATCo report, "Policy Aspects of the Smoking and Health Strategy in the U.S.A." In it, the observation was made, "The leadership of the U.S. smoking and health situation . . . lies with the powerful Policy Committee of senior lawyers advising the industry, and their policy, very understandably is . . . 'don't take any chances.' It is a situation that does not encourage constructive or bold approaches to smoking and health problems, and it also means that the Policy Committee of lawyers exercises close control over all aspects of the problems."

In 1978, the situation hadn't improved much, according to a memo prepared by Curtis Judge, then the president and CEO of Lorillard. "We have again 'abdicated' the scientific research directional management of the Industry to the 'Lawyers' with virtually no involvement on the part of scientific or business management side of the business," Judge wrote.

In 1985, a memo sent from B&W to parent company B.A.T.

Industries asked that all research materials destined for the U.S. subsidiary be first sent to the law firm of Wyatt, Tarrant & Combs in Kentucky. "This firm should not be listed as a distributee in the documents nor should B&W," the memo said.

In Jaffe's opinion, the CTR, the Tobacco Institute, and the Committee of Counsel played active roles in suppressing unfavorable research information and "were engaged in a systematic effort to try to make sure that smokers . . . did not receive information that would tend to confirm their fears about cigarettes, but instead would receive this message that the controversy is still alive, that causation has not been proven."

As to the third prong of his conspiracy theory—that cigarette companies agreed not to produce product warnings unless the government ordered it—Jaffe kept the story short. He used a June 13, 1983, letter from the U.S. Department of Health and Human Services to Tobacco Institute Chairman Horace Kornegay about warnings on cigarette packs. Among the conditions the industry had set forth: The warnings should not use the term "addiction" and that the new warnings should continue to reference the surgeon general, not the manufacturers.

"I think in the context of the agreement to suppress competition, the concern was that a warning that came from the tobacco companies themselves would have greater credibility with smokers than a warning from the government, and that was to be avoided," Jaffe stated.

The final chapter in Jaffe's story had to do with new product development. According to the professor, concerns about promoting "safer" cigarettes led several companies to drop promising improvements in their products.

Philip Morris developed the Saratoga cigarette, which featured a newly designed charcoal filter. However, according to a 1964 memo by communicative scientist Helmut Wakeham, Saratoga was not to be. "Physiologically it was an outstanding cigarette," he wrote. "Unfortunately . . . after much discussion we decided not to tell the physiological story which might have appealed to a health conscious segment of the market. The product as test marketed didn't have good taste and consequently was unacceptable to the public ignorant of its physiological superiority."

BATCo, in 1966, worked on Project Ariel, a series of smoking devices which allowed users to obtain a preset amount of nicotine either with or without cigarette smoke. The product was never introduced, and Jaffe could find no documentation to explain the reason.

For its part, in the late 1970s, Liggett worked on a project known as XA, that executives at the time predicted could capture a 1.6 percent share of the market—or more than $150 million—within a year of introduction.

A confidential Liggett document explained that the new process "consists of treating conventional tobacco with palladium and nitrates." Incorporated into the process was a newly designed filter that removed smoke irritants and thus, reduced toxicity. It also reduced "nitrate emissions to normal level."

Liggett scientists planned to test the new product to determine whether "tumor incidence in test rats and mice can be virtually eliminated," the memo stated.

While there would be regulatory hurdles to leap in bringing the product to market, the memo acknowledged, "They are not insurmountable."

In June 1979, a memorandum issued by the legal team formed to study Project XA tersely instructed readers to "please issue a memorandum to those concerned requesting that any materials which have not already been turned over to the Law Department related to XA, be it financial, scientific, production, or marketing, should be transferred to the Law Department no later than Thursday, June 28."

And that was the last of the documents related to Liggett's palladium cigarette that Jaffe could find.

Jaffe concluded that "the logical inference is that the reason the project was dropped was because they concluded that they couldn't successfully exploit it without relying on competitive exploitation that would rely on the health issue, and they couldn't do that because of the collusive agreement."

In Winston-Salem, RJR scientists worked on Project SPA, which eventually produced a breakthrough cigarette they called Premier. Premier heated tobacco, rather than burned it, which reduced carcinogens in the smoke. Like Liggett's palladium cigarette, scientists had determined through biological studies that the cigarette was far safer to smoke than existing brands.

A 1987 report to the RJR board of directors called Premier "the biggest technological breakthrough in the cigarette industry over the past 30 years."

That was the last good news about Premier. A subsequent RJR memorandum stated, "Premier is thought of in some quarters—both inside and outside the company—as the largest and most expensive marketing failure since the Edsel."

The author concluded that Premier had failed because "the smoking experience was significantly inferior to existing products on the market and the product advantages were prevented from being communicated effectively."

Although scientists at other companies examined Premier and concluded that the taste could be improved, RJR did nothing. That was a mystery to Jaffe, but its failure to tout the product's safer biological features again suggested a conspiracy, he said.

"They went after [Premier] walking a very fine line. They did it in a way that did not violate the collusive agreement, that avoided a competitive exploitation of the product in a manner relying on health fears. They were hoping that they could have it both ways."

Jaffe brought his story to a close by telling jurors, "It's my opinion that the collusive agreement . . . by preventing the transformation of the market that would have otherwise occurred into one in which there was a wider variety of products available and in which consumers would have had the information necessary to make effective choices among those products, was a significant contributing factor to health care costs in Minnesota."

During cross-examination, Peter Bleakley asked Jaffe how he could see a conspiracy when market share shifted dramatically among manufacturers between 1954 and 1994.

"There has been significant competition in aspects other than smoking and health," Jaffe acknowledged.

Bleakley's cross-examination nibbled around the edges of Jaffe's testimony, but produced little of value. Trial lawyers watching Bleakley's work in the courtroom that day commented that he seemed unfocused. There was good reason. The attorney had a bad case of stomach flu, a "number-six problem," he told the judge, referring to malady that struck Juror Number Six, Jim Otis, earlier that week. Court was adjourned early that Friday when Bleakley became too ill to continue.

Adam Jaffe had left quite an impression on some jurors. Dorothy Hallen said she took so many notes during Jaffe's presentation that she had a blister on her finger by the end.

"For me, he tied it all together," she said. "Before that, it had just been parts and parts and parts. He showed us what the gentleman's agreement was and what the Plaza Hotel was about. He was just the smoking gun. I thought, 'Wow, so this is where they had been leading.'"

Jim Otis agreed. "I didn't understand the whole conspiracy thing until he got on the stand."

In better health the following Monday, Bleakley began to probe the frailties in each prong of the antitrust expert's conspiracy theory.

Jaffe acknowledged that the tobacco companies had contracted for animal research at laboratories other than their own because "they thought it was important that smokers be reassured and that that would be undermined if confirmation on causation came from the laboratories of tobacco companies themselves."

Jaffe also conceded that "a number" of CTR-funded studies had been unfavorable to the tobacco industry. He also acknowledged that the Auerbach study had ultimately been published and widely disseminated. He didn't know whether or not the National Cancer Institute had ever funded additional work by Auerbach.

In the area of new product development, Bleakley wanted to know if Jaffe felt that "spending billions" on so-called "safer" cigarettes was significant. Jaffe didn't.

Jaffe responded that, over four decades, the tobacco companies spent about $3 billion developing new products compared to $47 billion during the same period on advertising and promotion. "I think if these firms were competing, there would have been much more," he said.

When questioned about his knowledge of Liggett's palladium cigarette, Jaffe also conceded that he knew public health authorities were concerned about the product's safety, given that palladium, a heavy metal, could increase carcinogens in the smoke. He acknowledged that he had no basis to determine whether or not the palladium cigarette would have been a safer product.

Bleakley succeeded in shooting some holes in the conspiracy theory by the end of his cross, but not many. The sheer volume of incriminating documents had been simply too difficult to overcome.

The attorney, who had few kind words for most of the plaintiffs' witnesses, would later acknowledge that Jaffe was "okay."

The state called Paul Much as its final scheduled witness to testify about the financial condition of the tobacco industry. A senior managing partner for the Chicago investment banking firm of Houlihan Lokey Howard & Zukin, Much was to give jurors a sense of the considerable profitability of tobacco manufacturers to support the plaintiffs' request for punitive damages—a sum to be unveiled during closing arguments.

"What you have here is consistent, stable, growing profitability and that will lead to strong financial condition," Much stated. It wasn't exactly a earth-shattering revelation.

Much told attorney Roberta Walburn that the defendants recorded operating profits, before interest and taxes, of $6.7 billion in 1996 from domestic sales alone. Globally, he said, the industry had earned $1.9 trillion from 1954 to 1996. In Minnesota, Much said, the defendants earned slightly more than $1.85 billion from 1954 to 1996.

On the second day of Much's testimony, Monday, March 24, B&W attorney David Bernick spent some of his time quibbling with Much over his use of operating profits—rather than net profits. However, Bernick, noting that Much's testimony included the $1.85 billion earned by defendants in Minnesota, sought to dive through the hole that statement had opened. Turning with his magic marker to the flip chart, Bernick quickly sketched a drawing of a cigarette pack, dividing it up into sections—seeking to show the jury how much money the state of Minnesota earned per pack of cigarettes.

Defense attorneys wanted to throw the figure into the mix in order to raise questions in juror's minds about the true harm to the state, when several hundred million dollars a year were entering state coffers from the cigarette tax. Walburn objected, and a heated sidebar with the judge ensued. Bernick was moving into a forbidden area. The judge was adamant that the jury not be told how much money the state earned from each pack.

That day, another drama unfolded out of range of almost everyone at the trial.

During lunch, Philip Morris' lead local counsel Peter Sipkins got a call from Michelle Jones. "The judge wants to see you in chambers, and only you—no other defense counsel," he later recalled her saying.

As Sipkins rode the elevator to the seventh floor, he had no doubt what the meeting would be about. "I immediately knew it was my letter." Sipkins had written to court observer Patricia Miller on March 22 regarding the latest monthly bill she had submitted to the defense for $20,953.14. After the early fiasco with Michelle Jones, Sipkins now reviewed each statement carefully. He characterized the latest bill as "light. The bills were typically

$60,000 to $80,000 a month."

However, the attorney had some questions about the latest sub-mission—and about Patricia Miller's exact duties.

According to Sipkins, Miller had originally been hired to act as an observer for the court during the parties' "meet and confer" sessions, after it became evident that the parties weren't communicating effectively.

"The judge said, 'I can't attend all of these things myself, so I'm going to have a court observer go, because I think it will have an influence on the way the parties tend to interact, then I can get an unbiased report back,'" Sipkins recalled. "And from that humble beginning of having somebody attend meet and confers once a month or once every three months, she became a fixture at all court proceedings."

Some of the problems Sipkins outlined in his letter had to do with Miller, who was charging $150 per hour for her services. That month, her total came to about $8,000.

In his letter, Sipkins noted that Miller's statements contained time entries for assistance to Special Discovery Master Mark Gehan. He then asked whether her time entries on the current bill reflected assistance to Fitzpatrick, in connection with the defense's appeals of Gehan's orders.

The letter asked what Miller was charging for attending the trial, noting that she frequently attended during "days when there are no meet and confers or other discovery issues, and when the regular court clerk is present and performing her duties."

In addition, Sipkins questioned the charge of $252.40 for cell phones, plus a separate charge of $116.52 for long-distance phone charges, and $5,500 charged each month for technology assistance.

Sipkins assumed the $5,500 represented the monthly salary of county employee Richard Parker, who was assisting the judge with the courtroom setup. Sipkins wondered "whether assisting in this litigation is the sole work being done by Mr. Parker. Will this be an ongoing charge each month?"

Last, but not least, Sipkins had been incensed by Miller's inclusion of a $116.06 interest charge for an unpaid balance. "As you are well aware," he wrote Miller, "Our check to cover the unpaid balance was deposited with Judge Cohen. Thus, we think your charging interest on the unpaid fees of Court Clerk Ms. Michelle Jones is improper, and defendants do not intend to pay it. You should raise the question of interest directly with Judge Cohen."

Sipkins and Ciresi, who had also been summoned, walked into Judge Fitzpatrick's spacious chambers, which—unlike his tiny judge's quarters at Ramsey County Courthouse—featured a wall of windows looking east over the city to Dayton's Bluff. Fitzpatrick stood with his back to the two of them, looking out the window.

"He was stomping like a horse in a stall because he was so mad. I thought to myself, 'He's lost control.' He was red-faced, this had so incensed him," Sipkins recalled. "Keeping his back to us, he started screaming. I recall his exact words. He said, 'I am considering moving this case up to my courtroom. I am considering allowing only two lawyers for the defendants to be in the courtroom. I am going to not allow the media in the courtroom at all. And you can explain to the public in this state why they can't watch or know about this very important trial.' Then he walked over and sat down at his desk."

Sipkins noted that Ciresi, "for the first time in this trial, was absolutely at a loss. He didn't know what was going on. He said, 'Just a minute, Your Honor. What the hell is this all about?'"

Sipkins proceeded to explain the letter to Ciresi, who had not seen it.

"Then I said, 'Look, judge, we paid these costs, but I think we certainly have a right to question them."

Again Fitzpatrick exploded, Sipkins said.

"'I know what you're doing. You're playing games.' Then he pointed his finger at me. 'If you want to play those games, I can play those games too. I can play those games better than you.' He just went on and on and on."

As for his opposing counsel, Sipkins recalled, "Ciresi, always Ciresi, immediately jumped to a position that I was wrong, without really knowing what my position was. But he skillfully said, 'Your Honor, I'm shocked that Mr. Sipkins didn't just pick up the phone and call me personally. That would have been the proper thing to do. If Mr. Sipkins was concerned about these things like cell phones, then we could have raised them at the end of the trial.'

"And the judge thought that was a great idea."

Ciresi, recalling the exchange, later described the judge as being "agitated that every time something was spent, the defense was going to question it."

Shaken, Sipkins rejoined his concerned colleagues downstairs. Sipkins chuckled as he recalled, "Here's the local counsel stuck by himself with nobody there monitoring what was going on, and not knowing if I'm going to suddenly settle the case, or what was going to happen."

But he wasn't laughing when he told his colleagues, "In 30 years of practicing law, I don't remember an incident ever quite like that one." For Sipkins, "It was bizarre and frightening."

Any doubts about whether or not to file a motion for reconsideration with Ramsey County Chief Judge Lawrence Cohen evaporated in the wake of Fitzpatrick's tirade. The defense team made plans to move ahead.

March 24 also marked the end of the plaintiffs' case. Ciresi provisionally rested, leaving open the possibility of calling additional witnesses, particularly if the anticipated release of the 39,000 documents led the plaintiffs in new directions. The plaintiff's case had been powerfully built on the testimony of 26 witnesses over nine weeks.

All eyes turned toward the defense.

Chapter Eleven

Where There's Smoke, There's Lawyers

The Defense Team

The defense team, which resembled little more than a large blur of white men in dark suits at the beginning of trial, sharpened into individual focus as the weeks passed.

While Ciresi and his team remained reserved and sequestered in their seventh floor war-room, the rented conference rooms for defense lawyers and the media stood side by side on the courthouse's first floor. For reporters, whose need for information, quotes, and sound bites was voracious, it was a perfect arrangement. As the trial progressed, the attorneys' different personalities slowly began to emerge, as they gradually grew more comfortable with their nosy next-door neighbors.

By dint of their trial experience and their clients' market shares, Philip Morris' Peter Bleakley, R. J. Reynolds Tobacco Company's Robert Weber, and Brown & Williamson's David Bernick were the undisputed kingpins of the defense team. The three spent months together in 1997 working on the Florida attorney general's lawsuit before it settled, and Bernick had moved from there to the Texas lawsuit. By the time the three arrived in Minneapolis, they'd experienced more tobacco litigation in a year than most lawyers see in a lifetime.

Although Bleakley was usually described as "lead defense counsel," he downplayed that designation.

"I didn't call all the shots, I didn't make all of the decisions. I didn't rule on whether a witness would or would not be called," he explained. "It was a collaborative effort, and we made those decisions by consensus in this case."

Bleakley, Weber, and Bernick shared leadership, similar clients, and reputations as top litigators, but that's where the common ground stopped.

Bleakley, at 61, was the team's grizzled veteran (without the grizzle), his craft honed by years of experience litigating on behalf of Philip Morris and other significant corporate clients. Angularly handsome, tanned, and detached, his mere presence lent weight to the proceedings. Philip Morris Associate General Counsel Greg Little described Bleakley as, "brilliant, insightful, and forceful." Philip Morris loved Bleakley. After all, this was the man whose Cipollone trial triumph on the tobacco giant's behalf had been dutifully recorded in a number of books written not only about tobacco trials, but in books about top litigators in general. He was diffident with the media—pleasant, but remote. He was there to do a job, one he had performed many times over the years on behalf of his clients. He knew the ropes, and could anticipate the probable moves of plaintiffs' attorneys and judges—at least he had in the past.

A graduate from the University of Virginia law school and a one-time lawyer for both the Federal Trade Commission and the Justice Department, Bleakley had been involved in complex litigation for the past 31 years as a partner in Arnold & Porter, a distinguished Washington, D.C., law firm.

A former smoker himself, Bleakley looked every bit the hired gun, brought in to do a job. Nothing more, nothing less. By trial's midpoint, he hadn't yet received a nickname from the jury, and, in fact, never would. He litigated like the wind, leaving little trace behind.

With his easy drawl and quick grin, RJR's Robert Weber, "The Duke," could have come from the south, although he grew up north of the Mason–Dixon line. Born in Pittsburgh, he was raised in Chardon, a small town near Cleveland, until he went off to college at Yale. He joked that he intended to major in football, until he was sidelined his freshman year with a shoulder injury. He ultimately graduated with an English major with the intention of teaching, but a year spent as a student teacher disavowed him of that ambition. Instead, he applied and was accepted at Duke University's law school. After he graduated, he returned to Cleveland and joined Jones, Day, Reavis & Pogue, where he quickly distinguished himself as a litigator.

He came to RJR's attention in 1985 with his successful litigation of the Galbraith tobacco trial in Santa Barbara, California. RJR's

Assistant General Counsel Thomas F. McKim described Weber
as "a tremendous trial lawyer. He's as close to the total package as
you're ever likely to see.

"He combines the power of prescient intellect with the kind of
street smarts you need to operate effectively in a trial environment, yet he has the kind of personality that makes it easy for him
to connect with the jury. You usually find one or two of those
traits in a trial lawyer, but Bob falls into the rarified atmosphere
of possessing all three," McKim said.

Weber's "aw-shucks" demeanor and his easy grin made him a
popular media figure. During most courtroom breaks—and at
least once during lunch—he could be found outside having a
cigarette, instead of holed up inside "150" (as their rented conference room had been dubbed), and was easily accessible. He was
the only lawyer whose comments invariably included literary references. An article he wrote for the *Cleveland Bar Journal* in 1995
on unpopular clients and their lawyers included an elegantly
written discourse on similar problems encountered by Thomas
More in the 16th century, as dramatized in Robert Bolt's *A Man
for All Seasons.*

Weber's prominence as a defense spokesman in the trial's media
coverage drew some unusual fan mail. One St. Cloud resident
sent Weber several letters offering his assistance at trial. "I have
information that would assure your case," he wrote Weber initially. A second letter guaranteed that the information "will turn the
tables for you if you choose to use it. The fee is seven million dol-

lars, so it must be good."

David Bernick, at 43, was the youngest of the three and also the newest arrival to tobacco litigation. However Bernick wasn't some rookie from the farm leagues. Although the number of cases the tiny attorney had tried in his career wasn't large, only about 20, they represented some of the biggest mass tort litigation cases in the country, if not the world: the Dow Corning breast implants, nuclear weapons plant litigation, the San Juan Dupont Plaza hotel fire. Big issues, big money.

And although other lawyers at the trial easily acknowledged that this case represented the biggest money case in which they'd ever been involved, Bernick actually had to think about it for a moment before answering, "I think that is probably right." Unlike the other attorneys, for whom this was also the longest trial they'd attended, Bernick had tried longer ones: "Gee, the San Juan trial lasted nine months, I think."

Bernick's love of litigation stemmed from his love of telling stories. "I love trying cases, and the more complicated and the more they are apparently difficult to defend, the better I like 'em," he said in an interview after the trial. "I think that all the cases that I've been involved with—and this one is no exception—present a very large picture of human conduct, in the sense of aspirations, ideas, goals, and actions that go way beyond this document or that document. They're part of a much broader canvas. I love telling those stories."

For Bernick, figuring out the actual story, then telling it to the jury, was his favorite trial task. "I love seeing the jury's eyes grow as they come to believe that the case really will have significance, that they'll go back over a huge controversy that occupied some of the best minds of the scientific community, involves the lives of tens of millions of people, and that they will sit in judgement of what was done."

For the jury's benefit, Bernick said, he always spoke extemporaneously, "because it's gotta be me, and once they see that I really do have my finger on something that's fascinating and important and something that I'm really convinced about, then you're into the pay dirt of the case.

That "pay dirt" involved "affecting the attitudes and ultimately the decisions of people who have no tie to you, no reason for being in your favor or loyal to you at all," Bernick explained. "I get onto the process, and I know when I try a case, that's what gives me confidence when things don't go well, because it's part of a much deeper and broader dynamic that's unfolding, and gives you the ability to weather the storm in the process."

Bernick got involved in tobacco litigation in 1994. His Chicago-based firm, Kirkland & Ellis (whose Washington, D.C. office was home to Kenneth Starr before his special prosecutor appointment) had a historical relationship with Brown & Williamson (B&W) over the years, but in commercial litigation, not cases involving smoking and health. When the Medicaid lawsuits began to be filed, B&W turned to Kirkland & Ellis, and, specifically, Bernick, because of his background in mass tort litigation. In the spring of 1995, he was designated B&W's national trial counsel.

Bernick's approach to the law was cerebral and precise, and that attitude extended to his day-to-day behavior in court. When the uproar about Judge Fitzpatrick was at its worst, Bernick was noticeably absent among those attorneys lining up to complain. It wasn't his style. He was totally focused on the case. He rarely let his eye leave the ball.

The out-of-town media, in particular, loved him. Bernick, who was staying at the St. Paul Hotel, was a creature of habit. He would descend from his room at about 9:00 each night for dinner and a cigar. Reporters from CNN, the *Wall Street Journal* and the *Los Angeles Times* would gather round and shoot the bull about the days events.

"He was a true believer," said CNN producer Tom Watkins, "It was interesting to hear his perspectives, since he'd covered the waterfront from breast implants to asbestos and tobacco. His perspective was absolutely the same as his employer's, and that was absolutely sincere. He had no veneer of phoniness."

Bernick, unlike some of his colleagues, appeared to have a genuine affinity for the media. "I've had a lot of cases that involve contact with the press and I enjoy talking to them," he acknowledged. "I'm not always pleased with what they write, but that's their business. There's almost nobody I won't talk to."

Accompanying each attorney was a coterie of local and national counsel, which corresponded in size to each companies' economic standing.

Philip Morris' entourage was the largest. Joining Peter Bleakley from Arnold & Porter was Murray Garnick, a quiet, solemn, 38-year-old attorney who appeared to be undergoing grooming for a tobacco trial of his own someday. During several early trial appearances before witnesses, his frequent restructuring of questions, midstream, earned him the jury nickname, "Strike That." He was a constant presence at Bleakley's side and seemed content to dwell in that shadow.

Local Philip Morris counsel, Peter Sipkins, a top litigator himself at the powerhouse Dorsey & Whitney law firm in Minneapolis, stood in cheerful contrast to his national colleagues. Bleakley and Garnick seemed to regard media questions with about the same pleasure as they would welcome a swarm of mosquitoes. The gregarious Sipkins often stopped in to socialize in the media room, or could be found chatting with reporters during courtroom breaks.

Ironically, Sipkins, 53, was Skip Humphrey's law school classmate at the University of Minnesota, and had been the youngest solicitor general to plead the state's cases before the Minnesota Supreme Court. His firm served as the liaison firm for all the defendants, and Sipkins played the most important role in the trial of any of the local lawyers. The small, bespectacled attorney's penchant for brightly colored neckwear made his jury nickname almost a given: "Bow Tie."

Philip Morris Associate General Counsel Greg Little, 43, was another favorite media target. Little, who joined the tobacco company in 1996, was a former commercial litigator for the Hunt & Williams law firm in Richmond, Virginia. Little spent most days seated in the gallery, directly in front of one of the media rows and was never averse to delivering the defense's point of view on a particular witness or legal ruling.

"Greg was one of the most well-connected attorneys in the group," said KMSP-TV reporter Lillian McDonald. "He was the hit man when things got tough."

Joining Weber on the RJR legal team was second chair Peter Biersteker, 42, who came from Jones, Day's Washington, D.C., office. Biersteker, a Harvard law school alumnus, was the tobacco team's damage model attorney. He'd been involved in tobacco litigation since 1985, but with the advent of the attorney general lawsuits in 1994, Biersteker's area of expertise shifted to studying the statistical models used to calculate damages in such lawsuits. He'd cut his teeth on the Mississippi damages model, moving from there to Florida and Texas. The Minnesota model, a new and vastly complicated version of the latter, would present his biggest challenge to date. Biersteker's Wisconsin birthplace was belied by his fresh-faced, ruddy countenance. The jury nicknamed him "Rosie."

Gray, Plant, Mooty, Mooty & Bennett was RJR's local law firm, which the tobacco company had been using for local tobacco litigation since 1984. Although senior partner James Simonson was the firm's longtime counsel on such matters, day-to-day court duty fell to associate attorney Jonathon Redgrave who was on hand to provide assistance to Weber and his team. Redgrave, 32, a Notre Dame law school graduate, was the youngest of the defense lawyers at trial. Although Redgrave had been involved in minor bench trials in Ramsey County, this was his first big trial, "probably the biggest I'll ever see," he later acknowledged.

Redgrave was one of the few defense attorneys who could recall a pleasurable experience with Judge Fitzpatrick. Redgrave's third son, George, had been born in August 1997. In honor of the event, Fitzpatrick issued a *"Pro Hoce Vice"* in his son's name—a document granting the newest Redgrave judicial permission to practice law in Fitzpatrick's courtroom.

"It was an extraordinary gesture," Redgrave said later. "Not many judges would do that."

B&W's second chair was held by the sole female defense lawyer to appear regularly at trial, Bernick's Kirkland & Ellis colleague Michelle Browdy. To Browdy, 34, fell the task of keeping Bernick's tonnage of research and scientific evidence at the ready, and she worked quietly and efficiently. Local counsel was provided by Faegre & Benson's Jack Fribley, 50, a skilled litigator who was no stranger to complex corporate litigation. He'd been involved in defending a number of Dalkon Shield IUD cases that were tried in Minneapolis, and had assisted in his firm's landmark trial representing Prince William Sound fisherman in the Exxon Valdez trial. At this trial, Fribley's considerable skills would go unused, and he remained a quiet player in the defense background.

The defense attorneys representing the smaller cigarette manufacturers would play little or no role in the upcoming defense portion of the trial. Lorillard's national counsel, Shook, Hardy &
Bacon attorney John Monica, was joined at the defense table by
local attorney, David Martin, from the St. Paul firm of Doherty,
Rumble & Butler. Martin, 52, joked, "Our job was to more or less
hide behind the big three, and hope the jury wouldn't notice us
too much."

B.A.T. Industries' national counsel was Michael Corrigan, 53,
from the powerful New York firm of Simpson, Thatcher &
Bartlett. His local colleague, Gerald Svoboda, 53, had planned
before the trial to retire from his firm, Fabayanske, Westra & Hart,
but agreed to stay on until the matter was concluded. The two
attorneys almost looked like brothers, with their full heads of prematurely gray hair. But it was Corrigan's unsmiling countenance,
and Svoboda's ongoing allergies, that earned them the jury nicknames of "Grumpy" and "Sneezy," respectively.

Svoboda, who had appeared before Judge Fitzpatrick in prior
trials, was particularly incensed by the way the tobacco trial was
unfolding. "These guys may not be going to corporate heaven, but
they deserve a fair trial," he told reporters in the media room one
morning.

"I'd never represented a tobacco company before and I'll never
represent one again, so I have no financial interest in the outcome whatsoever," Svoboda said in an interview after the trial.
"I've never smoked. I think it's a disgusting, filthy habit, and I per-

sonally believe it probably does have some causal relationship to lung cancer and certainly causes emphysema. So I have no sympathy for tobacco companies.

"But damnit, I feel entitled to a fair trial. And once we get to a point where—because of the type of defendant we're dealing with—they're no longer accorded due process, we're in big trouble in this country."

Other lawyers came and went, as circumstances dictated, but it was this group that became best known to reporters and other courtroom observers as they made their daily march down the long courthouse corridor, past the media room. Another corridor, off-limits to the press, led from their conference room to the courthouse lobby. Media wags noted that this alternate route was often taken on days they least wished to be pressed for comment.

"We liked the fact the press was there," Sipkins said. "We thought the press, at least at the beginning of the trial, was reporting far more fairly on the state's position than the defense's. Our location gave us an opportunity to develop relationships and trust, and try to get our message across. I don't think anyone viewed it as a problem of inconvenience, because, of course, we could always go the other way."

Somewhere in the no man's land between the defense and plaintiffs' teams were the lonely local litigators for tiny Liggett, Steven Kelley and David Sasseville from Lindquist & Vennum.

Liggett had once been a card-carrying member of the defense team. But, once Liggett CEO Bennett LeBow settled with the state of Minnesota, Liggett attorneys quickly found themselves personae non grata at the pretrial conferences and other gatherings.

When both sides consulted on the courtroom setup before the trial began, the Liggett attorneys were to be set up "at their own little table on the side," Steven Kelley recalled. "Nobody wanted to sit with us. It didn't work out that way, then they stuck us in between plaintiffs and defendants. They stuck us where, in order to be seated at the table so you could write, you'd have to have your back to the jury and to the court. It wasn't really a problem. But it was odd."

The rest of the "non-Liggett" defense counsel (as they subsequently described themselves in court pleadings, after Liggett's defection) congregated each day for a catered, buffet lunch in "150," where they could also avail themselves of the myriad office accoutrements and staff on hand. Kelley, on the other hand, "walked around the skyway. Ate here and there."

Of a much more serious nature was Liggett's periodic trouble getting necessary trial information, Kelley said. "As trial liaison, Dorsey & Whitney was supposed to, on behalf of all defendants, receive information from plaintiffs, receive information from the courts, and disseminate it.

"There got to be problems with that because we were basically shunned by all the other defendants. We were excluded from any joint communications or conversations, we were fed information only on a need-to-know basis by Dorsey. And, although Peter

Sipkins tried his best to keep us informed, in the mix of things we'd sometimes get left off a notice that an issue was going to be discussed in a 'meet and confer,' and we'd miss it, because nobody told us."

Kelley added, "There were a couple of times when we went to plaintiffs and said, 'Look, can you give us some information about what's happening here, because we can't get it elsewhere.'"

However, although Liggett had cooperated with the state, given Blue Cross' ongoing action against the company, the plaintiffs didn't much like Liggett either.

"We were not in the plaintiffs' camp. They treated us like adversaries," Kelley recalled. "They didn't go after us with the fervor of everybody else, but we were never considered to be on their side."

"It was awkward," David Sasseville agreed. "We were the friend of no one and the enemy of everyone." The tall, 41-year-old attorney spent his time watching the trial from "the perspective of the jurors themselves, since I wasn't familiar with a lot of the documents they were putting in."

Kelley and Sasseville alternated appearances at court, relying on the kindness of local defense counsel to share their real-time transcript computer monitors during sidebars and acting as, more or less, observers. "That was my principal job," Kelley said. "To sit there, watch what was happening, get my impressions about where things were going. I know all of the issues that impact Liggett very well. Any time anything came close to impacting those issues, I would pay particular attention."

However, Kelley did acquire something that even Peter Bleakley was never awarded, a jury nickname. The 41-year-old attorney wore his blonde hair in a stylish spiky cut once favored by a certain British rock star. The jury called him "Sting."

At night, the defense team scattered to various offices they'd established throughout the Twin Cities. Philip Morris used space on a floor near Dorsey & Whitney's offices in downtown Minneapolis. R. J. Reynolds had rented space several floors above its local counsel, Gray, Plant, Mooty in the Multifoods Tower. Brown & Williamson rented office space near the courthouse in St. Paul, and its holding company, B.A.T. Industries, maintained its own offices directly across the street from the courthouse. Lorillard's space, in the St. Paul Hotel, was kept under constant surveillance by a Pinkerton guard, reflecting the security consciousness of its law firm, Shook, Hardy & Bacon, whose Kansas City offices were among the most high-security operations in the country.

As the defense moved closer to the day when they would finally have their say in court, a reporter invited Bleakley and Weber to abandon the confines of Room 150 and have lunch out for a change, to provide a preview of their upcoming case. The two lawyers agreed, and, one snowy March day, ventured outside the courthouse via the skyways to a nearby local restaurant.

Once seated, their conversation quickly turned not to what lay before them, but to the hostility of Judge Fitzpatrick, the audacity of Mike Ciresi, and the strangeness of the trial in general.

"I don't think there's any question that we're facing a hostile court," Robert Weber said, as he munched on a salad. "But the surprise to me, so far, is the degree to which the state is unconcerned about an appeal. They have goaded the court into greater and greater error—a whole series of errors. This tells me that the state has absolutely no concern about its record on appeal. What this is, is a political show trial.

"After all," he kidded, "what else does A. G. stand for except 'aspiring governor?'"

But Weber really wasn't kidding. "The state basically has carte blanche for whatever it wants to do."

Were they being outmaneuvered?

"Sure," said Bleakley. "It's pretty easy to be more clever than your opponents when one side gets everything they want and the other side doesn't. I think we set forth pretty clearly in our motion for mistrial and for recusal how we think the deck has been stacked against us, and continues to be."

But what was really steaming Bleakley's soup was the "extraordinary lengths to which the state has gone to prevent this jury from hearing anything about their claims for damages. This case has not really been about their claims for damages. It has been a show trial to condemn the behavior of the tobacco industry. Lost in the shuffle has been a complaint that says, 'We, the state of Minnesota, and we, Blue Cross, have incurred increased health care costs because of the misconduct of the defendants.' No person has come in here and testified about Medicaid. No person has come in here and testified about the state. No person has come in here and even explained the programs or who the kind of people are who *are* in the programs."

Bleakley took a breath, but he wasn't done by a long shot. "What we have here is a show trial in which the plaintiffs are allowed to do whatever they want to convince the jury that the defendants have been bad boys. And then, because of that, they're allowed to write a number up on a blackboard and say, 'Give it to us.'"

Bleakley was particularly incensed that the defense was not being allowed to present its argument against the plaintiffs' damages model, the argument dubbed "the death benefit," by the plaintiffs.

"You can't do that, they say, because it would be horrendous public policy," he said angrily. "Forget that it's a fact that absolutely proves that they haven't suffered the increased health care costs they claim. We can't do it because it's bad public policy."

He stabbed at his lunch, shaking his head. "Well, that's not what trials are all about. Trials are about facts. But they don't want the jury to hear those facts."

Weber recalled the testimony of the plaintiffs' marketing expert, Robert Dolan. "He tries to leave the impression that advertising causes people to smoke. So you ask him some questions, like 'What about all this research and data in other countries where they've stopped advertising and people keep smoking at the same rates.'"

Mimicking Ciresi, Weber growled, "'Uuuuuhhhhhh irrelevant!'

"And the judge sustains it!" Weber, too, shook his head.

Bleakley moved on to another complaint. "And this only–one–lawyer–in–front–of–the–jury–thing," he said, laughing bitterly. "I mean, this case is supposed to be a conspiracy case. Requiring us to speak with one voice in a case in which part of the case is that we're conspirators, which makes us appear to be conspirators before the jury. That is inexcusable, and I think, by itself, is clear reversible error."

The two attorneys continued in this vein for some time, their thoughts turned more toward appealing the verdict than winning the case. It seemed, at this point in the trial at least, that they weren't anticipating much promise with the latter option.

One thing that *didn't* bother Bleakley, surprisingly, was the documents. "I went into this trial assuming that every document the plaintiffs were looking for would be introduced if it was any good," he said. "I made a decision that I was not going to sit during this trial and fret about what bad documents would come in."

When talk finally turned to what they *did* plan for their portion of the case, they acknowledged that they were going to try to put on the best defense they could.

"We're going to attempt to present our case exactly the way we think it should be presented," said Bleakley.

Weber interjected, "There will be enormous obstruction. Major daily battles."

Bleakley agreed. "I have never seen a lawyer object as much as Ciresi does. But we're going to move forward. We're going to start and end with what this case ought to be about, which is, have the state of Minnesota and Blue Cross incurred any increased health care costs as a result of the defendants' alleged fraudulent conduct? That's going to be the beginning and the end of our case. How much are we going to be allowed to present? I don't know. The moment our first witness finishes his credentials, Ciresi's going to be getting up, making up objections, making up rules of evidence that don't exist. Objecting on grounds of relevance, lack of foundation. . . ."

"And getting the judge to agree with him," Weber interjected.

"I think the change in atmosphere when we start our case will be palpable. I bet we won't do five questions in a row throughout our entire case without screaming and objections and absurd evidentiary rulings," Bleakley continued.

Said Weber, "If this were a pinball machine, the tilt sign would be blinking. Right from the beginning this whole thing has been on tilt."

Their lunch hour was up and, as the two attorneys strolled back to the courthouse, they talked of more personal matters.

Bleakley bemoaned the fact that in the past month, both of his daughters had become mothers, and he hadn't been able to see his new grandchildren yet. He had a wife and 5-year-old daughter at home. The trial was not only costing him professionally, it had become a personal matter as well.

Weber, who also had a family back in Cleveland, tried to get home as often as possible, but that wasn't much. On Friday nights, he sometimes went out with his staff, and mentioned a recent visit to the famed Northeast Nye's Polonaise Room, where he'd favored patrons at the piano bar with a rendition of "Danny Boy."

As they moved toward their first witness, most of the defense team seemed angry, dispirited, and almost driven to distraction by an exasperating judge and an infuriating local counsel.

One could almost picture Michael Ciresi smiling with glee.

Chapter Twelve

Tobacco Road

At 3:45 p.m. Tuesday, March 24, leadoff defense witness Hyman Berman took the witness stand and swore to tell the truth. Berman, a history professor at the University of Minnesota, seemed a crafty first choice by the defense. His credentials as a student of Minnesota history were unshakable; his grandfatherly presence a crowd pleaser. He could be witty and authoritative. On the stand, Berman taught, but did not lecture.

He would discuss the "common knowledge" Minnesotans had about the link between smoking and health risks. He would attempt to demonstrate that vast amounts of public information had thoroughly forewarned state residents about the possible consequences of long-term smoking. When he was done testifying, the defense hoped, the jury would find it difficult to believe that the industry had misled or deceived anyone.

The trial, now two months old, was exacting a toll. The judge looked weary, and at least one juror was faced with economic catastrophe caused by his loss of income during the trial.

As he began his testimony, Berman felt jittery. But he quickly relaxed and became comfortable addressing a jury that considered Berman to be a breath of fresh air after weeks of testimony about statistics and human anatomy.

The son of immigrant, working class-parents, the New York-raised Berman was the first in his family to attend college, graduating in 1948 from City College of New York with a degree in history. He earned a doctorate from Columbia University in 1956, and landed on the history faculty of the University of Minnesota in 1961.

Berman's first afternoon on the witness stand was mainly a warm-up appearance under the direction of Philip Morris attorney Peter Bleakley. At one point, Berman invited the jurors to visit his home to look in his den and see the volumes of material he reviewed in preparation for his testimony. "My wife will even make coffee for you," he said, bringing a round of laughter.

On the witness stand during his second day of testimony, Berman traced the growth of awareness in Minnesota about smoking and health, beginning in the 1870s. He quoted an 1876 book review in the *Minneapolis Citizen* newspaper where the author stated, "Smoking is a habit better not acquired."

He said the Women's Christian Temperance Union, the Anti-Cigarette League, and the No Tobacco League all mounted campaigns against smoking through the turn of the century and into the 1920s. Dr. Harold Diehl, who eventually became dean of the

University of Minnesota Medical School, wrote about the health risks of smoking in the 1930s, 1940s, 1950s, and into the 1960s, Berman testified.

The perils of smoking were present in popular culture, as well, Berman said, quoting Mark Twain's famous line: "Giving up smoking is easy. I've done it a thousand times."

Berman said Tex Williams had a hit song in 1947 called "Smoke, Smoke, Smoke," which included the lyrics, "Smoke, smoke, smoke that cigarette. Puff, puff, puff and you'll smoke yourself to death. Nicotine slaves are all the same."

Even Fitzpatrick was relaxed by Berman's entertaining history lesson, joking, "I don't think I'll allow this [song as evidence] unless the professor can sing it."

Berman replied, "Your honor, I'll be happy to, but if the jury isn't bored by now, they'll be tone deaf afterwards."

Beginning in the 1950s, Berman said, there was an explosion of material printed in the popular press about the dangers of smoking. He said *Reader's Digest* published as many as a dozen articles on the hazards of smoking with titles such as, "How Harmful are Cigarettes?" and "Cancer by the Carton." By the mid-1950s, the health debate had spilled onto television, including Edward R. Murrow's *See It Now* news program, which did two shows on lung cancer and smoking.

But the question about smoking and health was answered definitively in 1964, Berman stated, with the release of the first surgeon general's report on the subject. It concluded there was a link between smoking and disease.

"The surgeon general's report closed the debate for most scientists, most scientific observers, and led to an explosion of information disseminated to the public," Berman said, noting that 95 percent of the respondents in a 1970 *Minneapolis Tribune* poll said they considered smoking cigarettes unsafe. "For a historian, that is virtual unanimity," he claimed.

Minnesota schools also taught that smoking was harmful, Berman explained. A 1928 curriculum guide issued by the state education department said tobacco "contains poison," has a "harmful effect on the body," and called its use "costly."

But as smoothly as Berman's testimony was flowing, Philip Morris's Bleakley, who was leading the questioning, was slipping. A number of exhibits he offered as evidence were missing exhibit numbers and several copies of exhibits were illegible. Frequent objections by Ciresi slowed the pace of testimony. "I'm sorry," Bleakley said at one point. "I'm confused."

Outside the courtroom, members of the defense team privately wondered how Bleakley's performance was playing with the jury. "Do they think we're incompetent, or Ciresi is being an obstructionist, or something in between?" asked one attorney during a break in testimony.

During recesses, Berman chatted with reporters, many of them on a first-name basis. Berman was a valuable media resource when it came to history questions. Well into his 70s, Berman was still spry of mind, although a little hard of hearing. In court, questions frequently had to be repeated.

The small animated professor wore comfortable, soft-soled shoes and a suit that was slightly too large. He didn't feel right in the suit, he joked during recess. "I wish they'd let me wear my sweater because that's what I always wear when I teach," he said.

Berman had been approached by the tobacco industry in November 1995 to work as an expert witness for the defendants. He was at first skeptical about representing a client he wryly called "the evil empire." He even told defense attorneys during his first meeting with them: "I hope the other guys win."

However, Berman was challenged by the academic exercise of exploring the history of health awareness in the state when it came to smoking.

On the witness stand, Berman discussed teaching guides about smoking for Minnesota schools, state health department memos about campaigns to prevent smoking, and, ultimately, legislation that made Minnesota a national leader in smoking-control efforts.

The most significant legislative action came in 1970, Berman said, with passage of the Minnesota Clean Indoor Air Act, which segregated smoking from nonsmoking areas in public places. That was followed by the 1985 Omnibus Smoking and Health Act, which included smoke-free workplaces, education programs, and a higher cigarette excise tax.

But when the subject of the excise tax came up, Fitzpatrick intervened, concerned that the tax offset issue would rise again.

Fitzpatrick dismissed the jury 25 minutes early that afternoon, but kept attorneys in the courtroom and Berman on the witness stand. He warned the defense about going further with the excise tax issue, pursuant to his previous ruling that the tax could not be used to mitigate the cost of the health care damage claims. The defense considered Fitzpatrick's earlier ruling on the excise tax issue to be a critical blow to their case.

At issue was Berman's testimony about the proposed 1985 cigarette excise tax increase. With the jury absent, Berman said he would testify that a small portion of the additional tax was planned for smoking education programs, while the bulk was to be earmarked for sewer projects. The defense wanted to show that the state relied on the cigarette tax to fund basic state government services.

Fitzpatrick ruled that Berman could not testify about the legislative debate over the tax issue, noting he was not qualified to analyze the legislature's decision-making process. "No one has that expertise," the judge commented.

Meanwhile, tension between the judge and the defense team was growing—in court as well as outside it. Even as Berman was testifying that Wednesday, the defendants continued their attack on Fitzpatrick by filing a motion with Ramsey County Chief Judge Lawrence Cohen to have Fitzpatrick removed from the case because of perceived bias against the tobacco industry.

Physically, the 62-year-old judge was ailing, unbeknownst to nearly all in the courtroom. The efforts to remove him and the defense charges of bias were taking a toll. Two weeks earlier, the defendants had asked Fitzpatrick to remove himself from the trial. Now they were asking the chief judge of Ramsey County to remove him.

Some days Fitzpatrick looked dead tired, almost gray. Other days his face was flushed. He considered attempts to remove him as acts of betrayal.

The judge's deteriorating medical condition would not be known until after the trial. In an application for disability retirement, Fitzpatrick's personal attorney and long-time friend, R. Scott Davies, would write, "During the trial, [Fitzpatrick] experienced difficulties with heart rhythm which were exacerbated by the stresses of this prolonged, acrimonious, and complex litigation. The normal stress of lengthy litigation was significantly increased by personal attacks on the court, including motions for recusal midway through the trial. It was during this period, in March 1998, that [Fitzpatrick] experienced the most severe symptoms which included racing of the heart, irregular heartbeat, flushed face, and significant anxiety about the physical symptoms being manifested."

It was common knowledge that Fitzpatrick had a history of health problems. In the early 1990s, he had gall bladder surgery and did not work for nearly five months after complications to his digestive system. In a 1997 interview with the *Star Tribune*, he said, "Today I feel fine. What tomorrow brings, I don't know."

Ciresi later said he was shocked to learn of Fitzpatrick's condition. "His orders were well written. I thought he had a voracious appetite for work. I don't know how one guy could keep up with this case. It was unbelievable. We were all tired. He had so much going on and I think the personal attacks take something out of you."

But Fitzpatrick kept his taciturn visage in place and the marathon trial proceeded.

On Thursday, March 26, Berman came face to face with Ciresi. Ciresi began his cross-examination by gently challenging Berman's credentials as an expert witness on the smoking issue, noting he wasn't a behavioral scientist, a chemical engineer, or an expert on addiction.

Nonetheless, defense attorneys still felt comfortable with the decision to put Berman on the stand first, thinking he would give historical context to the smoking and health debate.

Ciresi believed Berman to be a crucial witness for the defense. Berman was their first witness and his testimony was the underpinning of their contention that smokers continued to smoke as a matter of personal choice, even in the face of adverse health information. But Ciresi also believed that a couple dozen newspaper articles about cancer and other diseases could not be allowed to sway the jury away from his contention that the industry lied and misled the public.

As the cross-examination wore on, Ciresi became more firm, asking Berman if he had access to the industry's internal documents about smoking and disease. "I have no idea what knowledge the tobacco industry had," Berman answered.

"In fact, sir, you feel it's not your concern about what the industry knows or did know, correct?" Ciresi asked.

"That is correct," Berman replied.

"And, in fact, I believe you said you're not interested at all in what the tobacco industry did, correct?" Ciresi pressed.

"That is correct," Berman answered.

"And you're aware there's 30 million historical industry document [pages] at a depository in Minneapolis, correct?" Ciresi continued.

"I'm aware of that, yes, sir." Berman answered.

Ciresi continued his offensive.

"Now you know that children, by and large, don't read medical journals, don't you?" he asked.

"I would assume that," Berman responded.

But children did watch television, see billboards, and go to convenience stores where they could be exposed to cigarette use and advertising, Ciresi countered.

"Yes, they do," Berman answered.

Berman said he was unaware of a rise in teen smoking in the 1990s, and did not know how much the industry spent on marketing and advertising. Once again, Ciresi brought out the enlarged copy of the Frank Statement, noting that the industry said in 1954, "We believe the products we make are not injurious to health."

"What the industry said to the general public was false, wasn't it?" Ciresi declared.

"I have no way of knowing that what the industry said was false, no, sir," Berman answered.

"Do you know if the industry . . . .has ever said smoking causes any disease?" Ciresi queried.

"I have not come across that, no, sir," Berman replied.

Ciresi then turned to a 29-year-old book to deliver a body blow to Berman's testimony. The jurors liked Berman and had listened intently to his history lesson about Minnesotans, smoking, and discussions about the health risks. They were about to learn that Berman's story might be incomplete.

One of Berman's underlying resources for his testimony was a 1969 book by Dr. Harold Diehl entitled *Tobacco and Your Health: The Smoking Controversy*. Berman used a chapter from that book in his testimony to underscore his conclusion about public awareness. A copy of Diehl's chapter had been supplied to the plaintiffs' team, as were all planned exhibits prior to a witness' testimony.

But Ciresi and his team located the entire book at the University of Minnesota's medical school library, and discovered that Diehl's treatise went far beyond the revelation that the public knew of the link between smoking and disease. Diehl's conclusion, it turned out, was a damning indictment of Big Tobacco's cover-up on health questions. Berman hadn't testified on that issue. Ciresi was about to change that.

Quoting from the book, Ciresi said Diehl believed that most people considered the health risk of smoking to be "small or remote" and that most knew "little or nothing" about heart disease, chronic bronchitis, emphysema, or other diseases brought on by smoking. Ciresi noted that Diehl made those observations five years after the landmark surgeon general's report linking smoking and cancer.

"He's the living practitioner," Berman acknowledged. "He was a participant/observer, as we would call it."

Ciresi continued with Diehl's determination that the industry used clever advertising techniques to encourage smoking and distributed "misleading propaganda." Diehl wrote about a public relations campaign in the mid-1960s funded by the Tobacco Institute to debunk the cigarette-cancer link.

According to Diehl, a public relations writer hired on behalf of the Tobacco Institute authored an article that appeared in *True Magazine* critical of the statistical evidence linking smoking with cancer. It was titled "To Smoke Or Not to Smoke—That Is Still the Question."

Diehl said reprints of the article, funded by tobacco interests, were sent to 600,000 opinion makers in the country, including doctors and teachers. The reprint said, "As a leader in your profession and your community, you will be interested in reading this story about one of today's controversial issues."

The reprint also said, "At the moment, all we can say for sure is that the cause of cancer isn't known and that there is absolutely no proof that smoking causes human cancer," Diehl reported.

The same *True Magazine* author, Diehl continued, used another name to write an article in a national tabloid several months later under the headline "Most Medical Authorities Agree—Cigarette Lung Cancer Is Bunk—70,000,000 Americans Falsely Alarmed."

Ciresi described Diehl's findings as a crass attempt by the industry to spread doubt, confusion, and uncertainty on the smoking and health issue at a time when public officials were finally making conclusions linking cigarettes with disease. Berman could not dispute it.

"I believe his account implicitly," Berman agreed, considerably weakening his previous testimony.

Several months after the trial was over, Berman acknowledged that Diehl's account of the planted stories was based on an article in *Collier's* magazine, which Berman had not verified. Why didn't Berman point that out during his testimony? "No one asked me," he said.

As Ciresi neared the end of what he considered the best cross-examination of his career, he asked Berman:

"You'd agree that the health of our nation is more important than the profits of an industry?"

"I agree," Berman answered.

"Without a doubt?" Ciresi asked.

"Without a doubt," Berman said.

"Unequivocally?" Ciresi persisted.

"Unequivocally," said Berman.

Ciresi then presented Berman with a 1998 article from the

Journal of the American Medical Association. It was written by Drs. David Kessler, C. Everett Koop, and George Lundberg. They wrote, "If the whole truth were known [and much more may come out during the Minnesota trial], we believe members of Congress would have to distance themselves completely from the industry."

Ciresi asked Berman, "And you, as a historian, knowing what deceit can do, believe the truth should come out, don't you?"

"I certainly do," Berman replied.

"You think it's absolutely necessary for the truth to come out, don't you?" Ciresi continued.

"Yes," Berman said.

"It's particularly necessary for the children of this country," Ciresi went on.

"For everyone," Berman responded.

"Thank you, professor, I have no further questions."

As Berman was preparing to leave the witness stand, Ciresi said, "Thank you, professor. You take care." Berman smiled and gave Ciresi a thumb's up.

At all times on the stand, Berman had presented himself as an honest, sincere academician. But he had not been the witness with which the defense had hoped to open its case. Berman, at best, had been neutralized. At worst, he'd just become one of the most effective witnesses the plaintiffs never presented.

Ciresi later characterized Berman's testimony as a disaster for the defense. "He ended up admitting much of our case," Ciresi recalled. "I thought he was a very, very important witness because he was their leadoff witness and in the end he gives me the thumb's up.

"Your first witness has to be good and he ends up being the other side's witness. It's devastating."

Some jurors agreed. Although they'd been charmed by Berman's chatty history lesson, they felt Ciresi cut major holes in his testimony. It was a critical blow for the defense, with their first witness sitting as damaged goods.

"I loved him, you know we all did." said Dorothy Hallen. "We just thought he was so cute. No one else invited us over for coffee. I thought he did a really good job at letting us know what was really out in the community about cigarettes and health and stuff. I didn't know all that was out there. It was fun watching him [when Ciresi showed him the book excerpt]. You know how he just kind of turned. He just became one of their witnesses and it was like he was flabbergasted at that stuff he was seeing. "

Berman felt good about his testimony and the factual basis for his conclusions. "I just let the chips fall where they may," he recalled.

The defense was circumspect. "His strength is his agreeability and affability and encyclopedic knowledge of history," said R. J. Reynolds' Robert Weber. "He was as agreeable on cross-examination as he was on direct. He emphasized things for the defendants just as he acknowledged things for the plaintiff."

Events outside the courtroom continued to draw attention

away from the workings of the trial. On Friday, March 27, as RJR Vice President for Product Development and Assessment, David Townsend, testified about cigarette design improvements, the Minnesota Court of Appeals refused to block the release of an additional 2,161 documents from the files of British-American Tobacco and affiliates, which Fitzpatrick ordered produced as a sanction on the company for failing to bring two former company scientists from Britain to St. Paul to testify.

Even worse for the industry, on the same day as the appellate decision, the Minnesota Supreme Court rejected its request to keep the 39,000 disputed documents sealed under the claim of attorney-client privilege.

Writing for the high court, Minnesota Supreme Court Chief Justice Kathleen Blatz stated, "We recognize [the companies'] concerns that effective review of discovery orders occurs prior to disclosure of documents, but the extraordinary relief they seek is, as a practical matter, an impossibility."

Brown & Williamson's David Bernick was incensed. Speaking to reporters, he said it would be a "sad day" if the principle of attorney-client privilege was "sacrificed to practicality."

Humphrey predicted the new documents would "tell the most devastating tale of corporate fraud and deceit in American history," even though he hadn't yet seen the disputed documents.

The industry had one last resort—the U.S. Supreme Court.

Tobacco's defense was off to a rocky start as the document cards continued to stack up in the state's favor.

Continuing his penchant for weekend orders, on Saturday, March 28, Fitzpatrick ordered the Minnesota document depository opened to the public, granting an industry request that was made with an eye toward a national settlement. All nonprivileged material would be available for public inspection in 15 days, Fitzpatrick ruled. The industry could now tell Congress and the public that this was a good faith effort to cleanse any sins of the past. But what was in the 39,000 documents protected by attorney-client privilege? Ciresi's team wanted to know.

When testimony resumed on Monday, March 30, RJR cigarette expert David Townsend continued to describe efforts to identify and reduce potentially harmful elements in cigarette smoke. The defense had high hopes for Townsend's appearance. He was a modern-day scientist. Even at age 50, he was young and articulate compared to fossilized scientists like Thomas Osdene and Helmut Wakeham, seen on videotape earlier in the trial.

The defendants considered Townsend to be one of the industry's foremost authorities on the science of cigarette design. His testimony was intended to demonstrate how cigarette manufacturers studied the smoking process and attempted to respond to health concerns. The goal with Townsend was to counter the plaintiffs' cigarette expert, Channing Robertson. Robertson testified that tobacco companies manipulated nicotine levels to keep smokers addicted.

Rather than creating suspicion by being elusive, Townsend was forthright in describing industry attempts to reduce tar and nicotine levels and identify hazardous compounds in smoke. Townsend explained how manufacturers experimented with different types of filters, cigarette paper, and tobacco blends in an effort to satisfy consumer demands for improved cigarettes, that still tasted good.

Cigarette designers, Townsend said, learned that consumers wanted lower-tar cigarettes, but were less enthusiastic about reduced nicotine levels.

"Maintaining consumer acceptance as tar and nicotine levels are reduced further and further becomes difficult," he said under questioning by Robert Weber. "The theory is to keep nicotine levels up while going as low as you can go with tar levels."

Townsend said the highest tar cigarette currently sold by RJR was lower than the lowest tar cigarette sold in the 1950s. The company was able to do that by improving the filter, placing microscopic ventilation holes in the paper, increasing the burn rate of the paper, and using less tobacco for each cigarette. Townsend also said reconstituted tobacco was incorporated into the tobacco blend to reduce tar and moderate nicotine levels.

But not all attempts to change the content of cigarette smoke were successful, Townsend acknowledged, pointing to a short-lived experiment with carbon filters. "The companies learned that consumer acceptance of modified products is essential in the marketplace," he said.

Townsend was an effective witness with plenty of trial experience. He'd testified in six previous smoking-and-health trials as an expert witness and had nothing but victories under his belt.

Townsend described numerous experiments by RJR to find sub-stitutes for tobacco in cigarettes, including lettuce leaves, cocoa bean hulls, peanut shells, fig leaves, corn cobs, and puffed grains. He talked about the addition of ammonia to the tobacco blend as a way to enhance flavor and reduce irritation as tar and nico-tine levels were altered. He denied, as Robertson had testified, that ammonia was used to increase the pH in smoke to provide the smoker with a nicotine kick.

"The design tools that have been developed have made a major reduction in tar and nicotine levels," Townsend emphasized.

Weber felt good about Townsend's testimony. He believed the jury understood that efforts were made to address health concerns and improvements were made to cigarettes through that research.

"David Townsend put a human face on the industry. I think it is important to have company people testify in cases like this," Weber said later.

Ciresi, however, considered Townsend to be nothing more than a full-time witness for the industry with little hands-on experi-ence in the research lab. "He was a talking head," Ciresi said.

Under a tough cross-examination by Ciresi, Townsend was unbudging in his defense of industry efforts to produce a less hazardous cigarette. He said the decision to reduce tar and nico-tine levels was done at the behest of the scientific community and the smoking public who felt "less is better."

But Ciresi argued that it never had been proven that reducing tar and nicotine produced a safer cigarette. Townsend conceded that there was no way to prove one cigarette was safer than another.

On his fourth day of testimony, Ciresi pressed Townsend on the issue of compensation: that smokers of low-yield cigarettes inhale deeper, longer, and smoke more cigarettes to maintain their desired intake of nicotine. Ciresi quoted from the 1981 surgeon general's report saying that lower-tar cigarettes reduced the risk of lung cancer, provided the smoker did not inhale a compensating extra amount of smoke. Studies, Ciresi said, showed no health benefit from lower-tar cigarettes.

"There are some studies that suggest there is, there are some studies that say there isn't," Townsend responded. "My common sense tells me less ought to be better."

Ciresi also appeared to score a key point with the admission from Townsend that RJR used Freon gas in the tobacco manufacturing process from 1970 to 1993, without studying the long-term impact on humans. Decomposed Freon, as would occur in the smoking process, produces phosgene, a nerve gas used in World War I.

When did the industry warn the public that they didn't know all the constituents in smoke?" Ciresi asked.

"I take great offense at the suggestion we don't know what's in smoke," Townsend replied. "We've spent an extreme amount of scientific effort to do exactly what you're suggesting."

Ciresi continued: "The question's very simple, sir. When did Reynolds warn people it didn't know all the constituents in smoke?"

"I'm not aware that my company ever warned people that we don't know all the constituents of smoke," Townsend said.

Townsend held firm to the industry position that a causal link between smoking and disease was not definitive, that people smoked of their own free will, and were well aware of potential risks. But a Ciresi cross-examination was always a demanding exercise and Townsend didn't leave the witness stand totally unscathed. Ciresi had hoped to neutralize Townsend. Seated at the crowded plaintiffs' table, Ciresi's team believed he accomplished his goal.

As far as colleague Richard Gill was concerned, Ciresi's cross-examination of Townsend was his best of the entire trial, surpassing even Berman.

"Townsend was an extraordinarily practiced witness," said Gill. "Mike spent two days dismantling his testimony piece by piece. Few attorneys would have conducted that cross as well. We were overjoyed with his performance."

Outside the courtroom, the eyes of the trial's attorneys and observers focused on Supreme Court Justice Clarence Thomas, in whose hands rested the industry's appeal to block the release of the highly anticipated 39,000 privileged documents. As Townsend was winding up his testimony, Thomas denied the appeal, but did so in such a manner that the industry could approach a second justice for relief.

Defense attorneys promptly asked Justice Antonin Scalia to step in. But time was waning.

Few believed the defendants would prevail with the Supreme Court, especially with an ongoing trial at stake. "It's an important question that's being presented," said Joseph Daly, a Hamline University law professor who was following the trial. "But I can't imagine that the Supreme Court would interfere with an ongoing case. The Supreme Court is a court that contemplates. They don't step in when the battle is going on."

Walking back to the St. Paul Hotel after court, Friday, April 3, Ciresi was confident that neither Townsend's testimony nor any part of the defense case was swaying the jury. "They're in disarray," he bragged to his trial team, wondering aloud about lead attorney Bleakley's absence during the last two days of testimony. "There's no leadership."

As attorneys for both sides awaited word from the Supreme Court on the disputed 39,000 privileged documents, other jurors faced more personal concerns. Juror Terry Zaspel was experiencing periodic chest pains, but kept that information to herself. Juror James Otis still was suffering from stomach problems. However, these didn't come from stomach flu, but from worry that he might get sick again. He was so distracted that he stopped taking notes, he said, for the next three weeks. "I didn't realize I was a nervous person until I got into that deal," Otis recalled.

James Livingston, known in the courtroom only as Juror Number Two, was concerned about court documents of his own.

Beset by debts and a sizeable cut in income because of his jury duty, Livingston now faced a financial meltdown. Earlier that week he and his wife had signed papers to initiate Chapter 7 bankruptcy proceedings in order to obtain protection from creditors. Their petition would soon be filed on the second floor of the same building where he was hearing testimony.

Livingston, the youngest person on the jury, was a welder and metal finisher who earned between $11 and $12 an hour. Before the trial, he usually supplemented his income with 10 or more hours of overtime each week at a rate of time-and-a-half. But when he decided to file for bankruptcy, Livingston had earned just $2,500 for the first three months of the year, and creditors were on the phone most evenings. Moreover, his mortgage lender was threatening foreclosure on his small St. Paul townhouse as Livingston and his wife had fallen three months behind on their $430 monthly mortgage payments.

The bankruptcy form was signed by Livingston and his wife on April 1. Even with a combined income of $2,300 a month, their bills exceeded their income by $300 a month. Livingston said later that—prior to the trial—they were a little behind financially from Christmas bills, but that he would have caught up with the overtime he normally earned.

Repeated attempts to communicate his plight to Judge Fitzpatrick were unsuccessful. He made copies of the foreclosure notice and sent them to the judge through Michelle Jones.

"And they didn't do anything," he said. "They didn't say anything at all."

The only comment he did get from court personnel was an

admonition to stay awake during testimony if he was going to work such strange hours, Livingston said. At the beginning of the trial, jurors had been warned that only a hospital admission would be cause for missing court. But, by now, Livingston had reached his breaking point. Although he took jury duty seriously, Livingston was ready to toss it in and stop showing up in court, even if it meant a visit from the Ramsey County Sheriff's Office.

One night Livingston told his wife, "I don't see why I'm still bothering to go. I might as well go back to work [full time]. We've only got a month to come up with the money [to prevent foreclosure]. "

His fellow jurors warned him about not showing up, telling him he'd probably go to jail.

"Yeah, but at least maybe I'll get off the trial then," he told them.

Ultimately Livingston's wife and juror David Olson talked him out of taking such drastic action.

"Dave just told me that it would create more problems," Livingston recalled. "He said, hopefully the trial would be over soon."

So Livingston kept working graveyard hours and worrying about his family's financial straits.

During jury selection, Livingston had warned the court that, if all he earned was the standard jurors' fee of $30 per day, he'd face financial disaster.

Now he was looking it straight in the eye.

Chapter Thirteen

Smoking Howitzers

Big Tobacco's last hope for a judicial intervention preventing the release of the 39,000 documents was dashed on Monday, April 6, when the U.S. Supreme Court took a big pass on hearing the industry's request. In a one-sentence ruling issued first thing in the morning, the court let stand Judge Fitzpatrick's March 7 order requiring the industry to produce documents sealed for decades under the seemingly inviolate claim of attorney-client privilege.

As attorneys milled around the courtroom that morning before trial, the difference between plaintiffs and defense teams had never seemed more stark. Mike Ciresi rocked on his heels and beamed as he and his colleagues awaited Judge Kenneth Fitzpatrick's impending order requiring tobacco attorneys to finally deliver the goods. Even the normally solemn Roberta Walburn grinned ear-to-ear.

The tobacco attorneys stood stiffly, separately, and quietly. Malaise hung heavy over Team Tobacco, their spirits at an all-time low in the trial. When a reporter followed a group of them down the hall seeking a comment on the Supreme Court decision, they stopped and looked at each other.

"Shit," said one of them, finally. "What am I supposed to say?"

Ultimately, Philip Morris Associate General Counsel Greg Little was elected to speak for the industry. "I think it's very unfortunate," he said. "It sends a very chilling message to any trial lawyer that attorney-client privilege is not as sacred as it once was. In eight weeks [of trial] there has been no proof that the state was misled in any way. These documents won't help." Although articulate, there was no fire behind Little's statement. His words spun as wobbily as a semideflated basketball.

His opponents, on the other hand, soared into hyperbolic heaven.

Attorney General Hubert Humphrey proclaimed the occasion "a landmark day" as he stood in front of the 110 file boxes of documents delivered to Ciresi's law firm. "This is the truth that we have been seeking. Now the American people will know, and justice is going to be done."

Blue Cross CEO Andy Czajkowski declared, "The iceberg has hit the Big Tobacco ship. The industry that has claimed invincibility for so long is sinking under the weight of its own words." (The movie *Titanic* was breaking box-office records at the time and the iceberg analogy would pop to the surface at the tobacco trial a few too many times.)

Ciresi said that with the documents, "we will now be able to commence the unraveling of the 40-year conspiracy of fraud and deceit. We will learn the full nature and scope of the abuse of the American judicial system and legislative process by this industry."

And in words that would prove to be prophetic, Ciresi commented on what he would do if he were in Big Tobacco's shoes. "I think I'd be looking at things other than continuing to try this case. But I'm not here to give them advice. That's up to them."

Of the 110 boxes delivered, 54 came from R. J. Reynolds Tobacco Company (RJR), 23 from Brown & Williamson (B&W), 18 from Philip Morris, four each from British-American Tobacco Company (BATCo) and American Tobacco Company, two from the Tobacco Institute, and one each from the Council for Tobacco Research and B.A.T. Industries.

Over the course of the plaintiffs' quest for the documents, Attorney General Humphrey and his staff penned a variety of appellations to describe the as-yet-unseen industry documents. From "treasure trove" to "crown jewels" to "smoking howitzers," Humphrey's terminology built high expectations for the contents of the files.

Ciresi pulled together two dozen attorneys from his firm to begin a systematic review of the material in his firm's Minneapolis offices so Ciresi could enter them as evidence as soon as possible. Not all of the additional lawyers had worked on the tobacco case, but they were experienced in complex litigation and were familiar with corporate document searches.

The Ciresi team quickly determined that the documents were

more damning of the industry than they could have hoped for. In eight days, the plaintiffs would be ready to begin showing new industry secrets to the jury.

"It was an amazing collection that confirmed your worst thoughts about the industry," recalled Walburn, who'd by now become one of the most experienced, and successful, tobacco document researchers in the country.

Walburn said she and tobacco team attorneys Tara Sutton and Gary Wilson began thumbing through boxes even as they were being unloaded in the firm's conference center. "We started finding stuff right away," Walburn said.

The road leading to the plaintiffs' acquisition of the closely held industry documents ran back four years, when the lawsuit was filed.

"We let the tobacco companies know and the judge know back in 1994 that we believed the privilege documents would be a defining issue in discovery," said Walburn. "Before we filed, we looked at the history of tobacco litigation and talked to the attorneys who'd fought the industry. It was clear to us that [industry] lawyers had played a pivotal role in the documents. It was clear that many critical documents were being withheld on claims of privilege. We knew those would not be easy to get and it would be a long, hard battle."

Through 1996, the plaintiffs battled to get logs of the documents for which privilege was claimed. But the few logs they did obtain contained inadequate descriptions of the documents under the privilege seal. Still, Fitzpatrick declined to waive the privilege protection just because the logs were unsatisfactory to the plaintiffs.

By early 1997, the plaintiffs and the defendants both agreed to resolve the matter by appointing a special master to review the disputed material. Fitzpatrick turned to local St. Paul attorney Mark Gehan for the job. At about the same time, the Liggett Group had settled claims with a number of states, including Minnesota, and would be turning over privilege documents from its files. Reviewing the Liggett privilege documents would become Gehan's first official task.

In the spring of 1997, Fitzpatrick held hearings on the documents. The plaintiffs intended to show that tobacco industry attorneys were controlling sensitive industry material improperly, in furtherance of a crime or a fraud. In May, Fitzpatrick agreed with the plaintiffs, ruling that *prima facie* evidence existed to support the crime-fraud exemption to the claim of privilege.

Gehan tackled the joint industry documents provided by Liggett and held hearings on the crime-fraud issue. In September 1997, he recommended that more than 800 of Liggett's documents were not covered by attorney-client privilege and should be turned over to the plaintiffs. He then turned to the rest of the industry, working through the fall and into the winter before recommending to Fitzpatrick in February that documents in four of 14 categories should be produced to the plaintiffs.

"The defendants had month after month after month, and

hearing after hearing to try and rebut the findings of crime-fraud and they couldn't do it," said Walburn.

The industry unsuccessfully appealed Fitzpatrick's adoption of Gehan's February report, and, by April 6, had no choice but to deliver the documents to the plaintiffs.

Once delivered, the documents were placed in a 28th floor conference room at the Robins firm in downtown Minneapolis. Attorneys sifted through them from before sunrise until midnight.

Each evening a box-load of the day's best finds was delivered to the trial team's 11th floor command center in the St. Paul Hotel. After returning from the trial each day, Walburn and Sutton would cull through the first cut of potential exhibits and make a second cut of the most useful. Walburn and Sutton then determined which documents were appropriate for which defense witness. Eighteen-hour workdays were the norm.

It was a labor-intensive task, but adrenaline ran high among the reviewing team of attorneys. They were plowing new ground, looking at yet more material never before seen outside of the industry. The potential for discovery of earth-shattering information fueled the pace of work. The atmosphere was like cramming for college finals, one participant said.

Meanwhile, politicians in the nation's capitol didn't waste any time muscling in on the Minnesota victory.

House Commerce Committee Chairman Thomas Bliley vowed that he would initiate proceedings to hold Big Tobacco in contempt of Congress "unless the documents in question are produced immediately to lawmakers working on a national settlement with the tobacco industry." That threat fell by the wayside as Bliley's committee received its own set of documents later that day.

"This disclosure of these 39,000 documents will be like 39,000 new lobbyists working against the tobacco industry in Washington," said Senator Frank Lautenberg, a New Jersey Democrat. "Once we in Congress start reading these documents, whatever little support the industry has on Capitol Hill will vaporize in a puff."

Something else would vaporize in a puff on Capitol Hill that week, but it wasn't exactly how Lautenberg pictured it.

On Wednesday, April 8, Big Tobacco, having watched the terms of its highly publicized national settlement expand from a $368.5 billion agreement reached with states' attorneys general in 1997, to a $506 billion settlement at the hands of Senator John McCain, an Arizona Republican, decided it had had enough. The gauntlet hit the ground with RJR's announcement that it was withdrawing from the settlement. The other tobacco companies followed suit. For some, this indicated that no settlement would be reached in the Minnesota case as well.

Humphrey was unfazed. "Congress does not need this outlaw industry's permission to enact legislation to advance the public health and to protect the future generations of kids. We have always expected to bring our case to the jury in order to get the truth out about this rogue industry and, by God, we are prepared to see it through," he said. "If they are willing to face the consequences about their actions and finally face the truth, not only are we able and willing to meet them in the courtroom, but other states are ready as well."

Still, Humphrey's statements fell short of outright rejection of a possible settlement. "I think that people of good will who have sincere interests in resolving differences can always find a basis for doing that," he said. Humphrey's conditions remained the same: that the industry disclose its secret documents, stop marketing to children, and pay for the costs of treating smoking-related illness.

If Big Tobacco's actions had irritated Congress, it was nothing compared to Judge Fitzpatrick's anger when he discovered that the industry furnished Bliley's committee with CD-ROM copies of the documents, a courtesy that had not been accorded the Minnesota plaintiffs. With a CD-ROM copy of the documents, access would be faster for reviewers.

During a day while jurors were in another courtroom reviewing defense documents, a red-faced Fitzpatrick demanded an explanation from the first attorney he could question — in this case, RJR's local counsel, Jonathan Redgrave.

Redgrave had not intended to make an appearance at court that day and was on his way to his Minneapolis office when he was paged and informed that he was needed in the courtroom. Immediately. Redgrave was dressed way down in a plaid lumberjack shirt and jeans. He was soon dressed down even further by

Fitzpatrick, who demanded to know, "Who was it who was so anxious to rush the CD-ROM to the congressman before it was provided to the plaintiffs? The understanding was clear in chambers that the plaintiffs would have the first opportunity to obtain the documents and the CD-ROMs. It appears that somebody decided that they would go on their own. And I would like to know who that person is."

Redgrave apologized for the confusion and said he didn't exactly know what went wrong, but that he would find out.

Fitzpatrick wasn't appeased. "What I'd like is the apology from that person who felt the need to violate the understanding of the parties in chambers. I'd like to have that person's apology."

Redgrave was puzzled by the judge's anger over the matter. On a scale of 1 to 10, he put Fitzpatrick's displeasure with the industry at 8. "It appeared that he was concerned that there was a conspiracy going on and that the plaintiffs were going to be cheated out of something — either credit or the documents," Redgrave recalled later. "What's the great concern if you don't get the CDs at the same time?" he wondered, noting that Bliley's staff had requested CD-ROM copies only.

During the next 24 hours, Fitzpatrick received a steady stream of apologies from defense attorneys, with various explanations, but it was clear the jurist's mistrust of the attorneys and their actions had only deepened.

And, in return for their legal maneuvering to try to prevent the release of the 39,000 documents, Fitzpatrick ordered them to pay

$199,619 in plaintiffs' expenses and attorneys fees.

The jurors, meanwhile, were getting an eyeful of documents the defense considered damaging to the plaintiffs. They included copies of magazine and newspaper stories from the 1950s and 1960s about smoking and health, intended to bolster the defense's claims that consumers had long been aware of smoking's dangers. Another document, a 1988 letter from the chief of volunteer services for the Minnesota Department of Human Services, thanked the state's Department of Revenue for providing 651 packs of cigarettes to a state-run nursing home.

Document days were a welcome break for jurors who were growing weary of sitting in court day after day struggling to pay attention to witnesses, or confined to their small room during breaks and lunch. Document day gave them a chance to move about and study evidence without the usual courtroom decorum.

By now, jurors had a sense of the tension that had built between the defendants and Fitzpatrick. They thought he was firmer in his rulings regarding defense witnesses than he had been with the plaintiffs' witnesses. While some of the plaintiffs' witnesses had rambled on with their testimony, the jurors sensed Fitzpatrick was less inclined to allow defense witnesses to answer similarly.

"I started keeping a tally on one side of my [notebook] pages as to how many times the plaintiff was overruled and how many times the defense was," said Jill Burton. "At one point the defense had a witness on and somebody objected. The defense attorney stood up and said, 'Your Honor, could the witness be permitted to finish his answer?' and the judge said, 'Well, he was nonresponsive and someone had to cut him off.'"

Although they were unaware of all the external commotion associated with the trial, the jurors also believed the judge looked fatigued.

"Tired, that's what I kept coming back to, just thinking he looked tired," recalled Dorothy Hallen, who sat in the front row of the jury box. "He was edgier some days. It was getting to everybody. . . . But you know, the defense wanted to throw us out the first day. Halfway through the trial they wanted to throw the judge out. He knew all of this was going on. I can imagine it was real hard for him to stay neutral."

On the witness stand when testimony resumed midweek was BATCo scientist Michael Dixon. But his presence in court paled by comparison to the week's events. Dixon, whose testimony had begun the week prior, returned to the stand Wednesday, April 8, telling jurors that tobacco companies didn't manipulate pH levels in cigarettes to increase the nicotine kick.

Plaintiffs' attorney Richard Gill attacked the bearded, disheveled scientist not so much on his theories, but on his credentials. Gill suggested that BATCo could have sent a higher ranking representative to be its expert witness.

But as Gill mounted his assault on Dixon's credibility, a different tobacco-related event was unfolding several blocks away in the courtroom of Ramsey County Chief Judge Lawrence Cohen, where attorneys gathered to argue the defense's motion for Judge Fitzpatrick's removal from the trial.

Though close in proximity, Cohen's courtroom environment seemed light years removed from Fitzpatrick's dark, heavy, security-ridden venue. The light maple benches and colorful red and lavender carpet in Cohen's airy, window-filled courtroom created a cheery atmosphere that was amplified by the judge's staff. As attorneys and observers filled the small courtroom, a friendly bailiff directed overflow attorneys to sit in the jury box. No credentials were necessary to be seated in Judge Cohen's courtroom, no rules of conduct were outlined, the doors remained unlocked during proceedings, and no security guard stood by, ready to pounce on noisy scribblers or pageturners. Looking around the courtroom, Minnesota Public Radio reporter Laura McCallum drew laughs when she declared, "I want to stay over here!"

When Judge Cohen arrived, he nodded pleasantly to those attorneys he recognized.

Attorney Peter Sipkins spoke on behalf of the defendants—a position few attorneys would covet, given Cohen's long-standing relationship with Fitzpatrick. Cohen was Fitzpatrick's boss in the 1970's, when he was mayor of St. Paul and Fitzpatrick was in the city attorney's office. The two were said to be close friends. Now, Sipkins would be required to stand less than four feet away from Fitzpatrick's long-time colleague and argue for his removal.

"Once you make the decision that this is the right thing to do as a lawyer, standing up there and arguing is not difficult, or doesn't cause incredible angst," Sipkins said after the trial. "I felt strongly it was the right thing to do."

Sipkins began his presentation by explaining that this was the first time in his 30-year career that he'd pursued such an option. "We come before you not because we are losing or to vent a collective spleen, but because we feel very strongly that what is going on in the court is beyond reason."

Sipkins reviewed the defense complaints about Fitzpatrick: the way the judge conducted jury selection, his rulings from the bench, and his courtroom behavior toward the defense. At one point, Sipkins discussed Fitzpatrick's "red-faced" demeanor as evidence of his hostility toward defense attorneys. Cohen jokingly acknowledged, "He is a red-faced kind of guy. He's that way even when he is not angry."

Cohen added, eyes twinkling, "But I suppose when he gets ticked off, it gets even redder."

"It's only if you were there that you could see the full panoply of abuses the defendants incur in Judge Fitzpatrick's courtroom," Sipkins responded quietly, adding, "It's something the jury perceives."

Plaintiffs' attorney Bruce Finzen was quick to counterattack. He denounced the defense attorneys' motion as "a shameless act by a shameless industry." He said tobacco lawyers were desperate because "their case is not going well."

"The defendants are prolific judge-shoppers," Finzen claimed. Praising Fitzpatrick as maintaining a "calm, evenhanded, judicial temperament," he added that any judicial display of "impatience, dissatisfaction, annoyance, or even anger" did not meet the legal definition of bias.

"This judge has endured 12 appeals to the Minnesota Court of Appeals, five appeals to the Minnesota Supreme Court and two appeals to the U.S. Supreme Court, and has not had one ruling overturned," Finzen concluded.

Cohen was more interested in the implications for the trial, if he did remove Fitzpatrick. "How long would it take a new judge to get up to speed, fit into the case, with the same jury?"

Finzen estimated several months and the empaneling of a new jury. Sipkins thought the process could be accomplished in a month.

But when Cohen got Sipkins to concede that, with or without a new judge, the defendants would still appeal any verdict brought against them, the defense motion seemed almost certainly doomed.

"With all the money involved here, and with all the people involved, why didn't you put the fire out much sooner than now, with just weeks to go?" Cohen wondered.

Sipkins explained the decision to remove a judge "is a very serious matter."

Before Cohen concluded the proceedings, he had harsh words for the defense attorneys, some of whom had criticized Fitzpatrick in newspaper articles and on a local radio show.

"When I went to law school over 40 years ago, that kind of

conduct was unheard of," he said. "[Minnesota law school ethics professor] Maynard Pirsig would have been offended by that."

"Maynard Pirsig was my professor as well," Sipkins acknowledged, and apologized to Cohen, although he and his local colleagues had no control over the national attorneys who had participated on the shows in question.

The judge promised a ruling, but he didn't say when.

With Cohen's criticism still ringing in his ears, Sipkins and his colleagues had no comments for the media as they left the courthouse and returned to the trial.

Seemingly forgotten in the flurry of events outside the courtroom were the trial's jurors, whose sequestered lives were becoming monotonous and, for some, painful.

By now, juror David Olson's financial problems had reached a crisis level. Utilities were threatening to cut off service. Unable to qualify for food stamps, feeding his two daughters was a roll of the dice. Because of his reduced income, the girls now qualified for free breakfast and lunch at school. Were it not for neighbors and friends who dropped off leftovers, however, dinner was a question mark.

The other jurors knew of Olson's plight. Despite admonitions from court security not to talk about personal problems, Olson still shared his home situation with his colleagues, who were sympathetic.

Efforts by Olson to communicate with Fitzpatrick were fruitless. Olson sent messages to the judge via Michelle Jones, but never heard back from anyone. He hoped the judge could help him get food stamps since Ramsey County officials had already denied his application because he had too many assets, including a snowmobile and an all-terrain vehicle.

He'd refinanced his house just three days short of foreclosure. Without a paycheck since February, Olson could not make ends meet on jury pay that amounted to $150 a week and was mailed to him twice a month.

Fortunately for Olson, the jurors as a group had bonded emotionally as well as intellectually. No one in the group was independently wealthy. They all were making sacrifices of some sort to perform this public duty. But Olson's plight as a single parent of two girls, ages 12 and 14, touched their hearts.

Shortly before the Easter recess, Olson returned to the jury room from a smoke break. He noticed a lump under his trial notebook. He picked it up and found a card with a gift certificate inside for $125 at Rainbow Foods. It was a gift from his fellow jurors who wanted the holiday to be special for Olson and his daughters. In the face of adversity, the 12 Ramsey County residents had demonstrated a solidarity and compassion that became their strength as the trial slowly moved along.

Olson turned to the juror who made the card and said, "Tell everyone 'thanks.'" The next day he walked into the jury room and said to the group, "My daughters really say 'thanks.'"

On the Monday following Easter, April 13, a huddle of reporters stood in the drizzling rain outside a nondescript building in

Northeast Minneapolis' Hennepin Business Center, waiting to be admitted to a operation that, until today, they'd only dreamed of entering.

For the past three years, the office suite inside had become the closely guarded haven for some 30 million pages of documents gathered by the Ciresi legal team for use in the tobacco trial. Today was the first day the Minnesota Document Depository would open its doors to the public. For the "grand opening," the public consisted of one individual, St. Paul law student Michael Ravnitzky. The rest of the 40-odd people assembled were reporters or attorneys. Ravnitsky, basking in the sudden media spotlights turned his way, happily typed the word "licorice" into the depository's computerized database. His one-word question about a tobacco ingredient produced myriad data responses. "Licorice is the key to this whole thing," Ravnitzky claimed, obtusely.

Given that the same documents were freely available on the Internet, the depository's opening was largely symbolic, but it was a grand photo opportunity for Attorney General Humphrey and Blue Cross CEO Czajkowski, who were on hand for the occasion.

Reporters wandered down the narrow aisles, packed to the ceiling on all sides with banker's boxes full of documents. Officials estimated that, if the boxes were stacked on top of one another, they would rise to three times the height of the IDS Tower, the tallest building in the Twin Cities.

Conspicuous in their unavailability were the newly released

39,000 documents. The only place to get a look at them would be in Judge Fitzpatrick's courtroom, where Mike Ciresi promised their imminent introduction. Secret document aficionados wouldn't have long to wait.

The first "smoking howitzer" made its debut at 11:41 A.M. on April 14, during Ciresi's cross-examination of defense witness Scott Appleton, a toxicologist for B&W, who testified about various toxicological testing methods and efforts to develop improved cigarettes.

During questioning, Ciresi quickly sought to undermine Appleton's credibility by gaining Appleton's admission that one of his principal current assignments was to testify as an expert witness in tobacco trials. Appleton acknowledged that, shortly after he was hired, he was given an orientation on tobacco's legal issues by Kansas City's Shook, Hardy & Bacon, the industry's longstanding law firm.

The first of the privilege documents was rather muted in comparison to those that would arrive later in the trial, but it demonstrated the close relationship between the scientific and legal sides of the business. The document was a 1993 letter from J. Kendrick Wells, B&W's assistant general counsel, to outside attorneys at Shook, Hardy & Bacon in Kansas City and King & Spaulding in Atlanta. And it was about Appleton.

"Is Scott Appleton's current practice regarding information about scientific developments adequate?" Wells asked in the letter. "Among other considerations, should he attend some of the scientific conferences normally attended by a toxicologist? Would it be helpful if he talked with scientists outside of the company?"

Referring to B&W's then–CEO Thomas Sandefur, Wells asked, "What answer do you recommend for Mr. Sandefur when asked how he knows causation has not been proven? Among other considerations, should the vice president of R&D be included on Mr. Sandefur's circle of advisers in addition to Dr. Appleton? Should Mr. Sandefur talk with some independent scientists on the question of causation? What routine communications should be occurring between Mr. Sandefur and his advisers?"

Ciresi didn't let Appleton catch his breath, hammering him with an explosive 1969 document from the files of RJR which discussed the removal and invalidation of potentially embarrassing documents. Written by science director Murray Senkus, the memo was addressed to the company's legal department.

"We do not foresee any difficulty in the event a decision is reached to remove certain reports from Research files. Once it becomes clear that such action is necessary for the successful defense of our company, we will promptly remove all such reports from our files," Senkus wrote, continuing, "As to the reports which you are recommending to be invalidated, we can cite misinterpretation of data as reason for invalidation. A further reason is that many of these are needless repetitions and are being removed to alleviate overcrowding of our files. As an alternative to invalidation, we can have the authors rewrite those sections of the reports which appear objectionable."

Appleton's direct testimony was largely ignored as Ciresi entered document after document written by tobacco industry attorneys regarding the suppression of smoking-and-health research. All carried the new imprint: "PRIVILEGED AND CONFIDENTIAL—Produced as required by the Court's March 7, 1998 Order in *State of Minnesota et al v. Philip Morris, et al.* Court File #NO C1-94-8565. Its use is subject to the PROTECTIVE ORDER in that case."

Ciresi made sure the jury noted that designation, an action that peeved attorney Peter Bleakley, even though Bleakley had prepared himself for the worst-case scenario in terms of documents in the trial. He called Ciresi's repeated referral to the designation as "truly outrageous."

They included:

• A 1966 memorandum from Brown & Williamson General Counsel Addison Yeaman outlining his concern about animal testing at England's Harrogate laboratory. "We would hope to be afforded the opportunity of consulting with the people on your side concerning the way Harrogate's work is presented, admittedly with the hope of 'slanting' the report," it said.

• A 1980 memorandum from Philip Morris scientist William Dunn stating that any research on the psychopharmacology of nicotine could be regarded as a "tacit acknowledgment that the nicotine is a drug." Wrote Dunn, "Our attorneys, however, will likely continue to insist upon a clandestine effort in order to keep nicotine the drug in low profile."

- A 1979 Brown & Williamson memorandum in which then–Assistant General Counsel J. Kendrick Wells discusses "alternatives for handling . . . scientific reports in a way that would afford some degree of protection against discovery."

Appleton acknowledged that some of the memos appeared to reflect improper conduct, but said he never saw communications like those at B&W, or with his former employer, RJR.

Ciresi characterized the behavior outlined in the documents as "outrageous" and part of a calculated strategy to keep industry documents secret.

"This is a top scientist saying, 'Tell me what to destroy,'" Ciresi told reporters after the court recessed. "Lawyers do not act this way. The tobacco company attorneys act this way. It's offensive."

David Bernick saw it somewhat differently. "I think the jurors will find it unremarkable that lawyers were involved in decision making," he commented dryly.

But one juror found the documents remarkable for another reason. Jill Burton, a paralegal familiar with the concept of attorney-client privilege and aware of its elevated status in law, was troubled that these confidential documents were being removed from any law office, let alone those of the tobacco industry.

"I'm picturing these guys in white suits coming into a law firm with big pallets, just loading boxes, you know, carte blanche. 'Let's take them all.' And that astounded me," Burton remembered thinking at the time. "If there is wrongdoing and if they felt that there was enough wrongdoing to show that the documents being held by the law firm were all pointing to some big conspiracy, why wasn't the law firm named [in the lawsuit]?"

By trial's end, the plaintiffs had entered 46 of the new "smoking howitzers" as evidence. As the defendants further pared their witness list in the waning weeks of the trial, attorneys for the state and Blue Cross lost potential vehicles for entry of the material into the record. But the attorneys who had sifted through them for more than two hectic weeks remained convinced of their power and their potential in the national tobacco debate.

"The full impact of those documents has not been felt yet," concluded Walburn.

On Thursday, April 16, as Appleton was completing his testimony, Fitzpatrick got a vote of confidence from Cohen, who refused the defense's request to remove the judge. Fitzpatrick had run the trial "in a fair and evenhanded manner," Cohen wrote in his eight-page ruling. "None of Judge Fitzpatrick's statements, expressions, or conduct displayed a deep-seated favoritism or antagonism which would make fair judgment impossible. At most, they were expressions of impatience, dissatisfaction, and annoyance with the defendants' tactics."

Cohen noted that Fitzpatrick dealt with 190 pretrial motions and issued more than 200 orders in conjunction with the lawsuit.

"Based upon a review of the transcript pages presented by the parties, the interplay between Judge Fitzpatrick and counsel constitutes ordinary efforts at administering the Rules of Evidence on the part of Judge Fitzpatrick," Cohen determined.

Few were surprised at the news. Seldom is a sitting judge removed from a trial. "The bias and favoritism of Judge Fitzpatrick could best be observed by sitting in court. It does not translate well on paper. All of us felt we weren't being treated fairly," Peter Sipkins reiterated.

At the time, Sipkins didn't know what defense's next move would be on that issue.

In the jury room the next day, Cohen's decision was the talk of the jurors, none of whom knew that an attempt to remove Fitzpatrick had been made. Per Fitzpatrick's instructions, the jurors were not to read, hear, or see any news about the tobacco trial. But that was a hard admonition to follow, given the widespread coverage of the case.

"Someone had seen a headline about removing him," recalled Burton. "They saw a story that said, 'Judge Stays.' We didn't know why." It was another mystery in their suspended lives.

However, something was afoot behind the scenes that could have a significant impact on the remainder of the trial. New York attorney Meyer Koplow, the top industry settlement negotiator, had been spotted in Minneapolis earlier in the week. It was a titillating piece of information, but one that remained a puzzle. By the time a *Star Tribune* reporter located him at Minneapolis' Marquette Hotel, where members of the Philip Morris national defense team had been staying, he'd already checked out.

It was the first scent that settlement talk was in the air, although Humphrey aide Eric Johnson was adamant that there were no negotiations under way.

However, there were other auspicious visitors in town who wouldn't remain so elusive.

On April 17, Peter Rowell, a nicotine researcher at the University of Louisville, testified that nicotine provided as much pleasure as coffee and chocolate, but far less than sex, marijuana, or alcohol. On hand to watch Rowell's testimony was a plaintiffs' entourage of stellar proportions. Accompanying Humphrey and Czajkowski to the courthouse that afternoon was the antitobacco king himself, former Surgeon General C. Everett Koop. During his tenure in the Reagan administration, from 1981 to 1989, Koop was the driving force behind legal attacks on the tobacco industry. Standing before a podium set up for the occasion outside the courthouse, Koop, flanked by American Lung Association Managing Director John Garrison, told the reporters assembled that the trial was "one of the most important things that has ever happened in the tobacco wars." Koop opined that the trial would affect the ongoing Congressional debate on the national tobacco settlement.

Garrison echoed Koop's remarks, "America is watching this trial. Public health needs to have this kind of trial happen to get documents out. . . . Every day new information is coming out that is a surprise to people."

The spin surrounding the trial, which had whirled steadily from its onset, was beginning to reach dizzying speeds. Czajkowski's and Humphrey's visit to the trial with Koop marked their third appearance in a week. Up until then, they had been relatively absent from the courtroom.

Ciresi had stepped up his posttrial appearances, as well, facing cameras and microphones sometimes as often as twice a day.

The defense wasn't taking this lying down. After 11 weeks of talking freely to the media without public relations assistance, B&W's David Bernick suddenly appeared in the media room during one noon hour that week flanked by Cyndy Brucato, a one-time Twin Cities television anchor and former spokeswoman for Governor Arne Carlson. As Bernick stood by, Brucato immediately launched into an uninvited lecture to the reporters who milled around the media room.

"People, you have to remember, don't focus on style over substance," she admonished astonished onlookers, who, cumulatively represented more than 100 years of reporting experience. "Don't focus on the director's cut."

Bernick took the presence of his new "handler" in stride. "I think the main purpose for (Brucato) was that my client wanted her to be the eyes and ears for what else might be brewing while I was inside the courtroom," he said.

Out of range of anyone's eyes or ears, juror Jim Otis was wrestling with some issues of his own. One of his former associates at work, a smoker, had died from cancer in the middle of the trial. Although it wasn't lung cancer, Otis held the defendants responsible. He decided he could no longer be fair, and wanted to be excused from the jury.

"I tried to get out of it. I brought in the obituary and showed it to (court personnel)," he recalled. "They were nice about it and said, 'Do what you have to do.'"

Otis thought it over and ultimately decided to stay on the panel, saying "It wouldn't be fair to the other jurors."

Bleakley was surprised, after the trial, to hear of Otis' actions.

"When a juror comes to the judge, whether it's in writing, or orally, the first thing a judge does is tell the (attorneys), ask their views, then makes a ruling."

In Kenneth Fitzpatrick's courtroom, neither trial team was informed about Otis' crisis of conscience. It remained another inexplicable judicial decision.

Chapter Fourteen

Joe Camel's Mom, Scientists, and Statisticians

Lynn Beasley was the Betty Crocker of the tobacco industry. Petite, attractive, and animated, she was wholesome in appearance and the only female defense witness to take the stand. She had deep Midwestern roots and a Horatio Alger background. She was executive vice president of marketing for R. J. Reynolds Tobacco Company (RJR) and had never before testified in a tobacco trial. RJR attorney Robert Weber wanted to put a human face on the industry. Lynn Beasley provided the perfect visage. Through Beasley's enthusiastic sincerity, Weber would attempt to dispel the state's allegations that cigarette manufacturers marketed their products to kids.

Weber's introduction of "Mrs. Beasley," as he referred to her throughout, was folksy, just short of corny. She grew up on a dairy farm in Richland Center, Wisconsin, a town of 5,000 near Madison. One of nine children, Beasley had worked since she was legally able. During her high school years, she was employed as a grocery store clerk. After graduating, she worked in a sewing factory for a year and attended night school at a local community college.

When Beasley decided to attend college fulltime, she also put in 32 hours a week as a janitor—and later as a mail carrier—at the town post office. Eventually she transferred to the University of Wisconsin at Madison and earned a business degree in 1981. With financial assistance from a fellowship, Beasley continued with her education and graduated with an MBA in marketing a year later. Although Beasley had originally planned to accept a job offer from General Mills, RJR called in the middle of winter and invited her to interview at company headquarters.

"It was pretty cold here, and I had never been to the South, so I thought it would be fun to go to North Carolina and interview for the day," Beasley recalled.

Her initial impression had been "a cigarette company," she said, grimacing. "But once I got there, the people were so nice and I felt like I would really fit in. The company explained to me their philosophies on how they market cigarettes and how they viewed them, and I felt good about it. And I came back home and I talked to my parents and the marketing professors, and I ultimately made the decision to go with R. J. Reynolds."

As a beaming Beasley proudly recounted her career history to Weber, who seemed proud just to hear it, the jury smiled. Ciresi did not. When Weber began to question his witness about her twin sister, who coincidentally worked as a marketing executive for Whirlpool, Ciresi interrupted.

"Your Honor, this is really irrelevant," he objected.

Judge Fitzpatrick agreed: "I'm not sure how interested we are in her whole family history."

But Weber had made his point, sappy as it was. Beasley wasn't some detached Ivy League intellectual. She was the girl next door from the state next door, whose hard work and perseverance had paid off. Even her parents approved of her RJR employment.

Beasley started as a marketing assistant assigned to RJR's low-tar Now brand. Moving up the company's marketing ladder she worked with the Salem and More brands, until, in 1984, she was named assistant brand manager for Camel, then languishing in the marketplace.

Beasley described Camel's advertising campaign at that time as "a flop." The campaign, entitled "Bob Beck," featured a single male with unruly blond hair who was shown in rugged outdoor settings. The problem, Beasley said, was that Beck was perceived as a loner.

"Smokers were seeing the campaign as a kind of—I hate to say it—bad imitation of Marlboro," Beasley explained. "It wasn't very compelling and motivating, particularly to younger adult smokers."

Beasley didn't stay long during her first run through the Camel marketing team. Again on the move, she became brand manager in 1982 for the discount brand Century, and assumed responsibility over the additional brands, Doral, Sterling, and Magna. During her tenure, RJR's percentage of business devoted to the discount brands rose from zero to 30 percent.

"It was a huge change," Beasley told Weber.

In 1987, Lynn Beasley returned to the Camel team, this time as senior brand manager, overseeing all Camel's advertising, promotions, and packaging. The Bob Beck campaign would have a limited future.

"We had to get rid of it. Smokers didn't like it. It made Camel seem old and harsh," she said.

In conducting research through focus groups of "smokers 18 years and older," Beasley emphasized, her team discovered that Camels suffered from a lot of misperception in the marketplace. Not only did few smokers know that Camels were available with filters, the perception was that they were also strong and harsh.

"They thought it was their grandfather's brand," Beasley testified.

In 1987, Beasley said, she came up with the idea of building a new advertising campaign to commemorate Camel's 75th anniversary in 1988. She said that, among focus groups, an illustrated French poster of a camel with a cigarette in its mouth was a big hit. RJR asked four advertising agencies to give the camel human characteristics of "someone who's fun, who you'd like to be around."

And Joe Camel was born.

Associated Press reporter Steve Karnowski, one of the trial media's master nicknamers, found his peg for Beasley. "She's Joe Camel's mother," he marveled, chuckling.

"Me and my team came up with the name," Beasley testified proudly. "My vision for him was that he was the kind of guy the average person could relate to. You know the phrase, 'Average Joe.'"

The name also coincided with that of the original camel used in 1913 as a model for the Camel package—a circus Camel named "Joe."

Beasley described how Joe Camel was fitted with the description, "smooth character," to portray him as being hip, while sending the message that Camel cigarettes were smooth in taste. The jury was shown advertisements of Joe Camel as a pilot taking off from an aircraft carrier, wearing a tuxedo, and standing in a T-shirt next to a convertible.

As Beasley described the birth of Joe Camel, she was nearly giddy with enthusiasm. The campaign was a monster success (That is, until it was dropped in 1997 after allegations that it targeted underage smokers.) Market share rose from 3 to 10 points in the coveted 18-to-24-year-old demographic, while increasing 3 to 5 share points among smokers 24 to 34, and 2 to 3 points for those 35 to 49, Beasley said.

That success propelled her even higher in the corporate ranks. By 1991, just nine years after arriving at RJR, Beasley was named a marketing vice president. By 1997, she was appointed executive vice president—one of only three—reporting directly to RJR President Andrew Schindler.

As she explained, "I review and approve all of the marketing we do."

Beasley testified that RJR executives took calculated steps to ensure the Joe Camel campaign didn't appeal to minors. Punk hairstyles were forbidden on the character and party favors were not used in conjunction with the 75th anniversary campaign because those might appeal to younger kids, she said.

Beasley was an effective witness for the defense, denying firmly that RJR ever targeted anyone under the age of 18. The company didn't use models in its advertisements who were younger than 25—or who *looked* younger than 25. In fact, she said, in 1992, the company stopped tracking the smoking habits of those between the ages of 18 and 21, to ensure they targeted only adult smokers.

"We definitely do not want underage sales at all. I don't want kids to smoke. I don't think any responsible adult wants kids to smoke," Beasley said. "Every time a kid lights up, we get blamed and it becomes harder and harder for me to market to adults."

Beasley rattled off a number of other companies that used cartoon characters to sell adult-oriented products: "like Speedy Alka Seltzer and the Michelin Tire guy, you know, who's all puffed up, white tire guy. And Exxon Tiger guy, you know, get a tiger in your tank. And Bugs Bunny advertises Holiday Inn. There's the Dow Scrubbing Bubbles; Garfield the Cat advertises Embassy Suite Hotels. And of course a classic in advertising is Mr. Clean. The Pink Panther is used to advertise Owens-Corning Fiberglass insulation. Met Life Insurance Company uses Snoopy to advertise their insurance products. The Sprint people use the Jetsons to advertise the Sprint products. The Vlasic Stork is used to advertise Vlasic Pickles."

With that established, Weber brought the issue right to the jury's doorstep. Pointing to an exhibit, Weber directed his witness to identify it.

"This is an ad for the Minnesota State Lottery that uses the Bullwinkle character," Beasley responded.

"What's the legal age for purchase of lottery tickets in Minnesota?" Weber asked.

Over Ciresi's objection, Beasley was allowed to answer: "Eighteen."

Weber's examination was constantly interrupted by objections from Ciresi, who argued that Beasley couldn't testify about advertising because she wasn't an expert. When Weber tried to introduce two surveys of 10- to 17-year-olds that presumably would have showed that children could identify the Joe Camel cartoon character, but that it had no impact on their attitudes towards smoking, Ciresi successfully had them excluded.

During a brief court recess, Beasley joined attorney Weber for a cigarette outside the courthouse. Joe Camel's mother turned out to be an Eclipse smoker, RJR's super-low-nicotine brand.

During his cross-examination, Ciresi had trouble denting Lynn Beasley's credibility, although she was at a loss to explain internal company documents about underage smokers and their importance to market share and future sales, particularly several from the 1970s and early 1980s, which referred to the 14- to 24-year-old age bracket.

"Do you have any idea what would motivate an 18-year-old [to smoke] as opposed to a 17-year-old?" Ciresi asked.

"I think 18-year-olds are different," Beasley replied. "They're moving out on their own. They have the right to vote, the right to smoke, they can join the army. We don't do any work with anyone under 18."

Ciresi wasn't satisfied, and turned to his trademark question: "Would you agree, ma'am, that when you put a product into the marketplace that's reported to kill over 400,000 people a year, that you should ascertain whether the marketing campaign that you're going to utilize would appeal to the youth of America? Do you think you have a responsibility to do that?"

Beasley was defiant. "No. I think that if advertising caused children to start smoking, which it doesn't, then that would be different. But advertising affects brand choice, and that's been well documented. And we only do research among adult smokers, we develop the campaigns among adult smokers, and we screen ads for appeal among adult smokers."

Ciresi also tried to show that—for all her involvement in the Joe Camel campaign—Beasley left few, if any, fingerprints. Where was her name on Joe Camel–related interoffice memoranda, he wanted to know?

Beasley had no clear answer, but suggested that memoranda weren't needed as evidence, because "I'm here. I did it."

In what came closest to a misstep for the attorney, Ciresi presented Beasley with a memorandum regarding the Joe Camel

75th Birthday campaign, wondering, again, about the absence of her name.

Beasley pointed to the name Breininger. "That's me; that was my maiden name," she explained.

Sensing the jury's enchantment with Mrs. Beasley, Ciresi kept his cross short. Defense attorneys believed he didn't put on sparring gloves out of concern that the jury would react negatively. Some jurors said later that the defense attorneys were right.

"I liked that little marketing gal," Terry Zaspel said after the trial. "I used to work in a marketing department. She was a very credible witness."

Dorothy Hallen agreed. "Although Ciresi said that you can't believe she's that innocent that the advertising went to kids, you can," she said later. "You can because she was so into it. She brought that company so much money. She deserved anything she's gotten from that."

Hallen's opinion reflected the success Weber had hoped to obtain from his witness: "I started to think, 'this is a business. These companies have a right to be in business and they have a right to advertise their business like everyone else does.' They weren't this big evil thing."

The defense team continued its efforts to put human faces on its business endeavors with its next witness, Dr. A. Clifton Lilly Jr., vice president of technology for Philip Morris and a 32-year veteran from the research side of the corporation.

Lilly, 63, was a user-friendly tobacco scientist, articulate and easy to understand. The kindly, gray-haired scientist represented the "Hey, we're not all bad" defense. He had been intimately involved in attempts at Philip Morris from the mid-1970s through the present to develop a cigarette with little or no tar and nicotine. All efforts failed, but Lilly's testimony was intended to demonstrate how cigarette manufacturers tried to respond to health concerns.

With project names such as Delta, Delta II, and Accord, Philip Morris attempted to develop a cigarette that would heat tobacco rather than burn it. Another project, ART, tried to remove nicotine from the tobacco in much the same way caffeine is removed for decaffeinated coffee. But the "de-nicotinized" cigarette failed when test marketed with consumers, Lilly said.

Philip Morris attorney Murray Garnick, who was questioning the scientist, couldn't get past a barrage of Ciresi objections when he tried to ask Lilly why the cigarette, called NEXT, had failed. Finally, he asked, "Did you ever smoke the cigarette?"

Yes, he had, Lilly replied.

"What did you think of it?"

"It tasted bad," Lilly said, simply.

All told, Lilly said, Philip Morris spent $440 million on the experiments. Only Accord was still being test marketed, he said. RJR's experimental Premier cigarette nearly broke the smokeless cigarette barrier, Lilly testified, but it too languished in terms of consumer acceptance.

In some respects, Lilly's testimony, while sincere, illustrated an industry charade. While publicly denying the link between smoking and disease, the industry was spending hundreds of millions of dollars hoping to develop a cigarette without the carcinogens contained in normal cigarette smoke. The industry was playing two hands at the card table.

After Lilly, the defense team began to pare its witness list, making noises that it would rest its case in a week or two. They dropped Brown & Williamson CEO Nicholas Brooks and Lorillard CEO Alexander Spears, saying they'd had enough executives testify already. Ciresi contended that the industry was afraid of damaging their witnesses for future trials if their credibility was impeached in the Minnesota case. More significantly, Humphrey and Czjawkowski had also been dropped as potential witnesses.

Humphrey was jubilant. "I think it was probably the happiest moment of my life. I figured they were going to tear me upside down, inside out, make me look like a wimp, a short guy, and a tall guy all at once."

While that may have been true, attorney Weber offered another explanation. "The judge would have been extremely protective of Humphrey when we crossed him. Then, when Ciresi had him, he basically would have been allowed to give his campaign speech."

As the defense began the final stages of its case, its most sensitive documents were entering the public domain via the Internet. The 39,000 reports, studies, and memos obtained by the state less than three weeks earlier were posted in cyberspace by Virginia Congressman Thomas Bliley. But, at the industry's request, Bliley withheld several hundred documents from distribution.

Fitzpatrick was angry. He felt he was the victim of an industry end run and wanted to know how the industry communicated with Bliley. He felt his protective order on the material had been compromised. He ordered a complete explanation from industry attorneys. Again, CLAD was flooded with letters of explanation to the judge that nothing sinister had been intended.

Fitzpatrick's ire reminded Robert Weber of Humphrey Bogart's famous *Caine Mutiny* role as the paranoid, ball bearing–clicking captain.

"Congress was completely out of our control," Weber said. "However, Judge Fitzpatrick seemed to think that somehow we were engaged in some conspiracy with Congress to get documents released before Humphrey could release them. It was really a theatre of the absurd.

"There were times when we turned to each other and wondered if he was rolling steel ball bearings around in his hands. It was real Captain Queeg stuff when he was going through all of this about who released what and why didn't it get released here first. It was very much like Captain Queeg—and that we'd taken the strawberries."

The Internet documents again stole attention from the trial. One of them was a damning study prepared by Weber's law firm, Jones, Day, Reavis & Pogue, which grabbed headlines on

Thursday, April 23, and gave Humphrey more fodder to rail about the industry's "darkest secrets."

That memo was compiled in 1985, to assist the firm in future tobacco trials. It reported numerous contacts between lawyers and researchers at RJR to determine which areas of the health issue could be studied and which could not. The 104-page report also stated that research was conducted in Germany to keep it out of the hands antismoking forces in the United States.

Humphrey charged that the industry had "systematically destroyed, suppressed, reworded, and concealed damaging research." RJR's chief counsel, Robert Blixt, was incensed by Humphrey's characterization, noting that the 1985 report covered events that happened as long as 30 years ago. "It's filled with inconsistent statements," Blixt said. The defense also claimed that the memo was one that was withheld from release by Bliley's committee, and accused Humphrey's staff of leaking it to the media.

In the courtroom, James Morgan stepped off the video screen—where he had been seen during the plaintiffs' case—and onto the witness stand. A consummate salesman with a keen eye toward cigarette marketing strategies, Morgan was the recently retired chief executive of Philip Morris, Inc., the domestic cigarette division of the Philip Morris Companies. During his two decades with the company, he had been the patron saint of the Marlboro Man and the brains behind Virginia Slims cigarettes

Morgan raised eyebrows several years earlier with comments in a Florida deposition that he believed cigarettes were no more addicting than caffeine, "or in my case, Gummi Bears."

Tanned, handsome, and extremely wealthy from his years of service to the tobacco giant, Morgan was an animated history book of cigarette trends in the United States, and how to take advantage of them. When Philip Morris determined that its Merit cigarette was extremely popular with male bowlers between the ages of 35 and 45, for instance, the company began sponsoring bowling events, Morgan said.

But the most significant marketing story told by Morgan involved Marlboro, which in the 1950s was doing very poorly and was viewed primarily as a woman's cigarette. To boost sales, the company sought to reposition the cigarette as a man's brand. The more masculine flip-top box was one of the first product innovations.

In the early 1960s, Philip Morris introduced the Marlboro Country campaign with the music from the *Magnificent Seven* as its theme. Sales doubled in a flat market, Morgan recalled.

"The decision was to focus on the American West as representative of this cigarette," he told Peter Bleakley, who conducted the questioning. "It was big, masculine. It was American. It was flavorful."

When cigarette advertising on television was banned, Marlboro developed a new type of outdoor billboard that would look to passersby like a magazine advertisement. It added "Light" cigarettes to the brand mix in 1972 to compete with the growing low-tar-and-nicotine corner of the market. But at no time, Morgan emphasized, did Marlboro target underage smokers, even though Marlboro eventually became the brand of choice among minors.

"I think it would be wrong," Morgan said at the start of his cross-examination by Richard Gill. "Smoking is a risk and the decision-making ability for that is 18."

Gill showed Morgan a 1979 memo on Philip Morris letterhead that said, "Marlboro dominates the 17-and-younger category, capturing over 50 percent of this market."

But Morgan said he had no idea where the 50 percent figure came from. "Probably some government number," he replied. "We do not market to people below 18. We do not do it."

If minors were attracted to smoking by Marlboro advertising, it was unintentional, Morgan said. "It was an uncalculated consequence," he said, sounding like a general describing civilian casualties from a military raid as "collateral damage."

Asked about the rise in teen smoking in the 1990s, Morgan replied, "That's something I could do nothing about, unless you wanted me to stop the way we were marketing to 18- to 24-year-olds."

Gill continued on the youth theme, knowing this was a sensitive area for the jurors, many of whom said they opposed youth marketing during their selection.

A 1985 Philip Morris interoffice memo, cited by Gill, referred to a comprehensive memo on smoking trends "among high school and college students." It was to be used to update forecast models in the business planning department.

Morgan continued to deny that it was company policy to seek underage smokers. "I am perfectly willing to take market share with people when they turn 18 and ignore the younger ones," he said.

Gill countered with another company memo from 1979 outlining a promotional campaign for Marlboro to be conducted during spring and summer school breaks at beaches, shopping malls, and other hangouts where teens would be present.

Morgan said that was an approach for marketing to 18- to 24-year-olds. He denied that his competitors, including RJR with its Joe Camel campaign, targeted youth. "I wouldn't be concerned about this ad," he said when shown a picture of Joe Camel standing next to a convertible.

Gill, at times strident, accused Philip Morris of cynically manipulating underage smokers into buying the Marlboro brand. "All that growth, all that wealth has been built on the back of Marlboro and the primary basis for the performance of Marlboro over the last 40 years has been the youngest smokers," Gill stated.

"The success of Marlboro is its ability to become a large brand across every age spectrum, men and women," Morgan replied. At another point, he said, "The happiest day of my life will be when the last underage kid smokes," noting that allegations of youth marketing had depressed Philip Morris' stock price.

As Gill neared the close of his cross-examination, he asked

Morgan about the actors who actually portrayed the Marlboro Man.

"Did they really smoke Marlboros?" Gill asked.

"The ones who smoked did," Morgan answered, acknowledging that one of the actors contracted lung cancer.

"Did you ever ask about the health status of the other Marlboro cowboys?" Gill continued.

"I asked how they were doing," Morgan said.

"They served Marlboro well?" said Gill.

"Very well," responded Morgan.

Some jurors interviewed later mentioned Morgan as a witness they liked. David Olson was impressed with him because "He knew a lot. He knew what his company was doing. He was really good."

"From the sounds of it, he turned that company around," James Livingston commented.

"After Morgan was done, I could have just about sold anybody on his product," Hallen said.

However, juror Jim Otis thought Morgan's testimony had changed by his second appearance at trial. "He said one thing on videotape and something different in person."

When court convened on Tuesday, April 28th, the 12 members of the jury, emboldened by their St. Patrick's Day performance, arrived in court wearing matching black T-shirts, each reading "Minnesota Tobacco Trial" and bearing the juror's individual number. The courtroom's normally tense atmosphere evaporated momentarily as attorneys and courtroom observers cheered the stunt. Grinning mischievously, they greeted the judge, who deadpanned, "Where's my T-shirt?"

The stunt, in particular, heartened some members of the defense team. "This was a group that still had a sense of whimsy to them about the goofiness of their position and they were able to laugh at it," Robert Weber commented. "They didn't strike me as people who were really outraged. It made me convinced that they weren't angry at [the defense]."

Also that day, trial lawyers for both teams gathered in Judge Fitzpatrick's chambers for a discussion about court procedures during the final days of trial. Item number six on Fitzpatrick's agenda read, "the proposed videotaping of closing arguments."

"Anyone want to comment?" Fitzpatrick asked the group.

"Who proposed it?" Bleakley wanted to know.

"I did," Fitzpatrick responded.

"Oh," Bleakley said.

"We were wondering," Weber added.

Ciresi told the judge, "I'm not a big fan of cameras in the courtroom."

"Well, I've got to tell you, I'm not either," the judge responded.

"And neither are we," said Bleakley.

The judge explained that the taping would be conducted, "fairly unobtrusively. The purpose is not to give it to the press, its purpose is for historical preservation, number one, and possibly CLE (Continuing Legal Education) interest. I would propose that there be one copy, it would be delivered to the court and held by the court and no other copies made available, and only used very cautiously."

The defense team was unmoved.

"We would want to be on record as opposing that," Weber said, explaining that, with all the jury had been through, "I just think changing the atmosphere of the courtroom in any way would be something I wouldn't want to do."

Fitzpatrick persisted. "Well, it would have to be done very unobtrusively."

Ciresi asked for a night to think it over.

Fitzpatrick continued to downplay the proposal. "I'll be glad to listen to your thoughts. And the world won't come to an end one way or another."

The conversation turned next to the issue of sequestration. The defense adamantly opposed sequestering the jury. "I personally believe that sequestration is coercive and inappropriate in civil cases," Bleakley told Fitzpatrick.

Ciresi agreed with the defense team, but told the judge that he was concerned about tobacco companies ongoing lobbying efforts in Congress and about plans for an extensive television and radio campaign in support of a settlement. "I guess I'd like to have some kind of assurances from the defense that if the campaign is going to run, it's not going to run here in Minnesota [during jury deliberations]."

Bleakley told Ciresi that he had no reason to believe there were plans for a campaign of that type in Minnesota, but that he didn't have a definitive answer.

Ciresi said he'd withhold deciding for or against sequestration until Bleakley provided such an assurance.

Fitzpatrick had the last word. "I will, on my own, sequester the jurors if I have any indications that there's going to be any publicity concerning the tobacco litigation." He added that the lawyers would be expected to keep quiet during deliberations as well.

In court, the defense team's antitrust answer to Adam Jaffe took the stand. David Scheffman, a Minneapolis-born economist who taught at Vanderbilt University in Nashville, would be questioned by Peter Bleakley about business strategies and marketing. Scheffman, 54, had an interesting former credential as well—he worked from 1983 to 1988 as an economist for the Federal Trade Commission, reviewing antitrust cases.

According to Scheffman, tobacco companies had motivation to conspire among themselves—given the wave of negative information on the health risks of smoking—but chose to remain competitive. If the companies were engaged in antitrust, he added, they did a pretty lousy job of it, given the industry's decades of declining sales.

"It makes no sense to have a conspiracy, the effect of which would be to dramatically reduce sales," Scheffman told the jury. "Cigarette consumption would have been much greater without information on smoking and health. If the industry could have introduced a safer product, the amount of bad information on smoking and health would have been significantly less."

Bleakley's direct examination was interrupted repeatedly with objections by Gill, and it appeared to be rattling him. Several times Bleakley referred to his witness as "Mr. Jaffe," and drew a sharp retort from the judge after one of Gill's objections had been sustained.

"I guess I've been outvoted," Bleakley joked.

Fitzpatrick wasn't amused, informing Bleakley, "*I'm* the only one here whose vote counts."

It was clear the Ciresi team perceived Scheffman's testimony as a threat. Gill objected to almost every question, citing lack of foundation, and to almost every exhibit as not being properly designated. The objections were usually sustained.

At one point, after Gill voiced an objection for leading the witness, Bleakley responded, "I'll try to make [my questions] less leading."

"No," Fitzpatrick told him, "Try to make them *not* leading."

Scheffman also outlined the various companies' failed attempts to develop safer cigarettes. In relation to RJR's Premier cigarette, Scheffman testified that one of the reasons it failed was due to the "abuse heaped on it" by the medical community.

Gill objected. Bleakley asked for a sidebar.

"No," Fitzpatrick told him. "I will not have a sidebar on the abuse. I'm not interested in that."

Scheffman proved to be a much more interesting witness on

cross-examination than he had been on direct. Despite Gill's best attempts, Scheffman refused to budge from his assertion that the industry hadn't violated any antitrust laws.

"Look," he told Gill at one point, "American Tobacco is out of business, Liggett is on the ropes, and Lorillard isn't much better. They're all worse off than they could have been if they'd engaged in such behavior."

Scheffman easily deflected exhibits that had mortally wounded other witnesses. When confronted with the "Gentleman's Agreement" document from 1953, in which tobacco executives agreed to pull health claims from cigarette advertising, the antitrust witness had an easy explanation—one not heard before at trial. Scheffman said that the tobacco companies pulled the health claims because the FTC was preparing guidelines requiring the tobacco industry to substantiate them.

"They were very bad health claims because they weren't substantiated," he told Gill.

A Brown & Williamson (B&W) document that Gill introduced into evidence surveyed the health claims made from 1927 through 1964 for individual cigarette brands. Although intended to show tobacco's fraudulent advertising tactics, it inadvertently supported Scheffman's contention—the claims *were* preposterous.

RJR advertised that "More doctors smoke Camels," "They don't get your wind," and "They never get on your nerves."

Philip Morris claimed in 1940 that its namesake brand was better for the nose and throat with "superiority recognized by eminent medical authorities." A 1952 ad proclaimed Chesterfield cigarettes "entirely safe for use in the mouth."

Liggett described its L&M cigarettes as "Just what the doctor ordered."

However, during the heated, objection-ridden cross-examination of Scheffman, the animosity that had been simmering beneath the surface between Bleakley and Fitzpatrick finally surfaced in front of the jury.

At one point, as the judge again admonished the witness to answer the question, Bleakley objected, declaring that Scheffman was trying to answer.

"Counsel," Fitzpatrick cautioned, his voice rising to a roar, "Counsel, COUNSEL!! I have ruled."

Frustrated, Bleakley became more and more sarcastic in his objections.

At the end of his cross-examination of Scheffman, Gill broached a particularly meandering and obtuse question, telling the witness, "In this courtroom, it should be up to the defendants to persuasively show that telling smokers in the '50s what the defendants knew about the causal link would not have had any effect."

Bleakley's objections—that the question was argumentative, speculative, and called for a legal conclusion—were overruled.

"It should be up to the *defendants* in this courtroom [to present the plaintiffs' case]?" Bleakley asked, incredulous.

By the end of the cross, Bleakley didn't even bother to get up when he objected. That drew another rebuke from Fitzpatrick.

"Counsel, would you please stand if you have an objection."

Moments later, during another flurry of objections. Fitzpatrick again grew testy. "If anyone wants my job, if you want to trade salaries, I'll be glad to trade with anybody. Otherwise, I guess I will decide what the law is."

After Scheffman's appearance, Bleakley was noticeably absent from the courtroom for the remainder of the defense's case. Bleakley recalled that he was out of court at one point, "because I had to go off and work on a totally different case for another client." However, he acknowledged, "I don't think there was a particularly warm relationship," between the judge and him.

With all the talk of experimental cigarettes, media requests were made to see one of the products. Philip Morris accommodated by furnishing several samples of its new product, Accord, which was being test marketed in several U.S. cities and Japan. It was hard to imagine the Marlboro Man out on the range smoking Accord. The new product, which came in a large cardboard kit featuring all the cigarette's "elements," included videotaped instructions on how to use it. Accord featured a small, pager-sized device into which a short, squatty cigarette was inserted. A micro-chip heated the tobacco, rather than burned it, which required that the whole apparatus be brought to the mouth each time a smoker inhaled. Broadcast reporters immediately took it outside for "smoker on the street" impressions of this cigarette of the future.

Someone else was interested in seeing the experimental cigarette as well. When one of the Accord kits was found missing
from the media room one morning, the security guard explained
that Judge Fitzpatrick had asked him to bring it up to chambers,
so that he could take a look. When the security guard brought it
back later that day, he said Fitzpatrick had "been amazed" by the
device. "He just shook his head and laughed at the thing."

Scheffman's strong performance went overlooked by many
members of the media as they scrambled to follow up on a story
broken by Dow Jones wire service reporter Meera Mahadevan,
which quoted Wall Street tobacco analyst Gary Black, who predicted a settlement by the weekend. He was only too happy to
repeat his remarks for any reporter who called.

"My guess is you'll see it by next week, maybe by the weekend,"
Black told Associated Press. "We've talked to people on both
sides" who "indicate they're not that far apart."

Black said among the unresolved issues were whether
Minnesota would get more money than other states got in settlements and what would become of coplaintiff Blue Cross.

Ciresi was furious. "Gary Black, to suggest he's talked to anyone
on the plaintiffs' side, is a flat-out lie—unless he found a state
employee in Waseca or Willmar or Duluth and asked them what
they thought."

But Ciresi didn't confirm or deny that settlement talks were
taking place.

Eric Johnson, a top Humphrey aide, was equally contemptuous of the Wall Street analyst. "Gary Black has been predicting a settlement for eight months and he's been absolutely dead wrong," Johnson told reporters. Johnson suggested that Black's interest lay in driving up tobacco companies' stock prices by suggesting a settlement was imminent.

It was true, Gary Black had been pretty bad as a settlement prognosticator—thus far. Black predicted settlement before the trial began in January. In March, shortly after the defense began presenting its case, he predicted the state would settle for $4.5 billion.

The pronouncements bedeviled Humphrey's staff, Chief Deputy Attorney General Lee Sheehy later acknowledged. "It was problematic in Washington," he explained, since Humphrey's staff had made it clear during visits with national politicians that they were not going to settle without strong concessions from the industry. Black's periodic statements undermined their credibility.

However, this particular Black prediction had a different feel to it. Even Johnson, who had steadfastly refused to confirm or deny any reports of settlement discussions, let go this time with some tantalizing hints.

"Between now and the end of the trial, this desperate industry is likely to make overtures for a settlement," he told a reporter for Associated Press. "But they should know by now that Attorney General Humphrey is not going to compromise his goals. If the industry makes overtures that still fall far short of our goals, we're not going to dignify it by calling it 'settlement negotiations.'"

Black was undaunted. "Have I talked with Michael Ciresi? No. But we're hearing it from people on both sides," he told the *Star Tribune*. "The attorney general is running for governor and I'm not. I've said for some time that when Hubert Humphrey fires his last publicity bullet, you'll see a settlement and that came last week when the 39,000 documents came out, revealing the 'smoking howitzer' that wasn't."

Black also predicted that the face amount of the settlement would be "$4.5 to $5 billion over 25 years."

And, as for the suggestion that he was engaged in stock manipulation, Black told Associated Press that his firm had "buy" recommendations on Philip Morris, RJR Nabisco, and U.S. Tobacco. "I'm not doing a good job, am I?" he asked. "They're not doing very well."

Black had more to say. He maintained that some jury members were leaning in a protobacco direction. "I think there could be three jurors who could find with the industry. I don't sense that this jury is all that angry."

How Black, who hadn't set foot in court since the trial's opening arguments, had his finger on the jury's pulse remained anybody's guess.

The defense attorneys responded as they traditionally had when the topic of settlement came up. They were the warriors, they explained, not the negotiators. When and if a settlement happened, they'd be the last to know. In the meantime, said

Philip Morris spokesman Michael York, "Every day in every way we continue to get more comfortable with our case."

Although Black's prognostications had, in the past, proved meritless, the Wall Street analyst had been on target this time. There were, in fact, settlement talks going on. And they were getting serious.

As the trial attorneys battled it out in downtown St. Paul, a few miles away, in the trustee's boardroom at the University of St. Thomas, negotiators for both sides were warily circling each other. The meeting place had been arranged by Ciresi, who was an alumnus and trustee of the school. Plaintiffs' representatives initially included Ciresi's law partner Bruce Finzen, who had successfully handled critical negotiations for Ciresi in his IUD and Bhopal settlements, Lee Sheehy, chief deputy attorney general and a former litigator himself, and Blue Cross assistant corporate counsel, Tom Gilde.

Representatives for the defense team included longtime industry negotiator Meyer Koplow, from the New York firm of Wachtel, Lipton, Rosen & Katz, representing Philip Morris; Arthur Golden, from the New York firm of Davis, Polk & Wardwell, on behalf of RJR; Steve Patton, from the Chicago firm of Kirkland & Ellis, representing B&W; and Ken Feinberg, an attorney described by Finzen as having "a knack for getting a corporate defendant into meaningful negotiations." Feinberg, Finzen, and Ciresi had crossed paths several times before, and the plaintiffs had requested his participation early on.

"St. Thomas was a good, quiet place to meet," Finzen, who was acting as lead plaintiffs' negotiator, recalled. "I don't know that we necessarily blended in with the students, but we might have looked just a bit professorial. We seemed to get away with it. Nobody asked too many questions. The good investigative reporters wouldn't even look for us there."

Finzen had been in Washington, D.C., late in April monitoring the progress of tobacco-related legislation when he got a call from Ciresi. "They want to meet," he told Finzen. "Come on back."

This time, it seemed serious.

The meeting wasn't a first. Ciresi, Feinberg, and Patton held an exploratory session at St. Thomas in October 1997. In November, both sides gathered for a series of negotiations. Ciresi, Finzen, and Sheehy met with Koplow, Golden, and Patton for two days in Atlanta, and an additional two days in New York. The parties met once more before the trial, in the Twin Cities on Super Bowl Sunday.

On the last occasion, among other issues they disagreed about, Golden recalled, "Ciresi said, 'We've got to have immediate disclosure of the documents.'"

That wasn't acceptable. The tobacco negotiators went home. "We were at loggerheads until April," Golden said.

In the past, Finzen recalled, the industry's occasional suggestions of settlement talks had lacked sincerity. There were too many roadblocks in the way. From the plaintiffs' standpoint, the three major issues involved: release of all documents, serious movement on public health issues, and, finally, damages commensurate with the harm caused.

"Although I think they recognized that what we wanted was significant beyond anything they'd ever done before, I think they were still trying to size us up," Finzen recalled of the early meetings. "They were trying to figure out first, what did we want; then, what did we *really* want? Where were we going to dig our heels in? Early on, it was information gathering almost as much as negotiations.

"They were having a very hard time understanding that we weren't interested in talking about money. That what we wanted to talk about was documents. And I think early on, they probably didn't really believe that. They figured it was a facade and would break away. That after a couple of meetings they'd soften us up and we'd be talking about money. But we never talked about money."

Sheehy recalled that, "At first, the discussions never really got much beyond the documents." The industry didn't want to waive its privilege claims over them.

During the trial, Finzen said, Feinberg would occasionally call to see how things were going. "He'd ask 'Anything different?'" Finzen said he told Feinberg, "'No, it's going great and we're killing you guys. We had another good day, another good week. More of the same, Ken.' Ken may have been the only one who was willing to somewhat acknowledge that that's what he was hearing. Everybody else tried to put a good game face on. There was really nothing beyond that."

After it became apparent that the documents would soon be released, the tobacco industry negotiators' tactics changed, Finzen and Sheehy said.

"We talked briefly with them about the kinds of things we wanted addressed on the public health stuff, but we really never got into anything substantive on it," Finzen recalled.

The industry's difficulty, Sheehy speculated, was that "they were trying to determine how much they were going to have to move off the cookie-cutter approach they'd taken in settling with Mississippi, Florida, and Texas. It was a time-consuming process for them."

Again, movement was slow. "Once the documents were done, I got the sense they were thinking, 'Do they feel the same way about public health, or is *this* a facade and are we really going to be talking about money? After a few meetings, they were pretty well convinced that this was just like documents. That this was going to have to be worked out or we were never going to get around to talking about money, and there would never be a settlement."

By the time the parties gathered at St. Thomas, Finzen felt "for the first time that now perhaps they were going to come around to serious treatment of the public health issue." Finzen thought the discussions might actually lead to a settlement.

But talks bogged down almost immediately. While Finzen and Sheehy thought they'd clearly laid out the parameters for discussing the issues, it was immediately apparent that uncertainty still existed.

"Our expectations had been that they were ready to talk," Finzen said, "and yet the first discussion showed that they still weren't. We told them, 'This is not good.'"

That statement was amplified by Ciresi, who stopped by the meeting one evening after court. One of the tobacco attorneys asked him for his assessment of the case.

Finzen recalled, "Mike said 'We're just going to bury you. We're absolutely going to bury you.' He laid it out in a very straightforward manner. He said, 'Here's where we are and, guys, your [trial team] is divided, you don't have a leader, your case is going terribly. Ours is going great. This jury is paying attention, they're with us, we're going to kill you.'"

Sheehy added, "He said 'We love your witnesses, bring on a couple more. Do you have any more like Geoffrey Bible?'"

Koplow chuckled when asked later about Ciresi's comments. "Mike started *every* session that way."

Steve Patton added, "That's Mike's negotiating style."

The plaintiffs' team concluded the meeting by telling the tobacco negotiators, "If you've got something that you really want to talk about, you know where to find us."

The tobacco negotiators were back at the table the next day, under much improved circumstances.

"We got to the point where we had a pretty good sense of the structure of what the public health piece would look like," said

Finzen, adding, "we weren't actually drafting, we were dealing with concepts."

Whereas, in the early days, the talks had been punctuated with long breaks, while the various tobacco negotiators called their respective offices, "those time periods got shorter and shorter," Finzen said.

By the end of the week, the parties had made significant progress. The tobacco negotiators flew back to meet with their respective employers, with an understanding that the parties would regroup on Sunday, May 3, and start drafting the actual agreement.

As the excitement over the latest Minnesota settlement rumors subsided from buzz to a manageable hum, attention turned back to the courtroom, where William Wecker, the first in a trio of defense statistical witnesses, arrived to attack the state's damages model. The normally tense atmosphere in the courtroom grew taut as the first statistician took the stand.

Judge Fitzpatrick had made it abundantly clear that if the defense took one tiny step—moved one inch—toward "the death benefit" theory, he would throw the book at them. In fact, Peter Biersteker, the defense team's damages attorney, recalled, "The judge was threatening that if I had Wecker testify, and if the plaintiffs could come back and show that it involved a 'death credit'—and it wasn't clear anymore what exactly he meant by that—that he was going to tell the jury to disregard the entire testimony."

Biersteker was worried. "There was a lot riding on that. I was concerned that the plaintiffs were going to come in with something that was a little gray. I was real nervous about it." He moved through his questions as if on eggshells.

Statistician and Stanford professor Wecker was immediately impressive. The graduate of the U.S. Air Force Academy had flown more than 100 combat missions in Vietnam. To Biersteker's remarks about his war record, Wecker said quietly, "Well, that was a long time ago."

The tall, soft-spoken, former Air Force captain came armed with facts and figures, none of which the plaintiffs' attorneys wanted the jury to hear.

Wecker got straight to the point, in a polite but authoritative manner. The plaintiffs' damages model was flawed. Deeply. In the model's attempt to capture the cost of treating smoking-related illnesses, it had roped in quite a few that had nothing to do with smoking at all. Wecker's examples included hemorrhoids, schizophrenia, and broken bones.

"These are not on the surgeon general's list of smoking related illnesses," he said, simply.

Wecker's analysis of the damages model concluded that male smokers between the ages of 19 and 34 accounted for the largest group of claims — $720 million. "These were young males with virtually no tobacco-related disease in the group," he told the jury. The cost of hospital treatment for this group was almost entirely attributable to expenses not connected to smoking-related disease as defined by the surgeon general. The costs included treatment for car accidents, wounds, fractures, back problems, epilepsy, and hemorrhoids.

"Whatever the source of the extra cost for the smoker, they added it up, and if it's more than the nonsmoker, they put it in the claim," Wecker said.

Wecker's methodology for reviewing the model may have soared over most of the juror's heads, but his conclusions were simple: the plaintiffs' formula was contaminated by bias, so-called "nonsampling error."

"This is due to putting auto accidents and hemorrhoids in where they don't make sense."

Wecker, speaking without notes in the soothing voice of an airline pilot, was the critical witness the defense had been hoping for—and needed badly at this point.

Biersteker referred to a subject he'd dangled before the jury once before, during his cross-examination of Timothy Wyant— the two 94-year-old nursing home residents. Wecker testified that the state's calculation of costs for smokers in nursing homes included $108 million for women between the ages of 50 and 94. According to Wecker, $87 million of that could be extrapolated from the cases of two 94-year-old women.

One woman smoked for only eight years—between the ages of 30 and 38—and only had smoked four cigarettes a day. She had been admitted to the nursing home at age 93 with dehydration, anxiety, psychosis, and other ailments—none of them on the surgeon general's list of smoking-related illnesses, Wecker testified.

The other 94-year-old started smoking rather late in life—age 80—and quit one year later. She entered the nursing home when she was 87, suffering from depressive disorder, paranoia, and other mental disorders—none of them smoking-related.

How could those two women end up included in the damages model?

"Plaintiffs use the age, whether they smoked or not, and how long they were in the nursing home. That's it," Wecker declared, saying, "It looks like another form of [statistical bias]."

In addition, he testified, when he ran the numbers, he found that smokers on public aid cost the state no more money than nonsmokers on public aid.

The jury was spellbound. Even Judge Fitzpatrick seemed captivated by the information Wecker was providing, uncharacteristically brushing away plaintiffs' attorney Tom Hamlin's objections like lint. Ciresi, usually seated directly below the judge, as close to the witness stand as possible, had moved to the far edge of the courtroom. When Wecker returned to the witness stand after lunch, Ciresi was missing from the courtroom entirely—the first occasion since the trial's onset.

During the noon break on Wecker's second day of testimony, Ciresi and his wife, Ann, were seen taking advantage of the gorgeous spring weather by going for a walk along the Mississippi River bluff. However, Ciresi looked distracted and distant. Later he would acknowledge that he and his wife were talking about the possible settlement.

"I had a real ambivalence about the settlement," Ciresi said. "We had gone so far and so long on this, and the issue extended so far beyond Minnesota. There's no question that a verdict could have had a very profound impact on these companies. It may have precipitated a more rapid changing of their ways than a settlement. On the other hand, the settlement went so far beyond what anyone else had done. I was just wrestling with my ambivalence as a trial lawyer as opposed to the merits of the settlement. I also had a tremendous feeling for this jury, and really felt they deserved to make this decision."

Wecker's cross-examination by Hamlin was tedious—and, ultimately, fruitless. As jurors yawned, Hamlin resorted to picking out miniscule errors in the numbers listed on some of Wecker's exhibits. They indeed were sloppy, but had little impact on Wecker's testimony. The 94-year-old women still accounted for $87 million in costs in the damages claim—that figure went undisputed. Hemorrhoids were included as a smoking-related illness. That's what jurors would remember.

Juror David Olson wrote in his jury notebook, "The model is a sham."

Even Jim Otis, who acknowledged after the trial that he detested the tobacco companies, couldn't get behind the plaintiffs model: "That's about the only thing I wasn't sold on."

Dorothy Hallen initially had accepted the plaintiffs' description of the model's calculations, "but the defense gave me doubts."

Attorney Hamlin expressed irritation with Wecker's testimony after the trial. "He attempted to send a false message to the jury with the 94-year-old women. He admitted he had little familiarity with health care costs."

The next defense witness, Donald Rubin, was even more untouchable. Rubin, a Harvard statistician, was considered to be one of the finest theoretical statisticians in the world, and a master at interpolating missing data. One of the plaintiffs' damages experts, Scott Zeger, had been a student. Rubin's testimony was dense with talk of probit models, propensity scoring, and regression analysis, but his points emerged clearly. He used an exhibit that reflected missing data from the plaintiffs' model. The missing data was evaluated in such a manner that it rendered the entire model invalid, Rubin said.

According to the eminent statistician, the model used "single imputation" to fill in missing values, rather than the more accurate "multiple imputation," which Rubin personally had developed.

During his cross-examination, attorney Hamlin tried to paint Rubin as an ivory tower theorist, whose methods had little or no bearing on practical statistical analysis. Hamlin tried to take Rubin to task on his evaluation of the National Health and Nutritional Evaluation Survey (NHANES), one of the data sources for the model (which included the controversial nursing home data). Wasn't it true that NHANES used single imputation, he challenged Rubin?

Rubin smiled thinly, "That's incorrect. . . . I just talked with them a few weeks ago. . . . They don't believe the old way of doing it was valid from their studies over several years." Rubin explained that the new NHANES survey "will contain multiple imputations for all the major variables that had missing values."

Hamlin was no match for the world-class statistician, and by the time Rubin left the stand, the damages model looked worse than ever.

The final defense witness, University of Minnesota econometrician Brian McCall said he'd rarely come across a study that relied on a confidence level of less than 95 percent. To do so, he testified, would render the calculation "not statistically different from zero."

According to McCall, the damages model failed to meet the 95 percent confidence level, which rendered the calculations "statistically insignificant." He proceeded to testify that the model didn't even meet a confidence level of 90 percent. McCall went on to examine the model's components, concluding that at least one of them didn't even meet an 80 percent level. McCall's lack of confidence in the model persisted through an objection-peppered examination and registered enormously with Juror Number Three, Terry Zaspel, who later declared McCall the best witness of the trial. "He was the smartest, he was awesome. He blew the plaintiffs' statisticians out of the water."

Zaspel was alone among jurors interviewed in her enthusiastic endorsement of the University of Minnesota professor, but none held much esteem for the damages model by the end of the defense's presentation.

"I think they blew holes in the damages model, big holes. It was their strongest point," Jill Burton reflected. "I had questions about that model before they even got to that point. It just raised again the question for me, 'I don't know how the state had been damaged.'"

Burton, and the others, as it turned out, would never have to confront that conundrum.

Chapter Fifteen

Settlement!

In the 11th hour, Big Tobacco was looking better than it had all through the trial. The last four witnesses—three statisticians and an anti-trust expert—had testified extremely well and suffered little damage on cross-examination. It might not be a slam-dunk plaintiffs' case after all.

But the trial's atmosphere would change dramatically on Monday, May 4, with a screaming headline in the *Saint Paul Pioneer Press* that a $5 billion tobacco settlement was on the table. From that point on, the relatively predictable rhythm of the Great Minnesota Tobacco Trial shattered permanently. Replacing it was a week-long, three-ring circus that rivaled Ringling Bros.

There, under the Warren Burger Big Top, was ringleader Judge Kenneth Fitzpatrick, trying his level best to conduct proceedings while all hell broke loose on the outside. On Monday, Fitzpatrick twice admonished the jury to avoid *anything* in the media as it "does not have much resemblance to reality." With the jury and attorneys preoccupied with administrative hearings and document reviews until jury instructions were delivered Wednesday, there would be little of interest going on in the courtroom. That was fine with the media. With settlement rumors at fever pitch, there was so much to do and see, nobody much cared.

The plaintiffs' negotiating team was furious about the leak that led to the *Pioneer Press* scoop, especially Ciresi, who told both clients as much in a meeting. Lead plaintiffs' negotiator Bruce Finzen scolded his defense counterparts that leaks wouldn't help the parties reach an agreement.

"Find out where the leaks are and knock it off," he told them.

"If they thought this kind of pressure would force a settlement, it wouldn't," Finzen said later. "It would have the opposite effect. If they kept it up, at some point we were likely to say, 'We just can't negotiate in this atmosphere, so goodbye.'"

For their part, defense negotiators were convinced the plaintiffs leaked the information—a trial balloon to test public reaction.

"It plainly came from the other side of the table," Philip Morris negotiator Meyer Koplow said later. "Why would the industry want to float a story in front of the jurors about its willingness to pay $5 billion?"

Sunday night, because of the imminent news report, the negotiators felt that it was time to let Judge Fitzpatrick know about the developments.

"We got on the speaker phone with the judge, and he was very matter-of-fact about the whole thing," recalled Tom Pursell, a member of the attorney general's negotiating team, now meeting at the Radisson Hotel in downtown Minneapolis. "Just before the end of the conversation, there was a long pause, and then he said, 'Good luck,' but he said it almost wistfully. While judges almost reflexively urge people to settle and wish them good luck, it took a minute for him to do that."

Koplow thought Fitzpatrick received the news unemotionally. "He was very passive. He just listened and said, 'Keep me informed.'"

The negotiators still had to resolve several issues, including the payment of attorneys' fees. But they felt it was time to start putting settlement language on paper to see what it looked like.

With the media now swarming to find ground zero, the negotiations moved to a more secure location, two smoked-glass conference rooms on the 27th floor of the LaSalle Building in downtown Minneapolis—in the heart of Ciresi's firm. Security was tight, not even the employees knew the identities of the suits who commandeered the floor for the next five days. The tedious drafting process continued Monday until three or four in the morning, but with good results.

"I thought we made significant progress," Finzen recalled.

Defense negotiators kept receiving analyses from their trial attorneys and believed their case was going well. Nonetheless, they felt that Fitzpatrick's rulings and demeanor had poisoned the courtroom atmosphere.

"We thought the judge had, in effect, prejudged the case against us and was doing everything he could to dictate the outcome of the case," said R.J. Reynolds Tobacco Company (RJR) negotiator Arthur Golden. "That was our overriding concern. When a judge appears to be very strongly against you, you have substantial concern about what the jury will do, because juries are very influenced by what they see the judge do."

By Tuesday morning, rumors circulated that Skip Humphrey would make a settlement announcement within 48 hours, giving local politicians ample time to publicize their plans to spend the money. Senate Majority Leader Roger Moe compared the clamor to greedy children waiting for their inheritance.

The negotiations hit a snag Tuesday night. "We were fighting over words and certain issues," Finzen said. About 7:30 P.M., the defense negotiators came in and said, 'This ain't going to work.'"

"The public health injunctive language was, ultimately, the devil in the details," Deputy Attorney General Lee Sheehy recalled. However, defense negotiators said they had other concerns, including lack of immunity from lawsuits brought by other political subdivisions in the state. And the money issue remained unsettled.

Both sides shook hands and the tobacco negotiators left. Sheehy, Finzen, and the rest of the team went to the trendy Palomino restaurant for dinner. Sheehy thought the negotiations were over. Finzen wasn't so sure. "We did a little postmortem about where we were, and then we went home to get a little sleep for the first time in a couple of nights."

However, before Finzen got to bed that night, he received a call from Ken Feinberg, who had not been present for the last few days of negotiations.

"What the hell happened?" he asked Finzen.

"You tell me,'" Finzen retorted. "Your guys said they can't do it. You find out from them.

"'It's ridiculous,'" Finzen recalled Feinberg saying. "'Meyer's still in town. You guys ought to have breakfast tomorrow.'"

Phone calls ensued. Feinberg called Koplow in his hotel room, and told him to expect a phone call from either Finzen or Ciresi. Shortly, Koplow recalled, Ciresi was on the line. "He was very complimentary. He said he didn't understand what had happened. He was extraordinarily friendly. He said if it wasn't going to work, it wasn't going to work. But he was not very happy that things had broken down."

Meanwhile, Finzen called Ciresi and told him about his conversation with Feinberg and the suggestion that he and Koplow should meet again. "Ken thinks there may still be some hope," Finzen told Ciresi.

"What could it hurt?" Ciresi replied. "Give him a call."

Finzen did. Koplow recalled that Finzen told him the plaintiffs were prepared to compromise on some disputed elements. The two agreed to meet the next morning for breakfast at the Minneapolis Hilton.

During their early Wednesday morning meeting, Finzen recalled Koplow asking, "Look, if we could make some progress on these issues, would it make any sense for us to get back together?"

Finzen wasn't sure. With media reports already leaking about
the settlement hitting a snag, he told Koplow, "We have to really
be able to make progress."

The meal ended with Koplow promising to get back to him
before the morning was over. The negotiator made good on his
pledge, and the parties went back to the bargaining table that
afternoon.

Over in St. Paul, the circus outside the courthouse featured a
new attraction—huge white satellite trucks from the major
national and local news organizations, bristling with electronic
equipment, and ringing the courthouse, with cables and wires
snaking through the crowd like so many elephant trunks in
search of peanuts. The nutty morsels, in this case, would come
from any trial-affiliated lawyer crazy enough (or mediaphilic
enough) to come through the front door.

With the arrival of any trial attorney, the media horde sprang
into a choreographed routine funnier than any clown act. While
a carefully placed, camera-ringed podium stood unused, camera-
men and reporters instead swarmed the victim until the result
looked like a giant rugby scrum. Lawyers would disappear in the
middle, released only after delivering a satisfactory sound bite.
Then, it being a beautiful spring day, the media would return to
their lounge chairs and soak up the rays until the next trial
participant tried to make a run for it.

By afternoon, it was back to the center ring for Judge

Fitzpatrick's jury instructions. Jury instructions provide the legal lenses through which a jury must focus on a case during their deliberations. The instructions are critical in any litigation. As Brown and Williamson's local counsel Jack Fribley, a former law clerk, explained, "Jury instructions are the one thing that can torpedo a verdict. Lawyers don't want [legal] error in their instructions. If there's error, the verdict goes out."

Both defense and plaintiffs' teams had submitted their proposed instructions to Judge Fitzpatrick during the trial, and had argued their merits before him earlier that week. It hadn't gone well for the defense.

"The plaintiffs had about five key things they wanted in those instructions, and they got them all," said Fribley. "It surprised me that the plaintiffs were pushing so hard for such a one-sided set of instructions. Either they knew during the last week that they could settle the case anytime they wanted and didn't care if there was error. Or, for settlement leverage, they just want the biggest verdict they could get."

As he read through the 50-plus instructions, Fitzpatrick told the jury that he had already reached a decision on one count, and it had to do with the Frank Statement.

He told them that, as a result of the 1954 advertisement, "defendants voluntarily undertook to accept an interest in people's health as a basic responsibility, paramount to every other consideration in their business." Fitzpatrick added, that, as a result of this "special duty" finding, he had already answered the first question on the jury verdict form.

He also told jurors that, even if defendants met all government regulations regarding sale of their products, "such compliance is not a defense if you determine that any defendant should have acted differently."

In an instruction about manufacturers' responsibility, he again told the jury, "the fact that the government or other organizations may have researched tobacco or issued warnings about smoking does not relieve the tobacco companies of their responsibilities."

For the defense, they were devastating. To some onlookers, they were inconceivable. To the plaintiffs, they were perfect.

Michael Ciresi called the instructions "powerful." Roberta Walburn described them as "solid."

However, RJR's Robert Weber described the instructions as riddled by "error incarnate. Trying to find the worst one of them is like trying to find the drunkest man in New Orleans at Mardi Gras."

Even the normally circumspect David Bernick spoke out about what he considered to be the outrageousness of what Judge Fitzpatrick had spelled out. "They were so *extreme*. They were wrong in ways that were almost gratuitous. The instructions themselves were a guaranteed appeal. I couldn't understand why a judge would work so hard to create a trial that had such visibility and then issue instructions that were so clearly assured of leading to a reversed result."

Hamline law school professor Peter Thompson, who later

reviewed several of the most disputed instructions, wasn't troubled by all of them. However, he found several to be problematic.

"The special duty instruction was controversial," he said after the trial. "It's commonly used in personal injury cases, but not consumer fraud. I wasn't familiar with any court buying into that theory."

Because the special duty instruction dealt with a legal conclusion, he added, "It is very appealable, and something an appellate court would give the judge no deference on, if it wasn't applied correctly."

Thompson also wondered about the instructions related to government regulation of a product: "This is a pretty appealable one too," he said, explaining, "Government regulations supercede any state requirements. By putting warnings on cigarette packs, they had fulfilled their duty to inform consumers."

That said, given the swirling settlement rumors, and the ongoing bias the defense already felt the judge had shown them, by the time they reached the controversial jury instructions, B.A.T. Industries local counsel Gerald Svoboda recalled, "It was sort of 'So what?'"

Meanwhile, the negotiations weren't making much progress. After spending six hours that afternoon revisiting issues and hashing over language, the plaintiffs' negotiators found themselves looking at a proposal they'd already seen. Finzen and his group walked over to the defense team's conference room. "We said, 'It's over guys. It's not going to work. Here's what we need, here's what you got. Whichever way this verdict goes, nobody can ever say that it was from lack of trying. We tried hard to settle, everybody worked in good faith. Thanks a lot.'"

The defense negotiators packed up their things and left. Finzen went home and called Ciresi.

"Kill 'em," he told his law partner. "Just bury them. We're done."

The media reported Thursday that the talks had broken down; the settlement looked precarious.

But early that morning, Wednesday's jury instructions were just being digested in the boardrooms of Philip Morris, RJR, and Brown & Williamson (B&W) at their respective headquarters in New York, Winston-Salem, and Louisville, defense negotiators said. A sense of urgency gripped the corporate attorneys and executives, as they realized the implications contained in Judge Fitpatrick's instructions.

A conference call was arranged, with Koplow—waiting to catch a plane at the Minneapolis–St. Paul airport—on the Twin Cities end of the line. Some decisions had to be made. Immediately.

The bustling activity that week around the courthouse had not been entirely lost on the jury, nor had widespread reports about the settlement.

"Early in the week we saw all these trucks and satellite dishes and cameras, a podium set up, and all the lights, and we thought, 'It's way too early for them to be there for our deliberation,'" Dorothy Hallen recalled. "There's settlement talks. This has to be what it is."

David Olson recalled the scene outside the courthouse being "just bonkers. There were a couple of camera guys and reporters standing outside one morning when we drove by, and we all waved at them. Their mouths just dropped."

After that, the van that brought jurors from the parking lot to the courthouse began to take an alternate route.

Other jurors had seen headlines announcing the breakdown in negotiations. That was just fine with Jill Burton, "I thought, 'Good,' because when you had come that far, you just wanted to be handed the baton and told, 'Now go do it.'"

So once again, attention refocused on the courtroom, this time for the start of the final act: defense's closing arguments. Six attorneys would provide summations for the defense. Tiny Liggett would lead the pack. Liggett local counsel, David Sasseville, who'd been sharing court-attendance duty with his colleague Steven Kelley, asked the jury to exonerate Liggett because it did not participate in the drafting of the Frank Statement. "If anything, Liggett was a lone wolf," he said, reminding jurors that the company's brands now carried warnings that smoking was addictive, and could kill.

Philip Morris' Peter Bleakley took the podium next. The seasoned litigator moved smoothly through his presentation, deftly underscoring the defense's perceived weaknesses in the plaintiffs' case.

"It's not about popularity," he said. "Believe me, the defendants are well aware of the fact that they're not very popular these days."

Bleakley told jurors that he didn't doubt that many of them might conclude by trial's end that the cigarette companies should have admitted years ago that smoking caused disease. "I said that some of you would undoubtedly conclude that these defendants have been stubborn and foolish."

What was up to the jury to decide, Bleakley said, was "whether something wrongful about the way the defendants made and sold cigarettes caused the plaintiffs to incur increased healthcare costs in Medicaid, GAMC, and Blue Cross insurance."

Over Ciresi's objections, he also managed to remind the jury once again that cigarettes were already heavily taxed by the state.

Bleakley argued that Minnesotans had long been aware of smoking's risks. "Not a consumer, not a smoker, not a Medicaid recipient . . . not a Blue Cross member came in and said, 'we were fooled.'

"Just look around you," he suggested. "Most of our parents smoked. They smoked in their cars, they smoked in their homes, they smoked in restaurants. What do smokers do today? They're outcasts. They have to sneak outside buildings to smoke cigarettes. Most of the buildings in most large cities are nonsmoking. There has been a complete social revolution with respect to smoking and it's all because it is generally and widely and universally perceived that cigarette smoking is bad for you and kills."

Bruce Finzen didn't attend the court session. With everything that had been going on for the past few months, he'd been neglecting things around the house. While he was outside watering the yard, his wife took a phone call. "Take a message," he told her. "Well, it's Meyer Koplow," she replied.

Finzen started toward the house, "I'll take that call."

Koplow had acted immediately on the instructions delivered to him on that early morning conference call. He had been told to return immediately to the bargaining table, if possible, and strike a deal before the jury began deliberating.

"It was not until the jury instructions were issued that Wednesday, and people had a chance to absorb them, that the companies came to the conclusion that, no matter what the jury wanted to do, the judge required them to find against the industry," Koplow said. "By Thursday morning, all the companies had realized that the judge was directing a verdict against the industry. There would not have been a settlement, but for those jury instructions."

Finzen listened to Koplow's request. "If we were to come to your position on these issues, does it make sense for us to get back together?" Finzen recalled him asking.

"Meyer, I don't know," Finzen said. By that time, news of the settlement's breakdown was widespread. Finzen wasn't sure whether or not his client wanted to revisit the matter again. "My whole personal view, Meyer, is we ought to do it," he told the defense negotiator. "I'm not sure the client's going to feel that way."

"My bag's already been checked," Koplow told him. "I've got to get it off the plane if I'm going to stay."

"That's your call," Finzen replied. "You do what you want to do."

However, the tobacco industry was not just concerned about an adverse verdict. Trial attorneys were convinced that they had some appealable issues on which to seek a new trial. Of crucial importance, however, were the so-called "judicial equity issues" that Fitzpatrick alone had the power to decide.

Even if the jury came back with a verdict entirely in favor of the defense, the judge still had the power to levy significant financial penalties on the defendants. If, for example, he determined that the industry's years of doing business in the state were illegal, it was possible that the judge could fine them for each and every tobacco advertisement run since the Frank Statement was published in 1954. Were those damages higher than $10 billion, only Philip Morris might be able to post the bond necessary to continue doing business while the matter was appealed. The rest of the tobacco companies would find themselves at immediate financial risk, and, possibly, facing extinction.

And given Judge Fitzpatrick's jury instructions, no one had any doubts about the direction he was headed.

"The judge could have entered not just fines and penalties, but injunctions that could have effectively destroyed the companies' abilities to do business," RJR's Arthur Golden acknowledged.

Koplow got his bag and returned to his hotel. Finzen talked with Sheehy, Gilde, and Humphrey.

"We came to a decision to get back together again," Finzen recalled, but issued cautionary words to Koplow when the two talked by phone. "If you're not coming to say, 'Fine, we're where you are on those issues,' don't waste our time."

Koplow replied, "No, that's the premise."

After the midmorning break, it became apparent that something was afoot. Industry negotiator Steve Patton, who'd been sitting among tobacco attorneys in the spectator section earlier that morning, had vanished.

Blue Cross Chief Executive Andy Czajkowski, meanwhile, was unaware just how quickly events were unfolding. During the morning recess, Czjakowski went before a battery of reporters and cameras to say that no talks were under way. He noted that the trial was in its "11.99th hour."

By noon, the talks had resumed on the 27th floor at Ciresi's firm in Minneapolis. Using two conference rooms and a vacant office, the two parties took a final stab at an agreement. Meanwhile, the warriors continued their summations. B & W's David Bernick delivered his elegant two-hour summation on the intricacies of Big Tobacco's scientific and research efforts without looking at a single note. Instead, the defense attorney, utilizing his ever-present magic marker and easel paper, emphasized each of his points by writing them down for jurors.

"We're prepared to be judged on the bad parts of our conduct," Bernick said. "But let's also get a little bit of credit for the accomplishments."

He spent a good deal of time on the Frank Statement, declaring that the industry had, in fact, lived up to the promises it made in that 1954 statement.

"If you actually look for what came out of this process and the way of the science that was the subject of the Frank Statement, is there any question about the quality of that science? Is there any question about the scope of that science? Is there any question about the Surgeon General's reliance upon it? Has anyone shown you that results were mischaracterized by the scientists who did them? Nobody has shown you that."

Bernick brusquely dismissed the charge that the tobacco companies had engaged in anti-trust activities. "Don't tell us it's cozy," he warned. "This is a competitive market. We haven't seen the warm and friendly feeling in this industry."

With surgical precision, Bernick carved up the plaintiffs' favorite documents, asking, "Where is the silver bullet? Where is the magical secret of biological research that these companies uncovered in the hearts of their laboratories and it's now come to light and we now know the secret about smoking and health? For a case that's driven by concealment and the claims of concealment, wouldn't you expect by this late date that that fact be identified? Where is it?"

Bernick offered an answer. "There will be no silver bullet. Nobody has unlocked the secret of the safer cigarette. Nobody has unlocked the secret of how smoking actually does cause disease. Nobody has withheld from the marketplace those critical facts and those critical elements. They're not here."

Lorillard's John Monica sought to put the actual number of documents entered into the trial about his company into perspective. He told jurors that the number of documents requested from Lorillard during the discovery process amounted to a stack of 1.8 million pieces of paper 666 feet high, the equivalent of a six-story building. Picking up a small handful of documents, he slapped them on the podium and declared, "This was all they used in their testimony." He would thwack them down once more during his presentation for emphasis, declaring, "The broom on the plaintiff's case sweeps up too much."

Michael Corrigan, the attorney for B.A.T. Industries PLC—the English holding company for British-American Tobacco Company and Brown & Williamson—emphasized the lack of attention paid to his client in the course of the trial.

"Did you hear a single witness come in here and testify that B.A.T Industries made any promise, any undertaking to anybody? No, you did not. That proof never came. Did a single witness come in here and testify that B.A.T. Industries concealed scientific evidence about the hazards of smoking? Not one. The proof never came. Did any witness come in here and suggest to you that B.A.T. Industries targeted adolescents with advertising? Not one. That proof never came. Did any witness take this witness stand and offer an opinion that B.A.T Industries manipulated nicotine in cigarettes? Not a one. That proof never came. And it didn't come because B.A.T. Industries is a *holding* company, not a tobacco manufacturer."

Corrigan also reminded jurors that the defendants in the trial weren't the "tobacco industry," but 10 separate companies or trade groups. "It won't just be a yes or no [verdict on the industry] and we all go home."

But it was The Duke, RJR's folksy and personable Robert Weber, described by Bleakley early on as the defense team's "cleanup hitter," who stole the show that afternoon.

Weber, like his colleagues, acknowledged that his company had made some mistakes over the years. "Tens of thousands of employees working day in, day out—it would be a miracle if some things hadn't happened wrong, if there hadn't been some misjudgments," he conceded.

"They've made mistakes in the marketplace, they've lost market share for years. As you've heard, they used to be the leader, now they're not," he said.

Among those mistakes, Weber said, was RJR's efforts with the Premier cigarette, "betting hundreds of millions of dollars. . . . and losing every nickel of it in the marketplace."

And he acknowledged marketing mistakes as well "when, as you heard, for a period of years up to about 1982, Reynolds used to collect data that gave them information on share of market of people under 18. Mistakes are mistakes. They did happen."

But Weber asked jurors to put those mistakes into a context he was sure the jurors would understand.

"I know for years everybody in the American League admired

the Twins because they had Kirby Puckett, who worked hard, put
out every day. But if someone were to take the films of all the
Twins games that Kirby Puckett played in and only brought out
the video clips of every error he made, every time he struck out,
every time he hit, missed the cutoff man, every time he didn't
deliver for the team, you could put together a pretty long set of
tapes.

"You could look at that tape and show it to somebody who
didn't really know and they'd end up thinking Kirby Puckett was
a pretty bad ballplayer. And in one sense the film would be true.
It's actually what happened, but I think of course we all know
there's something wrong with that film.

"It wouldn't be fair," Weber said. "It doesn't look at the whole
context. And that's the issue I want us to keep in mind."

Declaring the damages model to be bloated and inaccurate, he
asked, "How on earth can anyone expect a check to be written
on that type of evidence?"

Weber maintained that the state failed to prove that industry
directly marketed to youth, saying that kids had been sneaking
smokes since "Tom Sawyer met Huck Finn." He said that smoking behavior was more likely to be affected by a teen's environment than by Joe Camel.

"Two percent of overall sales are made to the underage group,"
Weber said. "What smart businessman and smart businesswoman
would put a company at risk to go after 2 percent?"

As court adjourned, Ralph Walker, a plaintiffs' attorney

involved in Iowa's Medicaid lawsuit who'd been in court observing most of the trial, shook his head in amazement. "That's the best closing argument I've ever seen delivered by any attorney. Period," he declared.

In the media room, the closed-circuit feed from the courtroom had been strangely different. Weber's performance was praised, but that wasn't the only conversation about the closing arguments. Several reporters laughed about the videographer's artistic leanings that day. Every other day of the trial, the camera beaming the proceedings into downstairs conference rooms had been fixed and unwavering in its focus. On this day, the camera had zoomed in and out on the various attorneys, prompting reporters to wonder if the courtroom cameraman was pondering a future career in the movies. Only later would a shocking and astounding answer to that question be revealed.

Late Thursday, reporters learned the talks had resumed. This time it looked to be the real thing. Although the media sensed movement, facts were sketchy. That's because the agreement was still developing, as negotiators worked through the night. If a deal wasn't reached by the time Ciresi began his closing arguments at 9:30 A.M. Friday morning, there wouldn't be one, according to Bruce Finzen.

"The minute Mike stood up, they knew we were done," he said. "We've always taken the position that we're never going to take a case from the jury once it's been submitted. That's the deadline, everybody understood it, and that was never in doubt."

Finzen later acknowledged another reason as well. Ciresi was expected to ask for huge punitive damages in the course of his summation and wouldn't want to look like he lost if the settlement was less than his total package of actual and punitive damages.

For the defense negotiators, the reason to settle had little to do with losing the case, and everything to do with Judge Fitzpatrick. Between the jury instructions and the possibility of huge fines and penalties imposed by the judge, despite any jury verdict, they had to settle, and settle fast.

The plaintiffs' negotiators were well aware of this fact; it was their ace in the hole.

"I think that was a motivating factor for them to get serious about where we were in damages," Finzen acknowledged. "We said to them, the $1.77 billion is a given. Now we're going to talk about the total. The $1.77 billion is just a component, that's past damages, which is going to be paid 100 percent on the dollar over a very short period of time."

Negotiators worked through the night. They tossed out immunity from county lawsuits and criminal sanctions for violating new youth marketing restrictions. Proposed new disclosure requirements for industry lobbyists and representatives were made less restrictive. A heath care fund was established. In one of the more bizarre terms, product placement fees for movies—something the industry had ceased to do years before—were prohibited.

Sleep wasn't an option that night. "The clock was running and everybody felt it," said Finzen.

Defense negotiators faxed language changes for proposed terms back to their corporate headquarters, and were in frequent contact with their clients throughout the night.

Humphrey called in "about every two hours," Sheehy recalled. "We'd tell him 'Here's where we're at and here's how we think the process is unrolling.'"

Sometime between midnight and 2:00 A.M., Finzen called Ciresi, who was at the St. Paul Hotel working on his closing argument.

"Look, Mike," Finzen said. "This thing is going to happen. I think we're there, but there's no way we're going to get it done by the time court starts at 9:30 A.M."

Peter Bleakley was also contacted. Bleakley and Ciresi agreed to call the judge first thing in the morning to alert him.

The final element of the negotiation involved the attorneys' fees. "Of course, we had to draft a separate agreement for that because it was going to be separate," Finzen recalled. "There never was going to be any fee coming from the state, out of the state's share, no matter what happened. It was always going to be that the tobacco industry paid our fees and we would waive our agreement with the state. They agreed. In fact, I think they not only agreed with that, they felt that was the right way to proceed."

An agreement in principal was reached at 4:30 A.M. Friday morning. Draft agreements were circulated to the principals shortly before dawn.

"There was a shared feeling of professional admiration for the way we had worked through this," Finzen said. "It was a good working relationship."

Although the bulk of the work was done, negotiators would continue to work throughout the morning finalizing details in the final document.

Skip Humphrey was in his office at 6:30 A.M. when he first saw the settlement draft. "It looked very good. When I understood the framework of the whole thing, it looked very good."

He turned to his staff, "Okay, We've won."

Humphrey later recalled being disappointed not to see some terms included, such as "look back" provisions which would further financially penalize the tobacco industry if underage smoking did not decline within a certain time period.

"But Mike was very good," he recalled. "He said '"Skip, this is a lawsuit. This is what we've sued for. I am telling you as your attorney, this is what we're able to do. We're beyond where we thought we could be.'"

As the parties reviewed the fruits of their labor, the 12 members of the jury finished packing their suitcases. Unbeknownst to lawyers for either side, Judge Fitzpatrick told the jurors on Thursday that they would be sequestered for their deliberations. The judge planned to sequester the jury immediately following Ciresi's closing argument Friday, grant them a brief visit home the following Sunday, Mother's Day, then have them returned to sequestration until their deliberations were completed.

The decision produced mixed feelings in the jurors. Jill Burton was all for it.

"I was glad they were pulling us away," she said later. "I needed a concentrated time of not being disrupted. I think it would have been difficult to deliberate and then come home every night. To try to do your other life with the weight of deciding. Plus, I figured we could spend more time talking in the evening if we wanted."

Jim Otis felt exactly the opposite. "It was stressing me out. I mean, I liked everybody there, but I had had enough of close quarters for that long."

The jurors would be picked up at their homes Friday morning, or at designated meeting places, and brought to the courthouse.

As the jurors were picked up at various locations in vans driven by Judge Fitzpatrick's squad of private security guards, Jill Burton was shocked at their sudden transformation. "Our guard was dressed fully in black and he had a gun and holster, handcuffs, and a billy club. It was kind of scary. I didn't want to get in."

Burton struggled with a number of emotions that day during the drive to downtown St. Paul, as she continued to wonder whether the case would settle. "The worse case scenario would be to listen to it all, then be told we can't even decide. I thought if we could make it through this week, we can talk."

Burton was ready to deliberate. "It was difficult not to be able to vent. I held it all in knowing that there will be a time and it's coming, it's close, it's soon."

As the van drove by the side of the courthouse, Dorothy Hallen spied new activity at the media's satellite trucks. "They weren't just sitting there anymore. The trucks were open and people were running in and out of them."

She began to get a funny feeling about what might transpire that day in court. "Is this it?" she thought to herself. "Is the axe going to come down?"

At 8:30 A.M., Ciresi and Peter Bleakley went to see Judge Fitzpatrick to inform him that a tentative deal had been reached. They asked for a few more hours to formalize it.

"I perceived a sense of relief on his part," Ciresi later recalled. "However, I also had a sense that he would have liked to have seen what the jury would have done. I sensed a definite concern for the jury. He didn't want to hold them long."

Bleakley recalled events differently. "He had no visible reaction to it. He asked one question, which is whether or not we wanted to go on with court that day. That was it."

Meanwhile, jurors were brought into the courthouse's underground entrance, their luggage gathered and locked up, and they, once again, found themselves in their cramped jury room, waiting for what, they weren't certain.

Still, their bailiff, who they'd nicknamed "Deputy Rhonda," kept their spirits up by telling them what she had planned for them at the hotel where they'd be staying.

"She said she had this one community room where we'd get to

watch movies and she had a buffet dinner and a buffet breakfast already planned," Dorothy Hallen recalled. "She said we were going to have so much fun."

Out in the courtroom, the security guards had just spent the better part of 30 minutes sandwiching observers into the packed-to-capacity courtroom. The room was hushed as Fitzpatrick and the jury filed in.

Court was called to order—for about a minute.

"I wish to announce that the case will be continued until 1:30 this afternoon," the judge announced tersely. "Court is recessed."

The deal was done. The media knew it, the attorneys knew it, the judge knew it. The only ones left in the dark were the six men and six women who'd spent the last four months giving the highly technical and often tedious proceedings their undivided attention. They would spend the next five hours in psychic limbo, as they were shuttled from one place to another, with little or no explanation.

Since no one would tell them anything, they looked for clues in every activity.

"We all wondered, 'Surely not. There is just no way they are going to take it to the 11th hour, 11th minute,'" said Burton.

Shortly after court recessed, law clerk Michelle Jones arrived and informed the jurors that they would be moving from their cramped quarters to a larger room downstairs.

"They moved everything: the microwave oven, the contents of the refrigerator, the coffee," said Burton, an activity that gave her hope. "Why would they take all our stuff and move it? Maybe there was some other issue going on."

The new room was spacious, with a huge table and plenty of windows. There was even a small adjoining room the smokers were told they could use—there would be no going outside for cigarettes that day.

Jurors were severely cautioned not to go near the windows, which looked across Jackson Street to a building that housed KTCA, home to Minnesota Public Television and the city's PBS station.

"We were told they were worried that the media had microphones that could pick up our conversations off the window panes," Dorothy Hallen recalled. "The paranoia was huge. And I never saw the need for that much secrecy."

As the smokers huddled, they were joined by one of the most antitobacco jurors on the panel, Jim Otis. His nerves had gotten the better of him, and he quickly bummed a cigarette from one of his friends.

The Scrabble players set up their board and began playing. At 11:30, their bailiff arrived.

"Come on, grab your purses, we're going out to lunch," she told them.

Another bad sign, thought Burton. Friday was traditionally pizza day, and the order had been submitted the day before. Lunches outside the courthouse normally were planned weeks in advance. "Is this going to be the 'Last Supper?'" Burton wondered. "After 16 weeks together, is this how it was going to end? I just had a knot in my stomach.

"They just kept playing us through these ups and downs, but they would never say anything. They just acted like everything was normal. I don't think they knew anything either."

The group proceeded to Awada's restaurant, a short drive from the courthouse. Despite the tension and uncertainty, some things hadn't changed. When one of the jurors asked to have dessert, he was told he couldn't, because it would place his order over the $10 limit.

Juror Terry Zaspel was exasperated. "You order dessert," she told her fellow juror. "*I'll* pay for it."

While the jurors ate and speculated, the media circus outside the courtroom was operating at full throttle, with broadcast news reporters practically elbow-to-elbow delivering news updates into their respective cameras. Yellow crime scene tape kept the throng away from the courthouse's front doors. The reporters who had covered the trial alone for the past four months were now flanked by teams of colleagues, who fanned out into the crowd of spectators in search of sidebars and color. One reportorial coterie gathered around tobacco analyst Martin Feldman, seeking Wall Street wisdom.

Philip Morris attorneys Peter Sipkins and Murray Garnick watched the spectacle from the safety of the courthouse lobby, discussing whether or not to go outside on their lunch run. "I think we should take the skylines instead," said Garnick. Sipkins laughed. "You've been here four months now and you're still call-ing them skylines," he said of Garnick's reference to the skyways that connected Twin Cities buildings. When asked what they'd heard about the settlement, Sipkins joked, "We're like mush-rooms—they keep us in the dark and feed us shit!"

When the Ciresi team exited the building for a lunchtime stroll, they were immediately surrounded by cameras, filming their every movement until they finally left the courthouse block to cross the street to the park. Ciresi looked exhausted.

He'd spent some of the morning tying up loose ends. Seeking out Liggett attorney David Sasseville, Ciresi got straight to the point. "We think we've reached a deal. We think everything's going to be done. But honestly, we've been so busy thinking about everybody else and all the terms of the settlement that we haven't given Liggett a second thought," Sasseville recalled Ciresi explaining. "He said, 'I don't want to release you guys and dismiss the Blue Cross case against you without looking at what other settlements Liggett has entered in the last six months to a year. Maybe you gave up something in those other settlements that I should be asking for here.'"

He told Sasseville, "Trust me, we'll do right by you, but we aren't going to do it now."

Sasseville contacted Liggett's New York lawyers, who tracked down Liggett CEO Bennet Lebow, who was somewhere in Russia on a business trip. Finally, the word came back, Liggett would agree to the delay.

Shortly before court reconvened, Fitzpatrick summoned Ciresi and David Bernick to his chambers. In the confusion surrounding the settlement, he'd forgotten, he said, to address the matter of sanctions he intended to levy on B&W for its failure to provide several witnesses at trial. While Fitzpatrick said he was inclined to sanction B&W about $900,000, "he said he would like to see the issue resolved, so he would not have to rule on it after the trial, and he encouraged both sides to settle the issue," Bernick recalled.

Bernick and Ciresi agreed on a figure of $400,000, which Fitzpatrick quickly okayed. That money, along with the $100,000-plus in previous fines levied against B&W, resulted in a half million dollar financial windfall for Ramsey Country District Court, the direct recipient of the court-imposed fines.

Bernick never believed the sanctions were legitimate, but Judge Fitzpatrick had heard his arguments and ruled against them. Bernick disagreed with the large amount of the fine, but said there were few options available to his client at that point. "What court of appeals is really going to take a look at that seriously?" Bernick later wondered, adding pragmatically, "We had very, very little in the way of negotiation leverage."

Sometime that day, Fitzpatrick also dismissed B.A.T. Industries from the plaintiffs lawsuit, four months after receiving the company's request that he do so.

Humphrey and Czajkowski spent the morning in the chambers of a U.S. Bankruptcy Court courtroom on the second floor of the courthouse awaiting final word of the settlement.

At 1:00 P.M., the two went to the plaintiffs' trial room on the seventh floor. At 1:20 P.M., the settlement agreement was placed before them for their signatures. Someone in the room had a camera, but decided against taking a photograph of the historic moment because of the ban on cameras in the Federal Building.

At 1:55 P.M., a solemn Fitzpatrick reconvened the courtroom. His words, as usual, were sparse. "At this time the court wishes to announce that there has been a settlement of this case and the court has just executed a consent judgment."

The looks on the jurors' faces was heartbreaking. Juror Number Three, Terry Zaspel, broke down in tears, Jill Burton looked close to it. After 80 days in court, Ciresi's closing argument was all that separated them from deliberating, and that vanished with the rap of the judge's gavel.

Before they were dismissed, attorneys for both sides thanked the jurors for their service. "I've never in my 51 years in this state been more proud of 12 people," Ciresi told them, his voice cracking. "I can only imagine your feelings that you cannot render a verdict."

Bleakley spoke for the defense. "I don't think any of us thought, especially after hearing some of the hardship problems that many of you had back when we chose this jury in January, that we would have 12 people still here today . . . . It is a real tribute to the 12 of you that, despite those burdens, you stayed with us, and paid very, very close attention day in and day out to the evidence that was presented to you."

It didn't help Dorothy Hallen. "It was so hard to sit in that jury box and, again, not show anything on our faces while they both did their little 'thank yous.' All I wanted to do at that point was flip off the attorneys and leave."

Burton felt the same. "I just can't tell you how angry I was. I felt like standing up and walking out. Although I appreciated what everyone had to say, it was kind of 'thanks, but no thanks.'"

For David Olson, whose personal finances lay in shambles as a result of his jury service, the news was "a shock. We were going to be the ones who were going to be deciding this whole thing and all of a sudden they took it away. Then the anger set in. I was really pissed. But then, I was kind of relieved, too, that I didn't have to make the decision. I was torn both ways."

As Jim Otis left the courtroom, he ripped off his badge. As the jurors recongregated in their old jury room, Otis recalled, "all the girls started crying. They were just nuts. What a crappy way for it to end. It was kind of emotional."

Before the jurors had a chance to compose themselves or comfort each other, there was another intrusion. The bailiff arrived. The judge wanted to see the jury in chambers. Now.

"All the females were in tears. The men were in shock," Terry Zaspel recalled. "We shouldn't have been forced to do that."

Hallen was incensed. "We wanted some time. We wanted to be able to express how we were feeling. To talk to each other. You know, anything. We were really mad, but they were insistent, that we had to go right now."

Burton agreed. "My regret was not being able to be alone for half an hour, and just say goodbye to these people that I'd built a relationship with. As different as we were, we truly cared about each other."

The jurors silently filed into the judge's spacious chambers. Judge Fitzpatrick, his wife, his law clerk, and several others awaited them. He greeted them with a speech. He understood the hardships that many of them had endured during the trial, jurors interviewed recalled him saying. He had been raised extremely poor, and had undergone many hardships. In short, he felt their pain.

As it dawned on several jurors what he was talking about and whom he was referring to, their shock was replaced by growing anger at his words.

"Everyone was kind of looking at me, because they knew what he was talking about," said David Olson. "But my situation was totally different. Okay, fine, so he started out as a poor kid and had to work through all this stuff, and what his dad did, and him having to wait tables through college and all this stuff. But it's not the same thing: coming from nothing and going to something. It's a little bit different when you got everything and all of a sudden you're going to lose everything. It's not the same as almost losing everything you worked your whole life for."

Olson was angry, really angry. But he said nothing. After all, he was in the presence of a judge. "I wish he wouldn't even have said that. I really would. I didn't like it."

Neither did Jim Livingston, faced with both bankruptcy and foreclosure. "I think he was trying to say, 'Oh, don't feel bad.' But that doesn't cut it."

To Terry Zaspel, little about meeting Fitzpatrick "cut it." To her, the meeting was little more than spending two hours with the judge while "he was trying to explain away his behavior during the trial."

Hallen recalled Fitzpatrick expressing hurt at the defense team's efforts to recuse him. "He said in his 25 years that had never happened. I think by the end of the case, he was pretty mad at them. He was mad at them for not releasing documents and about witnesses not coming over from England."

Court observer Patricia Miller took pictures of the judge with his jury, and the judge passed out copies of the settlement for the jurors to keep.

Meanwhile, over at the nearby Radisson Hotel, a much more upbeat presentation was just beginning. Some 200 reporters, supporters, and onlookers marched behind Attorney General Humphrey to the hotel, where a victory celebration was about to take place. As Humphrey aid Eric Johnson walked along, he proclaimed, "Skip may never walk the 18th hole at the Masters, but this is pretty good."

Humphrey's day in the sun had finally arrived. Inside the Radisson, the gathering of health antitobacco activists, Humphrey staffers, Blue Cross employees, trial attorneys, and the

media resembled a religious revival much more than a postlitiga-
tion press conference.

"When we launched this historic lawsuit against the tobacco
cartel, the critics said we'd never prevail against this powerful
industry," Humphrey told the frenzied crowd. "Today, the
tobacco industry has surrendered—and they have surrendered
on our terms!"

As he was followed at the podium by Czjakowski and Ciresi,
volunteers worked the room, handing out T-shirts that declared
"The Secret's Out! We've Won against Big Tobacco."

During a live broadcast, WCCO-TV veteran political reporter
Pat Kessler would reflect that the occasion marked the day the
attorney general "stopped being Skip," and stepped out from
behind his father's long shadow.

Reporters were given copies of the settlement itself, a 35-page
document that many would have only minutes to digest and
report upon. As reported that day, the terms of the settlement
including the following:

—The state of Minnesota would receive $6.1 billion over 25
years beginning with $240 million by September 5, 1998.

—Blue Cross and Blue Shield of Minnesota would receive
$469 million over five years, commencing with a $160 million
payment by September 5, 1998.

—The Ciresi law firm, instead of receiving its contracted fee of
25 percent of the settlement amount, would be paid 7.1 percent of
the total settlement by the tobacco companies. No total amount

of payment was listed.

—A ban on marketing cigarettes to children. By court order, the industry was permanently enjoined from using marketing techniques aimed at minors.

—A halt to cigarette advertising on billboards, buses or transit areas. No tobacco-related merchandise could be distributed or sold in the state.

—An end nationally to placement fees for cigarette products in movies.

—Creation of a $102 million smoking-cessation fund and establishment of a nonprofit foundation to develop programs to reduce teen smoking.

—Closing the Council for Tobacco Research, an industry trade group accused of controlling unfavorable research.

—Additional disclosure rules for tobacco interests in the state to increase the amount of financial reporting of lobbying activities.

—Maintaining the Minnesota Document Depository for 10 years and transferring key documents from a depository in England to Minnesota.

The rest of the Ciresi team stood quietly to the side of the podium, looking shell-shocked. Only Richard Gill hung far back in the crowd. "Oh, this is their celebration," he said mildly.

Negotiators Finzen and Sheehy stood in the back as well, only, as Sheehy put it, "leaning against the wall" in their fatigue.

"It was great to come together and watch the folks in the room.

I can still close my eyes and see it," Sheehy said.

Finzen agreed. "It was almost like not being there, sort of watching from afar. Watching everything else going on in the room. Mike and Skip up at the podium . . . . the public health people. It was a very satisfying feeling."

Back at the courthouse, tobacco representatives warned about overreacting to the settlement. "Today's settlement does nothing to help establish a nationwide, uniform program to combat underage use of tobacco products," said spokesman Scott Williams. "Today's settlement is a reminder about the limitations of state suits. Another state has settled, but there is no resolution for dozens of others."

An RJR corporate press release reiterated its claim of bias. "We agreed to the settlement because we concluded that it would be extremely difficult to reach a fair outcome. When the government decides to use its coercive powers against a politically unpopular industry, it can ultimately produce any result it wants, regardless of the merits."

For the defense litigators—the warriors—the settlement represented an unsatisfying, though understandable, end to a trial most thought they had a chance of winning, against all odds.

"A lot of lawyers make the mistake of thinking cases are their cases. These aren't my cases. They're my client's cases. And if my client wants to fight or not fight or give away everything or give away nothing, that's their decision," Robert Weber said. "But, personally, did I want to see what the jury said? You're goddamn right

I did. I really did. There was a lot of sweat put into that effort. Did I want to see what those people would really do? Yeah. I didn't think they were angry. I didn't think they'd be overcome by emotion. I thought they were resentful of the plaintiffs overplaying their hand. Does that mean I thought we would have necessarily won? I don't know. But if we had lost, I think we'd have lost a heck of a lot less than they were asking for."

Weber returned to his Minneapolis trial office and began breaking it down. He would depart for Cleveland the next morning.

"It was frustrating," Peter Bleakley acknowledged. "I believed by the time this case was over that we were going to end with a hung jury." Bleakley left the press conference and went straight to the airport, where he flew to the Four Seasons resort on the Caribbean island of Nevis to join his family for a vacation.

David Bernick wasn't far behind, heading instead for his home outside Chicago. "There wasn't much point in sticking around," he said dryly.

Defense negotiators, their task completed, slipped out of town just as quietly as they'd arrived two weeks earlier.

In a conference room at the *Saint Paul Pioneer Press*, yet another media event was taking place, this one far more subdued. Five jurors—Dorothy Hallen, Jill Burton, David Olson, Jim Otis and Jim Livingston had agreed to attend the press conference.

"The rest were very adamant that they didn't want to go,"

Hallen said later. "They didn't want to talk that day. They didn't know if they would ever talk."

For those reporters who had attended the trial day in and day out, it was fascinating to see these individuals—so expressionless during the past 15 weeks—suddenly come to life, offering up real names to replace the nicknames they had been given and opinions where they had been mute. As court liaison Rebecca Fanning moved alphabetically through the press list, allowing one question to each news organization, it didn't take long for the jurors' frustrations to emerge.

"Where have the people spoken?" wondered Jill Burton, "I think what's frustrating is you assume it's government of the people by the people and for the people. You get here, and you are the people selected to represent Minnesota. So you fulfill your obligation, only to have the carpet pulled out from under you."

Dorothy Hallen chimed in, "We went through a long process and we didn't get closure. I was very disappointed, not a little. A lot of emotion went into this."

James Livingston declared, "The public has a right to know what we've been through the last four months," although he never mentioned, during that press conference, the financial problems that now plagued his family and him.

"It's not something you just want to go on TV saying," he said later.

David Olson told the media he figured he'd lost about $13,000 in wages by serving on the panel. He'd fallen behind in his house payments, refinanced, and now faced uncertainty about how he would cover his higher monthly payments. Olson had been trying to quit smoking before the trial began. "Due to the stress of all of this, I've kind of picked it back up," he confessed.

James Otis told those gathered that the worst part of the trial was "rearranging your whole life because it's your civic duty."

Otis also acknowledged that the trial had taught him a lot. "I think we now know more about how a courtroom operates than any of us ever wanted."

The jurors gathered said they hadn't formed any conclusions about the trial, as they'd followed the judge's instructions to the letter, and had refrained from discussing the case. "We never got to hear the other half of closing arguments so we didn't have the whole story yet," one juror explained.

They did, however, have some opinions.

Several jurors were surprised by the amount of the settlement.

"I was not leaning in that direction," said Burton.

Livingston agreed. "I don't think I would have awarded anything extra [in punitive damages]. I honestly myself don't think there was that much of an antitrust conspiracy going on. I think that they did what the consumer wanted. They made low-tar-and-nicotine cigarettes and they tried to keep products on the market that people wanted. So I don't condemn them for that. Yeah [the tobacco companies] talked among themselves, but I guess that's expected."

"It would have been hard to decide," said Olson.

Said Otis, "I personally hadn't thought about [damage awards] yet. I think maybe it was better off for the defense that they did settle."

The press conference broke up and the jurors went their respective ways.

Driving home, Otis was thrilled with his first, and possibly last, press conference, "I was on Cloud Nine. I was smiling so much, I'm sure other people were looking at me thinking I was crazy."

From President Clinton on down, everybody had a comment about the settlement.

In a formal statement, Clinton focused on smoking and children. "Today we have learned that Minnesota has won important new concessions from the tobacco industry. The Minnesota settlement, like those reached earlier in Mississippi, Florida, and Texas, will help us combat tobacco industry marketing to kids. This action provides still further momentum to our effort to pass bipartisan, comprehensive tobacco legislation this year."

Senator Paul Wellstone said the settlement was "very good news for Minnesota." He claimed the settlement would spur Congress on to "strengthen comprehensive tobacco legislation to protect the health of our children."

While Governor Arne Carlson said he was pleased with the settlement, he wasn't about to praise Humphrey. Instead, he maintained, "I have made it abundantly clear that any money recovered should go into the general fund of the state, and the legislature and the governor in 1999 should decide how it is going to be spent."

That night Ciresi, Finzen, their spouses, and several other friends and relatives celebrated at D'Amico's over dinner. Finzen, whose twin daughters were attending their senior prom that night, wasn't even sure he could make both events and stay awake. At that point, he'd gone almost 48 hours without sleep. However, he returned home from his daughters' "grand march," to find a message from Ciresi on his answering machine.

"We have reservations at D'Amico at eight. Meet us down there. You can sleep tomorrow. Tonight we're going to have a little celebration dinner."

Ciresi and his team returned to the firm's Minneapolis office, where a victory celebration was held. Ciresi went off to dinner; the rest of the trial team dined at the Capital Grille, then hit several night spots.

Lee Sheehy and other Humphrey staff members who weren't accompanying their boss around town for his various media appearances, gathered at Sweeney's in St. Paul. "There was a little garden area out back, where there was less smoke," Sheehy said. At least for the chief deputy attorney general, the celebration was short. "I didn't last long. I had about one beer, and then realized I was going to go to sleep. It wouldn't look good for me to go to sleep here at Sweeney's, because I'll be accused of passing out."

Sheehy headed home.

RJR damages lawyer Peter Biersteker headed right to the airport. "The first thing I decided was to buy a book. I'm going to buy a book! I'm going to read a book! It was as if somebody had stopped beating me in the head with a hammer. But it wasn't really until that moment—when I actually did something normal—that it occurred to me how screwed up the last several months had been."

With a brand new copy of Steven Ambrose's *Undaunted Courage* under his arm, Biersteker boarded his Washington, D.C., plane and flew off into the night.

In his south Minneapolis home, Andy Czjawkowski cracked a bottle of Dom Perignon he'd been saving for the occasion.

Juror David Olson stopped off at the White Bear Bowl on his way home, had a couple drinks, and thought about his future.

Chapter Sixteen

Aftermath

Once the high-tech trial equipment was dismantled, Courtroom Two in St. Paul's Warren E. Burger Federal Building, for 16 weeks home to case number C1-94-8565, went dark. The Minnesota Tobacco Trial was over, but it was far from done.

In the days immediately following the settlement announcement, trial attorneys, the jury, and the judge faded quickly from the media spotlight. Smoking activists, politicians, and pundits quickly took their place.

Dr. Stanton Glantz, a professor at the University of California's medical facility in San Francisco, was ecstatic about the Minnesota settlement. Glantz, whose receipt and subsequent release of secret Brown & Williamson (B&W) documents four years earlier cracked Big Tobacco's wall of invincibility, e-mailed smoking activists around the country the day after the settlement announcement.

He called it a "triumph of truth and justice for taxpayers," and "a monumental advancement for public health."

Glantz had been a constant resource for the Humphrey team throughout the lawsuit. An outspoken opponent of the industry, Glantz kept colleagues apprised of the fight against tobacco through his Web site, www.smokescreen.org.

"The Minnesota case goes beyond my wildest expectations," Glantz's e-mail said, suggesting that supporters of Mike Moore's proposed attorneys general settlement "should apologize to Hubert Humphrey for not supporting his position that the June 20, 1997 deal was a disaster."

Richard Daynard, head of the Tobacco Products Liability Project in Boston, called the outcome of the Minnesota case "a humongous tobacco control settlement."

"The fact that the documents are out there is playing a crucial role in the [national] debate," he said.

However, as Attorney General Hubert Humphrey III and Blue Cross Chief Executive Andy Czajkowski basked in the afterglow of their precedential settlement with the tobacco industry, controversy threw a slight chill on the news.

Humphrey's DFL opponents, Governor Arne Carlson, and other, predominantly Republican members of the state's legislature went on the offensive, attacking the terms of the settlement. They complained that the attorney general had misled the public by using inflated figures for how much the state would actually receive from its $6.1 billion share of the settlement. In "present-value" dollars, depending on whose calculations were used, the actual settlement over 25 years would be more like $3.4 billion to $3.6 billion, they said.

Humphrey aide Eric Johnson compared the criticisms to "getting the biggest birthday present in Minnesota history, then complaining about the color of the ribbon." He freely acknowledged that the settlement amounted to about $3.426 billion in present value dollars. Regardless of accounting principles, Johnson said, Minnesota still fared better in the settlement than any of the three states that had settled with the industry so far.

Fueling much of the carping was Humphrey's posttrial elevation in polls surrounding the ongoing gubernatorial race. The *Star Tribune's* Minnesota Poll, done in conjunction with KMSP–TV, found him beating candidates from both parties in head-to-head races. His strong showing was assisted in part by the tobacco settlement, the survey showed. A poll in the *Saint Paul Pioneer Press* showed similar results.

Humphrey's political foes also raised a stink about the $550 million in attorneys' fees awarded to the law firm of Robins, Kaplan, Miller & Ciresi for its work representing the state and Blue Cross, even though the amount paid to the Robins firm was considerably less than originally promised.

The fee, which was never specifically outlined in the public portion of the settlement, totaled $550 million for the Robins firm; $440 million for representing the state, and $110 million for representing Blue Cross.

Right-wing Republican Alan Quist called the attorney's fee

payment "obscene." Quist asserted that, because Michael Ciresi's firm would receive payment in full within three years, their share of the settlement would amount to 14 percent, rather than the 7.1 percent figure announced after the trial. Regardless, the amount was far less than the 25 percent that Ciresi's initial contract with the state stipulated.

Ciresi supporters were quick to point out that, unlike other states which had settled (and were still battling with their respective attorneys over much higher fee payments), Ciresi's team had worked for four years, providing the nation with a treasure trove of documents that would be used in future litigation, nationally and internationally.

In Florida, where he was vacationing at his home in Boca Raton, Ciresi was livid at the criticism, noting the fees would be paid by the tobacco companies and did not come from the considerable pot of money he had helped to negotiate for his clients.

"Nobody hid anything," Ciresi protested angrily. "I resent any suggestion otherwise."

The out-of-pocket cost to Ciresi's firm for pursuing the tobacco industry was $40 million. Nearly $30 million of that was in attorneys' time; $5 million was spent on expert witnesses and their reports; and an additional $5 million covered various other expenses. During the course of the lawsuit, Blue Cross covered between $4 million and $6 million in expenses for the firm and was reimbursed when the case was over.

Meanwhile, the health insurer was facing problems of its own.

Blue Cross created its own legacy as the first private insurer to take on the industry and, against great odds, obtain favorable results. "This case will be remembered for getting out the truth and changing the way tobacco products are marketed and perceived by the public," said CEO Czajkowski. "I hope this is a step toward making the tobacco industry a much smaller industry over the next 30 years."

However, within weeks of the settlement announcement, Blue Cross was hit with a lawsuit filed on behalf of policyholders who wanted the insurer to use its $469 million award to cut premiums rather than fund smoking cessation programs.

The industry was more reflective about the outcome in Minnesota. Scott Williams, a Washington, D.C.–based media consultant who served as spokesman for those companies seeking a national settlement, acknowledged that the trial documents would be "part of the record forever. The documents didn't change public opinion. Maybe they confirmed opinions or reaffirmed opinions. But they didn't make it easier in Washington."

Indeed, Congress could not agree on legislation to fundamentally alter the presence of tobacco in American society. A $516 billion tobacco bill moved haltingly, as the Minnesota documents came under scrutiny, and eventually died after the industry walked away from the table. Steven F. Goldstone, chairman of RJR Nabisco, ultimately placed part of the blame for the legislation's collapse on antitobacco crusaders in the public health community, including those who supported Humphrey.

But the industry would later put out feelers to attorneys general with pending Medicaid cases, and settlement talks resumed. More than three dozen states had filed claims against the tobacco industry to recover costs for treating smoking–related illnesses. They were joined by additional health insurers and labor unions, who stepped up to the plate as well.

Business at the Minnesota Document Depository was brisk. Cindie Smart — whose firm, Smart Legal Assistance, administered the depository — and her staff received telephone calls from around the country and the world to make reservations to visit the facility and search the 30 million document pages obtained from Big Tobacco's files. Attorneys, scientists, and students kept the depository's 12 computers occupied to capacity as they pressed to review material.

Some of those documents revealed curious little secrets about industry conduct within Minnesota's borders over the years. Among the disclosures: Wes Lane, a veteran lobbyist for the Teamsters Union, had for years acted as a $2,500-per-month tobacco industry consultant, without his union's knowledge, according to the *Saint Paul Pioneer Press.* Although union officials were upset by the reports, the semi-retired Lane called it "old news."

The Minneapolis *Star Tribune* reported that a foundation controlled by R. J. Reynolds Tobacco Company (RJR) made contributions to pet charities of legislative leaders, including former House Speaker Irv Anderson and former Senate Minority Leader

Dean Johnson. Senator Steve Novak, a DFLer from New Brighton, asked RJR to contribute to the Ramsey Foundation, where he served as vice president for development, the newspaper reported.

The effects of the Minnesota documents were seen elsewhere as well. In Florida, the family of a deceased smoker was awarded $950,000 in a trial that relied heavily on Minnesota-produced documents. The verdict contained the first-ever award of punitive damages against the industry—$450,000.

The documents also made their way across the ocean and surfaced in smoking lawsuits in Great Britain.

The national defense attorneys returned to other cases, taking some vacation time with their families as well. Robert Weber took his wife to Venice, then took the entire family to South Carolina. David Bernick traveled with his family to France and Switzerland. Peter Bleakley went to the beach for a month. He informed Philip Morris that, while he'd be happy to stay involved in tobacco litigation, he wouldn't take another trial that took him away from home for so long.

Attorneys remained divided over the legal significance of the case.

"It's an aberration. There'll be nothing like it again," said Gerald Svoboda, who represented British-based B.A.T. Industries and retired to Bayfield, Wisconsin, when the trial was over.

B&W's David Bernick disagreed. "It showed that the industry was prepared—in one of the most unfavorable settings—to go all the way through a very lengthy and arduous trial," he said. "Even in the worst of circumstances, significant numbers of jurors buy what we have to say and believe that it's not just a situation where it's time for the industry's comeuppance. They really want to listen to the evidence and rule on the evidence."

Ciresi, Roberta Walburn, and Humphrey were honored as trial lawyers of the year in Washington, D.C., by the advocacy group, Trial Lawyers for Public Justice. Among the many speaking invitations Ciresi received was a request to address the World Health Organization in Geneva, Switzerland.

Ciresi, who was torn between a settlement and sending the case to the jury, believed, ultimately, that the state and Blue Cross did the right thing.

"We felt it should be done from the standpoint of social good," Ciresi said, after the postsettlement euphoria had died down. "We were not trying to outlaw smoking. We were trying to get them to come clean. We wanted to give people a better opportunity to decide whether or not they want to smoke."

The intense competition between the attorneys who fought the case dissipated as time went on. Midway through the summer, Bernick, who enthusiastically used a large sketchpad and magic marker to emphasize points during the trial, received a letter and a box of crayons in the mail.

"Dear David," the letter began. "Please accept my apologies for the delay in getting the enclosed crayons to you. I'm certain that by now you've gone through every magic marker in the United

States and I wanted to make certain that you had a backup for your next trial. Give me a call if your travels bring you back to the Twin Cities and I will do the same when in Chicago. Best personal regards."

It was signed by Ciresi.

Meanwhile, the Minnesota Tobacco Trial jurors worked at putting their lives back together. Juror David Olson bought new clothes to fit his now-20-pound-heavier frame, and finally got a haircut, the first he could afford since the trial began in January. Juror Terry Zaspel immediately went out and purchased a book she was told she couldn't read during the trial—John Grisham's *Runaway Jury.* The lawyer's tale of jury tampering on a tobacco trial kept her riveted. "I should have read it the first week," she said. Referring to the fictional jury's cushy treatment, she added, "I could have been eating on china."

Jurors soon discovered there was keen interest in what they thought about the trial, even though they never returned a verdict. Attorneys for the defendants and at least one national jury consulting firm for plaintiffs' attorneys sought their impressions of witnesses on both sides of the case. The information would be used to plot defense and plaintiff strategies in tobacco trials to come.

The jurors who participated in the interviews were compensated for their time, a common practice after a complex trial, and generally received $100 an hour. The interviews were thorough and time consuming. David Olson stayed on the telephone so long with a Chicago-based jury consultant that the battery in his portable phone went dead as the three-hour conversation wound to a close.

James Livingston used the financial windfall from his posttrial interviews to get his house out of foreclosure. His bankruptcy proceedings continued.

Some jurors, though, declined to participate in the exercise. The juror known as "Free Spirit" was so upset by the way the case ended that she refused to talk about it even in the company of other jurors.

Toward the end of May, Zaspel was hospitalized with chest pains. The mild pain she'd experienced during the trial returned after she resumed her job in 3M's Post-It Note division. During one day at work, the pain grew worse. "I went home and told my husband, Bob, 'I think I should go to the hospital.' He said, 'What's the matter.' I said, 'Chest pains.' We went to the emergency room and they admitted me, bingo." Zaspel was hospitalized for three days, but suffered no heart damage.

She felt the stress she underwent during the trial was a contributing factor to the incident. "I'd never had any chest pain before then," she said.

In the weeks following the trial, Fitzpatrick fast became a judicial enigma. No one knew exactly where he was or what he was doing. Courthouse gossips long had speculated that the tobacco case would be his swan song before retirement. But Fitzpatrick, if he was going to go, was not going to go quietly.

Fitzpatrick informed Chief Judge Lawrence Cohen that he intended to return to the bench on July 6. He told Cohen that if his situation were to change, Cohen would be the first to hear about it—after Fitzpatrick's wife.

As he issued posttrial rulings and orders, Fitzpatrick pursued another goal, very quietly. Two weeks after the trial ended, each juror received a letter from Fitzpatrick's law clerk, Michelle Jones.

On May 20, Jones wrote, "You may recall on Friday, May 8, 1998, following the announcement of the settlement, Judge Fitzpatrick indicated to you in Chambers that he would try to arrange an opportunity for Plaintiffs to deliver their final summation in order to assist in closure in this matter. I hope to contact you shortly to update you on this prospect."

Jones added, "I must remind you that in the event this opportunity is possible it will be a private affair and for your benefit only. Any disclosure of this event may jeopardize this rare opportunity."

Jurors waited, and wondered.

During the last week in May, Liggett local counsel David Sasseville received a phone call from Mike Ciresi with some other trial-related news. "Blue Cross has decided to dismiss all its claims against Liggett," Ciresi told Sasseville. He told the Lindquist & Vennum attorney to draft a stipulation of dismissal and settlement and hurry it over to Roberta Walburn.

Sasseville recalled, "He said she wanted to orchestrate the timing of the filing to be done no later than June 1." Only later would

Sasseville understand the importance of that date.

On Sunday, May 31, Michelle Jones called jurors and told them that a county van would pick them up and take them to Ciresi's office the next morning, thus sparing them steep downtown parking rates. That wasn't the only information to come from Fitzpatrick's chambers that weekend.

In an order filed late Sunday night. Fitzpatrick ordered the release of the now-infamous 39,000 privileged tobacco documents and indexes, in their entirety, to the Minnesota Document Depository. Since the documents were already in the hands of Congress and on the Internet, Fitzpatrick ruled that the issue of privilege was moot. He also ordered the release of 2,000 documents from other defendants as a sanction for failure to comply with previous orders. Fitzpatrick, the godfather of the Minnesota Document Depository, was now finished with document production. The depository stood filled with millions of pages of material available for public inspection.

On Monday morning, June 1, Liggett's dismissal was filed via the CLAD electronic filing system and was instantly signed by the judge. It would become his last official act in the case.

Meanwhile, a Ramsey County van drove silently through the streets of St. Paul and its suburbs, picking up Fitzpatrick's 12 guests from various locations. Its final destination was the downtown Minneapolis law offices of Robins, Kaplan, Miller & Ciresi, where, inside one of the firm's conference rooms, Ciresi and his trial team waited to make up for a date they had abruptly broken almost a month ago. That morning, Ciresi would deliver his closing argument before a group of people he'd come to know well in 1998: the 12 members of the Minnesota Tobacco Trial jury, Fitzpatrick, the judge's wife and sister, and Fitzpatrick's court personnel.

It was a very private affair. Notably absent that June morning were members of the defense team, as well as the trial's coplaintiffs, Blue Cross CEO Czjakowski and Minnesota Attorney General Hubert H. Humphrey III.

Defense attorneys had learned of the closing argument session late Sunday evening, during an interview with a juror, but did not know where or at what time it would occur.

As the jurors arrived to hear Ciresi's unofficial summation, they found a mock courtroom awaiting them in the firm's conference room. Twelve chairs had been set up as an erstwhile jury box. Ciresi would address them from a podium, as he would have in the courtroom. The judge was seated at one end of the room, Ciresi's team of lawyers sat nearby. The judge's court reporter was on hand as well, though his stenographic equipment was not. This was not official court business, not by any stretch of the imagination. A video camera, however, was on hand to record the event.

Some jurors immediately noticed the absence of any defense attorneys, and found it odd, though none of them raised an objection. After all, they were guests here.

Ciresi delivered a four-hour closing argument, pausing only for a lunch break. In a setting more relaxed than a courtroom, Ciresi summarized the evidence to support the consumer fraud and antitrust charges against the tobacco industry. He did not, however, tell the jurors how much he thought should be awarded in the form of punitive damages, as he would have done in the scheduled argument three weeks earlier. "He said we should really hit them where it hurts," recalled juror James Otis.

Jurors enjoyed the day, even though they knew it was only a play and they were the audience.

"I'm glad I went to hear everything that was going to be said," said Jill Burton. "I'm sure it didn't have the thunder or vigor it would have had in the heat of the moment."

At the conclusion, the jurors, the plaintiffs' lawyers, the judge, and his guests gathered at an informal reception in the firm's offices. Dorothy Hallen remembers telling Ciresi that a one-year anniversary party for the jurors had already been set for May 8, 1999. "I want to be there," she remembered him saying. "And the defense attorneys should come too." She recalled being puzzled by the statement. If he wanted them at the party, she thought, why hadn't he invited them to hear his closing arguments?

The jurors were delivered home about seven o'clock that evening, after what they thought had been an enlightening day. Ciresi and his wife left town for an Alaskan cruise—just ahead of a firestorm that was just gathering force.

When defense attorneys learned more details of the closing argument session, they expressed outrage that the judge would arrange it without contacting them. They claimed it was an improper *ex parte*, or one-sided, contact between the court, the jurors, and the plaintiffs, without the defendants present. All of the parties should have been involved in the matter, the defendants asserted. Later, half-jokingly, the event would be referred to as the *ex parte* party.

On Wednesday, June 3, defense attorneys filed a motion seeking Judge Fitzpatrick's immediate removal from the case on the grounds of judicial misconduct. "By any ethical or judicial standard, it was totally improper and indefensible of the court—while still sitting in judgment of defendants and deciding motions against them—to be secretly furnishing its services to plaintiffs' counsel," the defense motion stated.

"In short, within 12 hours after deciding the first of a series of postsettlement applications against the defendants, this court, its law clerk, and the court observer spent the day collaborating behind closed doors with plaintiffs' counsel," the defendants argued, adding, "In a transparent effort to keep the meeting secret, the jurors were then advised not to disclose to defendants that the meeting had taken place."

Philip Morris' local counsel, Peter Sipkins, filed the motion. He simmered with disbelief. "The cardinal rule of lawyering is that lawyers and judges communicate with each other openly and with full access by both sides to the court." He said the meeting "more clearly reflects the bias" that the defense had alleged, almost from the trial's onset. "There was no chance for us to stand up and object. There was no chance for us to say that's not what the facts are," he said.

The defense motion demanded a record of all *ex parte* communications involving Fitzpatrick, the plaintiffs' lawyers, and the jurors. It also wanted any orders issued after those communications began to be set aside. The defendants also wanted to see a copy of the videotape of Ciresi's closing.

Juror Hallen didn't understand the fuss. Contacted by a reporter for a comment Wednesday evening, she said the case was over and it was silly for the defendants to protest.

With Ciresi on a cruise, Roberta Walburn rose to the judge's defense. Defense attorneys had known of the meeting in advance, making it far from secret, she said. Fitzpatrick was no longer considering the case, so there hadn't been a conflict.

"The jurors requested that Mike give closing arguments, and we understand they wanted it to reach closure in their minds," she said. "They gave four months of their lives to this case. We felt they were entitled to hear it. It was the right thing to do and we did it."

Ciresi later defended the gathering as something he agreed to do out of compassion for the jurors.

"I didn't know if I wanted to do it," Ciresi recalled. "It was like yesterday's news. The case was over. I was moved by my sense of obligation to the jury. I had only one condition—I didn't want any media around. I didn't want any publicity. I didn't want it to appear as if it was some ego gratification for me. . . . I would have invited one defense attorney but they would have told the other ones and they would have made a big deal out of it."

Fitzpatrick denied the defense's request for a record of contacts between the court and Ciresi, and for the videotape of the faux closing argument. In an unusually defensive order, Fitzpatrick said his work on the tobacco case had been completed by the meeting.

"It is and has been the Honorable Kenneth J. Fitzpatrick's intention to no longer participate in this litigation from the time of hearing the plaintiffs' final summation onward," the judge said.

Fitzpatrick denied that the jurors had been told to keep the meeting secret and, in a odd jab at defendants, stated that he found their motion "ironic" because local defense attorneys had been interviewing jurors and paying them $100 an hour.

The legal grapevine thrummed with the latest development. Even those attorneys who had faulted the defense for its recusal motions during the trial were shaken by Fitzpatrick's actions—and by the fact that Ciresi, under attack himself for the size of his attorneys fees—would allow such an unusual meeting to take place.

On June 9, at the same time Fitzpatrick asked to be removed from the case, Chief Ramsey County judge Lawrence Cohen ordered Fitzpatrick instead to cease all further involvement. In a stinging rebuke to his friend, Cohen, who denied defense attempts to remove Fitzpatrick from the bench during the trial, this time noted that Fitzpatrick's neutrality "might now be called into question if he continued to preside over the case."

Fitzpatrick's removal came a week after he had been granted permission by Governor Carlson to take an early retirement. Cohen learned about the retirement plans like everyone else, in the media. Apologetic, Fitzpatrick informed Cohen that he planned to retire from the bench at the end of July.

But the controversy with Judge Kenneth Fitzpatrick wasn't over. Members of the media who had observed the strange gyrations of the video camera during the defense's closing arguments discovered the answer to that mystery in a defense motion filed June 11. In it, defense attorneys demanded a copy of a videotape Fitzpatrick ordered made of their closing arguments, without their permission or their knowledge. Under Minnesota law, such taping under such circumstances was illegal. No one was certain how Fitzpatrick intended to use his two-volume video set.

Furthermore, the motion accused Fitzpatrick of continuing to work on the case, after claiming he was through. According to defense attorneys, Fitzpatrick issued directives to officials of the Minnesota Document Depository two days after meeting with Ciresi and the jurors. Finally, defense lawyers asked that Fitzpatrick's May 31 order releasing more documents to the depository be overturned.

The attorney general's office was quick to disparage the latest defense motion. In a statement released that day, Humphrey said "They have a hard time accepting the fact that they lost, that their deceit and lies are exposed, and that it is time for a new era of truth and reform."

However, the defense found an ally in a most unusual place—the office of Ramsey County's chief judge. "I wanted to just tell him to shut up!" Judge Lawrence Cohen said later, recalling Humphrey's statement. Cohen was livid over the last Fitzpatrick action, which he characterized as plain "wrong."

Cohen had assumed responsibilities for post-settlement issues in the case, after the *ex parte* fiasco. Now he assumed control of the disputed tapes as well, collecting all copies from Fitzpatrick and Ciresi and placing them under seal in the court administrator's office. During a subsequent meeting in June, he told attorneys for both sides to tone down their rhetoric, and to keep their acrimony out of the media.

While Cohen still voiced support of Fitzpatrick's trial rulings, he called the unauthorized taping and the *ex parte* gathering "unexplainable."

"How can you say a $6 billion case is done? It's never done," Cohen said. The court still had authority over many settlement terms, including use of the funds to establish an antismoking foundation, and the industry's compliance with advertising restrictions.

It was an inglorious finale for a public servant of 35 years. Having presided over perhaps the state's most significant and provocative legal proceeding, Fitzpatrick now found his closing performance under review by the state Judicial Standards Board. And to the end he maintained his silence, sending only a letter to colleagues and staff in the Ramsey County Courthouse thanking them for their years of service with him.

In a 1997 interview with the *Star Tribune*, Fitzpatrick reflected on the role of a judge in particularly contentious litigation where appeals are likely and numerous. He made it clear his decisions were based on the issues before him, not some exterior force.

"Some judges are concerned about their rulings being overturned," Fitzpatrick said. "A different philosophy is to do what you feel is the correct thing to do and if the [higher court] decides something different, then I'd be more than willing to listen to their guidance."

Fitzpatrick's request for a disability retirement revealed an emotionally and physically stressed individual whose health suffered when the trial became acrimonious. Fitzpatrick had decided to retire even before the trial ended. His physician wrote Carlson with the request on April 20, nearly three weeks before the case settled.

"Apparently the stresses that the judge is experiencing in his current trial situation is adversely effecting his health and heart rhythm, and it is our conclusion that his health will not allow him to continue working on a full-time basis as a judge once his current caseload is completed," wrote Dr. Frank Indihar to Carlson.

Patricia Miller, who served as Fitzpatrick's court observer and helped him administer the case, had a farewell dinner with the judge in early June. She said Fitzpatrick, a carpenter by avocation, told her he wanted to work with his hands and start pounding nails again.

Not long afterward, Fitzpatrick and his wife, Mary Ann, quietly left the Twin Cities and moved to a small town in eastern Tennessee to build a retirement home. Fitzpatrick never responded to requests to talk about the trial.

Shortly before the long Fourth of July weekend, the 12 jurors each received a business-size envelope in the mail. Inside the envelope were two color photos of the jurors as a group. Although the jurors had gone on two picnics during the trial, and had gone out for lunch several times, no one had ever taken a picture of them together. The photos were taken in Fitzpatrick's federal courthouse chambers shortly after the settlement was announced on May 8.

Jurors 1 through 6 were standing in the same order as they were positioned in the jury box. Seated in folding chairs in front of them were jurors 7 through 12 in their same order. And in the middle, sitting with the jury he'd taken on a four-month odyssey, was Kenneth Fitzpatrick.

Recalled Otis, "He told us he had more faith in us as a jury than any other jury he had ever had."

The Minnesota Tobacco Trial lasted 79 days. Nearly 3,000 documents were entered as evidence. Forty witnesses testified. The trial transcript covered 15,943 pages. And in September 1998, the state of Minnesota received its first $240 million payment from the settlement.

The case presented a powerful courtroom drama that ultimately released a torrent of information on smoking and health. In the end, the four-month legal battle provided considerable insight into the mindset and strategies of an industry once so powerful that it seemed invincible. People would continue to smoke cigarettes, but the tobacco industry would never be the same.

There were about 30 million reasons why.

The End.

Sources

Chapter One

Authors' interviews with Hubert H. Humphrey III, Eric Johnson, Andrew Czajkowski, Tom Gilde, and Roberta Walburn.

David Phelps' interviews with Doug Blanke, Michael Ciresi, and Mike Moore.

Peter Pringle, *Cornered, Big Tobacco at the Bar of Justice*, New York: Henry Holt and Company, 1998.

Carrick Mollenkamp, Adam Levy, Joseph Menn, and Feffrey Rothfeder, *The People vs. Big Tobacco, How the states took on the cigarette giants*, Princeton, N.J.: Bloomberg Press, 1998.

Trial transcript, February 9, 1998.

ABC *Nightline*, August 6, 1997

Chapter Two

Authors' trial notes.

Trial transcripts: January 20-23, 1998.

Authors' interviews with jurors Dorothy Hallen, Jill Burton, David Olson, James Livingston, Jim Otis, and Terry Zaspel.

Peter Pringle, *Cornered, Big Tobacco At The Bar of Justice,* New York: Henry Holt and Co., Inc., 1998.

Authors' interviews with attorneys Peter Bleakley, Robert Weber, Peter Sipkins,and Jack Fribley.

David Phelps' interview with attorney Michael Ciresi.

Chapter Three

David Phelps' interview with attorneys Michael Ciresi, Tara Sutton, Richard Gill, and Bruce Finzen.

Authors' interview with attorney Roberta Walburn.

David Phelps interview with attorney Michael Berens.

David Phelps, "Ciresi's Biggest Case: Taking on Tobacco," *Star Tribune*, June 16, 1997.

Julia Flynn Siler, "Winning With Hard Work and Histrionics," *New York Times*, October 9, 1988.

Michael Serrill, "Kings of Catastrophe; A Little Known Minneapolis Firm Gets The Largest Bhopal Suit," *Time*, April 22, 1985.

John A. Jenkins, *The Litigators: Inside the Powerful World of America's*

High-Stakes Trial Lawyers, New York: Doubleday, 1989.
Richard Solbol, *Bending the Law: The Story of the Dalkon Shield
Bankruptcy,* Chicago: The University of Chicago Press, 1991.

Chapter Four
Authors' trial notes.
Trial transcripts: January 26-27, 1998.
Authors' interviews with jurors Dorothy Hallen, Jill Burton, Terry Zaspel,
David Olson, and James Livingston.
Authors' interviews with attorneys Peter Bleakley and Robert Weber.
Deborah Rybak's interviews with attorneys David Martin and Gerald
Svoboda.
Joseph Nocera, Wilton Woods, and Henry Goldblatt, "Fatal Litigation,"
Fortune, October 16, 1995.
Richard Kluger, *Ashes to Ashes, America's Hundred-Year Cigarette War, the
Public Health, and the Unabashed Triumph of Philip Morris,* New York:
Alfred A. Knopf, 1996.

Chapter Five
Authors' trial notes.
Trial transcripts: January 28-February 6,1998.
David Phelps' interviews with attorneys Michael Ciresi and Roberta Walburn.
Authors' interview with attorney Peter Bleakley.
Deborah Rybak's interview with attorney David Bernick.
Authors' interviews with jurors David Olson, Terry Zaspel, and Dorothy
Hallen.

Chapter Six
Authors' trial notes.
Trial transcripts: February 6-11,1998.
Authors' interview with attorney Robert Weber.
Authors' interview with Special Master Mark Gehan.
Authors' interviews with jurors Dorothy Hallen and Jim Otis.
David Phelps' interview with attorney Michael Ciresi.
Deborah Rybak's interview with attorneys Richard Gill and Steven Kelley.
Carrick Mollenkamp, Adam Levy, Joseph Menn, and Jeffrey Rothfeder, *The
People vs. Big Tobacco, How the states took on the cigarette giants,*
Princeton, N.J.: Bloomberg Press, 1998.

Chapter Seven
Authors' trial notes.
Trial transcripts: February 12-27,1998.
Authors' interviews with jurors Jill Burton, Dorothy Hallen, Jim Otis, David
Olson, and Terry Zaspel.
Authors' interviews with attorneys Peter Bleakley and Robert Weber.
Authors' interview with Ramsey County Chief Judge Lawrence Cohen.
Deborah Rybak interview with attorneys David Bernick, Gerald Svoboda,
Greg Little, Peter Biersteker, and Thomas Hamlin.

David Phelps' interview with attorney Michael Ciresi.
David Peterson, "Order in the Court,"*Star Tribune*, February 22, 1998.

Chapter Eight
Authors' trial notes.
Trial transcripts: March 2-6, 1998.
Authors' interviews with jurors Dorothy Hallen, Jim Otis, James Livingston, and Terry Zaspel.
Authors' interviews with attorneys Robert Weber and Peter Bleakley.
David Phelps' interview with attorney Michael Ciresi.
Deborah Rybak's interview with attorney Gerald Svoboda.

Chapter Nine
Authors' trial notes.
Trial transcript: March 13,1998.
David Phelps' interview with attorneys Roberta Walburn and Michael Ciresi.
David Phelps' interview with Cynthia Lehr and Patricia Miller.
Deborah Rybak's interview with U.S. Representative Henry Waxman
Authors' interviews with attorneys Peter Sipkins, Peter Bleakley, and Jonathan Redgrave.
Authors' interview with Ramsey County Chief Judge Lawrence Cohen.
Authors' interview with juror Dorothy Hallen.
David Phelps, "Tobacco Loses Evidence Ruling," *Star Tribune*, March 8, 1998.
David Peterson, "For The Defense: Tobacco Firms' Lead Attorney Finds Trial 'Absurd,' 'Grossly Unfair,'" *Star Tribune*, March 11, 1998.
David Phelps "Judge Kenneth Fitzpatrick: Order In The Court," *Star Tribune*, January 27, 1997.
Thomas J. Collins, "Tobacco Trial Judge Known for Handling Tough Cases," *Saint Paul Pioneer Press*, January 20, 1998.

Chapter Ten
Authors' trial notes.
Trial transcripts: March 9-24, 1998.
Interviews with jurors Dorothy Hallen, Jim Otis, Jill Burton, and David Olson
Authors' interviews with attorneys Peter Sipkins, Robert Weber, and Peter Bleakley.
Deborah Rybak's interview with attorneys David Bernick and Richard Gill.
David Phelps' interview with Michael Ciresi and Roberta Walburn.

Chapter Eleven
Authors' trial notes.
Authors' interviews with attorneys Robert Weber, Peter Bleakley, Jonathan Redgrave, Jack Fribley, and Peter Sipkins.
Deborah Rybak's interviews with attorneys Peter Bleakley, Robert Weber, David Bernick, David Martin, Gerald Svoboda, Steven Kelley, David Sasseville, and Peter Biersteker.
Deborah Rybak's interviews with Lillian McDonald, KMSP-TV, and Tom

Watkins, CNN.

Richard Kluger, *Ashes to Ashes, America's Hundred-Year Cigarette War, the Public Health, and the Unabashed Triumph of Philip Morris*, New York: Alfred A. Knopf, 1996.

John A. Jenkins, *The Litigators, Inside the Powerful World Of America's High-Stakes Trial Lawyers*, New York: Doubleday, 1989.

Chapter Twelve

Authors' trial notes.

Trial transcripts: March 24-April 3,1998.

Authors' interview with attorney Robert Weber.

Authors' interviews with juror Dorothy Hallen, Jim Otis, Terry Zaspel and James Livingston.

David Phelps' interview with Hyman Berman.

David Phelps' interview with attorney Michael Ciresi and Roberta Walburn.

Michael Ciresi address to the Minnesota Trial Lawyers Association, August 14, 1998.

Henry Weinstein, "RJR Scientist Testifies On Safety," *Los Angeles Times*, March 31, 1998.

Chapter Thirteen

Authors' trial notes.

Trial transcripts: April 8-17,1998.

Authors' interview with attorney Roberta Walburn.

David Phelps interview with attorneys Tara Sutton and Michael Ciresi.

Authors' interviews with attorneys Jonathan Redgrave, Peter Sipkins, and Peter Bleakley.

Authors' interviews with jurors Dorothy Hallen, David Olson, Jill Burton, and Jim Otis.

Chapter Fourteen

Authors' trial notes.

Trial transcripts: April 20-May 4,1998.

Authors' interviews with negotiators Bruce Finzen, Lee Sheehy, Meyer Koplow, Arthur Golden, and Steve Patton.

Authors' interview with attorneys Robert Weber and Peter Bleakley.

Authors' interviews with Hubert H. Humphrey III and Eric Johnson.

Authors' interviews with jurors Jill Burton, Dorothy Hallen, Jim Otis, Terry Zaspel, and David Olson.

David Phelps' interview with attorney Michael Ciresi.

Deborah Rybak's interview with attorneys Peter Biersteker and Thomas Hamlin.

Doug Glass, "Analyst Predicts Minnesota Tobacco Settlement Imminent, *Associated Press*, April 28, 1998.

Chapter Fifteen

Authors' trial notes.

Trial transcripts: May 4-8, 1998.

Authors' interviews with attorneys Peter Bleakley, Robert Weber, Peter Sipkins, and Jack Fribley.

Authors' interviews with jurors Jill Burton, Dorothy Hallen, James Livingston, David Olson, Jim Otis, and Terry Zaspel.

Authors' interviews with negotiators Bruce Finzen, Lee Sheehy, Tom Gilde, Meyer Koplow, Arthur Golden, and Steve Patton.

Authors' interviews with Hubert Humphrey III, Eric Johnson, and Leslie Sandberg.

Authors' interviews with Professor Peter Thompson.

David Phelps' interview with attorney Michael Ciresi.

Deborah Rybak's interview with attorneys David Bernick, Peter Biersteker, David Sasseville, Gerald Svoboda, and Steven Kelley.

Chapter Sixteen

Authors' interviews with jurors Terry Zaspel, Jill Burton, James Livingston, David Olson, James Otis, and Dorothy Hallen.

Authors' interview with Andy Czajkowski.

Authors' interview with Ramsey County Chief Judge Lawrence Cohen.

David Phelps' interview with attorneys Michael Ciresi and Roberta Walburn.

David Phelps 'interviews with Patricia Miller, Richard Daynard, and Scott Williams.

Deborah Rybak's interviews with attorneys Gerald Svoboda and David Bernick.

Tom Hamburger and Greg Gordon, "Tobacco Gave to Pet Charities of 3 Legislators," *Star Tribune*, June 24, 1998.

David Hanners and David Shaffer, "Documents Say State Teamsters Official Lobbied for Tobacco," *Saint Paul Pioneer Press*, May 17, 1998.

David Shaffer, "Tobacco Frims Say Judge Secretly Taped Trial's End," *Saint Paul Pioneer Press*, June 12, 1998.

David Phelps, "Judge Kenneth Fitzpatrick: Order in the Court," *Star Tribune*, January 27, 1997.

Index